GOLFERS GUIDE

GUIDE

TO MENTAL FITNESS

HOW TO TRAIN YOUR MIND AND
ACHIEVE YOUR GOALS USING
SELF- HYPNOSIS AND VISUALIZATION

John Weir

Praise for the
GOLFERS GUIDE TO MENTAL FITNESS

"As an up-and-comer in the world of professional golf I've always wondered what the true difference is between guys that make it and guys that don't. We all hit the ball equally well, chip it close, and make putts. However, some make millions while others sleep in their cars. In the book, John Weir not only explains in easy to understand terms how the brain works and how the guys who make it think, he gives you the tools to start thinking like a champion. Through the use of self-hypnosis and affirmations in this book I've really turned my metal game around. I might not play like Tiger, but now I certainly think like him."

** --   Jacques Ungerer, Professional Golfer**

"As a former LPGA Tour Player, I am very strong in my opinion of the importance of the mental side of the game of golf and really any sport. John Weir takes the reader on an amazing journey into the mind and its impact on the athlete's success. I could not put the book down as I found ways to delve into my own brain through a plethora of lessons with Weir. He allowed me to minimize stress by truly knowing myself on and off the course. Through the pages of helpful training exercises, I began to synchronize with my body and brain for optimal performance. As a matter of fact, when I finished the book, I teed up in a tournament the following day and fired a solid even par round and felt nothing but a relaxed awareness and focused mind.

In the past, I was not a real proponent of hypnosis. (I just brushed it off as something weird that other people do.) However, as I read John Weir's book, the message is clear that positive mental programming is exactly what is needed for each of us to reach our competitive goals.

Well done, Mr. Weir and thank you for giving us the tools to perform at our best consistently and with true internal confidence."

** --   Kate Hughes, Founder Vision Fore Success**
**   Former LPGA Tour Player, Certified Mental Coach;**
**   University of Minnesota Hall of Fame for Golf;**
**   Director, Women's Golf at Bunkers Paradise**

"As a former mini-tour player for 4 years, I understand the importance of the mental side of the game. I really enjoyed *GOLFERS GUIDE TO MENTAL FITNESS* and found it to be a wonderful resource to help me in my own game as well as enhance my overall teaching program. This book has taught me the tools that apply to the 90% of the game, your mind, and they are easily applicable to all golfers. I found the book to be very beneficial and look forward to sharing it with my students. Excellent work!"

> -- **Pete "The Squire" Drotar,**
> **CEO of Drotar Golf Center in Murfreesboro, TN**
> **USGTF Master Professional,**
> **SW Michigan Top 100 Teaching Coach's Award, 2 years in a row.**

"What I liked about *GOLFERS GUIDE TO MENTAL FITNESS:*

- This is an incredibly comprehensive book. John Weir covers all aspects of Mental Game training in this book as well as any other author on the market today.

- John provides excellent, step-by-step, on course and off course drills that will help golfers stay positive, confident, and focused on the shot at hand.

- I really liked John's chapters about Visualization, Self-Talk, Affirmations, and Mental Rehearsal. These are skills that ALL golfers must train in order to lower their scores. These skills also improve a golfer's attitude and help him or her have more fun on the course. These tips will help a golfer enjoy the game more.

- John does an outstanding job of describing the importance of a Pre-Shot Routine and how golfers must immerse themselves in it to maintain a focus on the Shot that they want to hit, rather than the shot that they want to avoid!

- John's scripts for developing confidence and positive mental images are ones that golfers should definitely use to help them perform at their peak during tournaments.

- John does a great job of reminding golfers that their Mental Game skills need to be practiced consistently, just like they need to practice their Golf Swing on a regular basis.

- John superbly describes the Mind-Body Connection and how powerfully a golfer's thoughts (positive or negative) can affect his or her performance. Specifically, John gives many excellent techniques and drills for golfers to lock in their best shots into their subconscious mind and to rid their minds of the negative images caused by bad shots. A Post-Shot Routine to anchor the positives and flush the negatives is critical for any golfer.

- John reminds golfers that they need a Mental Game plan to maintain their poise and confidence when faced with adverse situations and tough course conditions. He reminds them that they have the best chance to succeed if they can control their thoughts, immerse themselves in their pre-shot routines, and remain present and patient during the entire 18 holes.

- John gives important drills and techniques (breathing, progressive relaxation, etc.) to help them release tension and negativity before during, and after a round of golf."

   -- **Ted Sheftic, Owner/Operator, Ted Sheftic Learning Center Golf Magazine Top 100 Teachers, 2003-Present; Golf Digest #1 Teacher in PA, 2000-Present; 3 Time PGA Philadelphia Section Teacher of the Year**

GOLFERS
GUIDE
TO MENTAL FITNESS

Learn More About Mental Fitness for Golf From John Weir, BCH, CI, mNLP

You are personally invited to connect with John Weir online.

Come and get involved on Facebook, Twitter, and YouTube.

Please share your success stories, ask your questions, and discover more about the mental game of golf.

Facebook: www.facebook.com/mentalcaddie

Twitter: www.twitter.com/mentalcaddie

YouTube: www.youtube.com/thementalcaddie

Download a FREE golf hypnosis session by going to www.mentalcaddie.com.

Learn more about private mental coaching by visiting www.mentalgolfacademy.com.

GOLFERS GUIDE

TO MENTAL FITNESS

HOW TO TRAIN YOUR MIND AND
ACHIEVE YOUR GOALS USING
SELF- HYPNOSIS AND VISUALIZATION

John Weir

Mental Golf Academy Press, Orlando, Florida

First Edition --June 2014

ISBN: 069223649X
ISBN-13: 9780692236499

Library of Congress Control Number: 2014910882
Mental Golf Academy Press,
Orlando, Florida

Published in the United States by: Mental Golf Academy Press, Orlando, Florida

www.mentalgolfacademy.com

I dedicate this book to the wonderful woman

in my life, Sevan.

You are my love, my partner, and my best friend.

Since the day we met, you have been my muse behind the scenes

who has provided an endless stream of inspiration,

encouragement, and support.

This dedication is just a small way of saying thank you

for who you are, all you have contributed,

and all you continue to do in my life.

I love you.

CONTENTS

FOREWORD

I first met John Weir through my golf coach. My coach could not understand why I was not achieving more with my golf swing and neither could I. I was open to anything that could make me a better player. John Weir confidently accepted the challenge to help me improve my mental game. I knew it would take some faith and trust but I was eager to do something new. The road to my first professional win was not paved in gold, it had its ups and downs but with faith and trust I knew it would all pay off.

My coach and I were admiring my golf swing on camera the week before I went to a tournament. We just knew that I was going to have a top finish given how good my swing was. I got down to the tournament and had some great practice rounds on a tight golf course and was excited for the event to start. The morning of the event everything was going great, but when I got on the first tee, I sprayed my tee shot way left. I thought "no big deal" but then the next shot went way right. I then proceeded to hit the ball in every direction that day and somehow in the process I lost all confidence in my great golf swing. I lost so much confidence that I was debating if I even knew how to play this game. I proceeded to withdraw and thought that maybe this should be my last event. I had people that I was letting down and maybe the easy thing to do was just get a job. This is the same person that a week ago was admiring how good his golf swing was.

So after a long talk with Ted Frick, my swing coach, he suggested that I talk with John Weir. I knew my golf swing was great, I was working my butt off, and yet I wasn't producing the results. Needless to say, I was extremely frustrated. However, in my heart I knew I was meant to be a professional golfer. My love of the game, my strong desire to get better, and play golf for a living, trumped my pity party that I was having for myself. I knew something had to change and I thought that, just maybe, this John Weir guy could be the answer. I was ready to commit and trust whatever John Weir had to say.

The process took a lot of commitment but something as powerful as learning how to control my mind on the course was surely worth putting a little of my trust and faith into. Not only did my golf game begin to improve as our sessions continued, my life off of the golf course was also slowly changing for the good. The next tournament I entered, I did not magically make the cut but I did see some improvements. So I continued to trust him, and a couple months down the road I started to see some real results. I proceeded to make 5 consecutive professional cuts in a row with every event finishing under par and I even had a stretch where I went 53 holes without a bogey in tournament golf. My game was back, I was excited.

Then I got side tracked and I started working harder on my golf swing and less on what John and I worked on. I was getting a little cocky and it showed. I proceeded to miss 3 cuts in a row and was struggling. I had gotten back in a similar position where I was loving my golf swing but couldn't get results when it counted. I immediately got back in touch with John Weir and we worked on some visualization exercises and getting back into being the master of my mind on the golf course. John Weir helped me make some mental adjustments and then the big week came, the week that put the icing on the cake of me knowing that I can play golf for a living.

I got my first professional win by committing to certain hypnotic techniques that I had put so much energy, faith, and trust into. John Weir knew I was ready, my swing coach Ted Frick knew I was ready. The week started off great. John Weir said to me the night before the first round, "If I told you that if you trusted 100% of everything we talked about, that you would win this tournament, would you do it?" I thought for a brief moment and said, "Absolutely!" So off I went on the journey to trusting and committing 100% to what we worked on. I had the 100% trust before and during practice, but tournament rounds seemed to be different. I hadn't been able to say that I trusted 100% yet, during any point of my season so far. Sometimes I would get to 90%, but I knew that the other 10% of the time, when I didn't trust my techniques was costing me strokes.

That 100% conviction went great for me the first 2 days. I put myself in contention to win my first professional golf tournament heading into the final day. Little did I know, my conviction was about to be put to the test. The final day started with a poised front nine scoring 34 without one blemish of a bogey. However, a quick bogey on the 10th hole jolted me into a sudden reality check. Was I going to be able to keep this spectacular play going? Could I avoid the treacherous water holes to come? Sudden flashes of my old way of thinking started creeping back into my head.

My racing mind had to be quieted and, at that moment, all my training set in. I had to trust 100% of what John and I had worked on. I had to conquer my mind. I knew I was the one that controlled my thoughts. I immediately knew I had to go into a brief self-hypnotic state and utilize what I worked on. I did a relaxation technique, known in this book as the 3-6 method. I immediately felt my racing mind and body begin to slow back down. I used the power of visualization and saw the ball flying down the middle of the fairways and then I saw myself holing out my approach shots.

My confidence was coming back. I kicked that confidence into high gear with some positive self-talk and positive affirmations. In the matter of the 5 minutes between the green on the 10th hole and the tee on the 11th hole something changed within me that my playing partners failed to notice. I had become the master of my mind. I was now committing 100% to my hard work with John, on the golf course, for the first time. I was ready to execute great shots with confidence and win this golf tournament. I had 100% faith and trust that these techniques would work coming down the stretch. I proceeded to birdie 4 of the next 5 holes to catapult me into the lead. It was a lead that I never relinquished. There are defining moments in people's lives, and that was mine. That is a memory I will never forget. I will connect with those emotions and draw off of them the rest of my life.

I am very thankful that I met John and that I am able to be a student of his. I was very excited to hear that he was coming out with a book and I have found the book to be very insightful, educating, and spot on the truth. Yes, you have to trust it and believe in it 100% to get the results that you want. It's not easy to master your mind, but everything in life worth achieving does not come easily.

I can relate with this book and I hope you will enjoy it and learn from it as I have.

Paul Woodbury
PGA Tour Canada

INTRODUCTION

YOUR GUIDE TO MENTAL FITNESS IN GOLF

*"We know so much about technique that
the last frontier in golf is mastering the mind."*

-- Gary Player

It is no mystery that golf is a mental game and the mind plays a pivotal role in peak performance on the golf course. The legends in the game have all come to the realization that success and high level performance on the course stems from positive thought and a strong focused mind.

Bobby Jones once said, "The game of competitive golf is played on a 5 1/2 inch course...that's the space between your ears." Ben Crenshaw also echoed this truth when he said, "I am about 5 inches from being an outstanding golfer. That's the distance my left ear is from my right." Renowned golfer Arnold Palmer said "What separates great players from the good ones is not so much ability as brain power and emotional equilibrium." The thing that unites all the greats in golf is not similarities in their golf swing or putting stroke, but their emphasis and intense focus on the mental side of their game. The historical legends like Byron Nelson, the modern-day superstars like Tiger Woods and the future champions to come, all share the same unique perspective: a positive, disciplined mind is the key to reaching the highest level of success in golf.

Many fall prey to the idea that a positive, disciplined, and focused mind are qualities that some are born with and others are not. There are a lot of golfers that believe the intangible qualities of a champion like mental toughness, the ability to 'will' the ball to their target, and the nerves of steel to execute in the clutch are unique to a select few elite golfers. *The fact is confidence, optimism, mental toughness, and the intangible qualities of a champion are not natural gifts. They are qualities that all the legends have worked on, developed, and cultivated in themselves.* The only difference between them and you is that they discovered how to harness their mental power quicker than most people.

For many decades, the mental game of golf has been an elusive thing for most golfers. Many have read books on golf psychology yet had minimal, if any, results. That is because even some of the books on golf psychology leave out key pieces of information in order to keep the elite golfers elite and the rest of us searching for the missing link that "only they can provide" to bring it all together.

At last, the road map to success is being revealed and in this book you will discover the ins and outs of the most fundamental lessons to developing a solid, positive mental golf game. You are about to learn ***how to harness the tremendous power of your subconscious mind and direct this power to achieve your goals, create higher levels of performance, and lower your score.*** This book goes way beyond just positive thinking and shares with you the secrets to actively taking control of the supercomputer between your ears to produce greater success on the golf course.

THE ***GOLFERS GUIDE TO MENTAL FITNESS*** provides a step by step guide for developing your *total mind* for success in golf. You will learn:

1. The mind-body connection in golf and the results of the latest research on how your thoughts are influencing your performance.

2. How your total mind functions on and off the golf course. This involves understanding both the conscious and subconscious parts of the mind. These two parts of the mind have completely different functions to fulfill in order to play peak performance golf.

3. The science behind the greatest performance secret in the mental side of golf: hypnosis. Finally, you will learn the truth about what hypnosis is, what it is not, and why it is the key to training the subconscious mind to improve your golf game.

4. The keys of effective communication to program your mind using affirmations and autosuggestion. You will also discover the best times of the day to use these tools for increased receptivity and acceptance of the suggestions.

5. Relaxation training to eliminate harbored tension in your body to swing your best and manage your mental game and emotional state on the golf course.

6. How to focus your mind for greater execution on every shot and perform without conscious effort.

7. Mental fitness exercises to improve performance and goal achievement including mental rehearsal, visualization, anchoring, conditioning and more.

In addition to all the above, you will learn the most effective ways to do self-hypnosis to accelerate the learning process, enhance the effectiveness of mental fitness exercises and, most importantly, lower your score. You will learn how to apply self-hypnosis to do positive mental programming and train your mind off the course as well as on course applications to keep you consistently performing in the zone.

This book follows the K.I.S.S. model which stands for "Keep It Super Simple" so that it is easy for any golfer to implement these techniques immediately and effectively. The goal of the ***GOLFERS GUIDE TO MENTAL FITNESS*** is to provide golfers a way to enhance their mental golf game all on their own by educating you on the mind and teaching you the process of self-hypnosis in as simple a fashion as possible. In the pages that follow, you will find nothing but straight forward information on self-hypnosis, the mental game of golf, and how to use your mind to achieve peak performance, without any fluff or needless information.

It is important to note this book is not intended to replace or eliminate physical practice from the road to developing the skills to succeed on the golf course. Peak performance comes from the combination of physical skills and a strong mind. Just about every golfer knows the importance of physical practice and developing the proper technique to execute on the course, yet very few have incorporated mental training into the mix.

The **GOLFERS GUIDE TO MENTAL FITNESS** was written to fill this void in golf improvement and provide you a guide for mental development. Regardless of your skill level, the mind must be developed if you want to take your golf game to the next level. Your mind is just like any other muscle -- it requires exercise to get stronger. **Neglecting the mental aspects of the game and focusing solely on physical development is a surefire way to stay at the skill level you are at, stuck at the same handicap, and only perform in the zone on random days.**

However, cultivating the skill of self-hypnosis and learning how to maximize your subconscious mind will help you breakthrough the old mental barriers that are preventing your best from consistently being released on the golf course. Mental training is essential for every golfer, not just the professionals, because the mind is involved in every shot on the golf course and at the range. When you know how to operate your mind, like you know how to swing a golf club, your performance immediately and steadily improves.

The information shared in this book reveals the ultimate secret in the mental development of the elite golfers and *NOW* it is available to you. *When the information in this book is applied and developed, you will find it to be the golden ticket to the zone and ongoing success in golf.*

You are reading the **GOLFERS GUIDE TO MENTAL FITNESS** because you are ready for a breakthrough in your game and, finally, you have found what you have been searching for. Commit to the techniques, apply them in your golf game, and enjoy the satisfaction that comes with better results and higher levels of performance.

Get ready to discover the greatest secret in the mental game of golf. Enjoy the book and harness the power between your ears to be the best golfer you can be. Your true potential awaits. The journey of empowerment begins now.

ONE

THE MIND-BODY CONNECTION IN GOLF

"Golf is a science, the study of a lifetime, in which you can exhaust yourself but never your subject."

-- David R. Forgan

Let's begin this journey into mental empowerment by first exploring the mind-body connection in golf to learn more about the mind's role in performance. To the unknowing golfer, the thoughts we have on the course are random and meaningless. Many golfers believe performance is simply all about the swing and neglect the power and the role of their thoughts. This is one of the main reasons why so many golfers stay stuck in their current skill level and have performance capped by their handicap, even though they may spend hours every week practicing, but without any improvements.

However, you will see a different trend the higher up you go in skill level. The elite golfers are all well aware of their mind's influence on their swing and putting performance as well as on their overall results. Because of his awareness, the majority of the elite golfers actively work with professionals to help them strengthen their mental game to harness the power of their mind on every shot and throughout the entire round.

The elite golfers realize that it is impossible to separate the mind from performance because it is our minds that are directing the body on how to perform and produce the results we want to achieve. One thing that makes golf such a special game is that every shot we take clearly reflects the pictures and thoughts we are holding in our minds.

In this chapter, we are going to explore research in the mind-body connection in the game of golf to provide evidence of the mind's influence on performance. Then we will conclude this chapter with a few simple exercises that will give you a personal experience and demonstrate the mind's impact on the body.

In 2012, I had the privilege of conducting an interview with one of Golf Magazine's Top 100 PGA Instructors, Dr. David Wright.[1] During the interview, Dr. Wright made a simple yet profound comment:

"All golfers think in pictures."

For example, every golfer has tee boxes, that regardless of how poorly they are playing, they stripe the tee shot with confidence and perform at a high level. There are also tee boxes that no matter how great we are playing, the moment we get on the tee box we feel timid, tentative, or even fearful of the result. ***The reason this occurs is due to the pictures in the mind and it is these pictures that dictate what the body will do.*** The pictures and visualizations that are maintained in the mind during performance, play a major role in the execution of every shot that we take.

In the interview, Dr. Wright said that according to the Brain Imaging Center in San Antonio, Texas when we visualize, we create up to 80% of the neural pathways needed to perform a task.[2] *Another way of saying this is when you maintain positive outcome images and visualize your success, you are 80% of the way to achieving the goal. However, when you are holding onto negative pictures or visualizations of your performance, you are 80% of the way to achieving that negative result.*

Dr. Kay Porter and Judy Foster, authors of *Visual Athletics* wrote:

> "The reason visual imagery works lies in the fact that when you imagine yourself performing to perfection and doing precisely what you want, you are in turn physiologically creating neural patterns in your brain, just as if you had physical performed the action. These patterns are similar to small tracks engraved in the brain cells that can ultimately enable an athlete to perform physical feats by simply mentally practicing the move. Hence,

mental imagery is intended to train our minds and create the neural patterns in our brain to teach our muscles to do exactly what we want them to do."[3]

Jon Finn, PGA tutor and one of the developers of the Golf Psychology Programme in Great Britain, had this to say about mental imagery:

> "When we make a movement, such as hitting a golf ball, specific areas of our brain are activated. Research evidence suggests that when we imagine making a movement, very similar areas of our brain are also activated as when actually making a movement. The idea that similar brain areas are activated when physically executing a skill and imagining physically executing a similar skill is termed shared neural circuitry. If, by generating images in our minds, we can access similar areas of the brain as when we physically execute a movement, imagery can be a very diverse and powerful tool that can be used to facilitate skill acquisition and motivation in golfers."[4]

Visualization and the Mind-Body Connection

Researchers at the Olympic Training Center in Colorado Springs, Colorado put visualization to the test. They wanted to find out how visualization affected putting performance. So here is what they did. They took 30 college-aged golfers and divided the golfers into 3 groups. The golfers were told to practice putting each day for a week. The first group was the control group and they were instructed to practice physically putting, but without any visualization instruction. The second group was instructed to practice physically putting *and* to also visualize sinking the putt before putting the ball. The visualization process they were instructed to do was to mentally rehearse the entire putt. They visualized the backswing, the stroke through the ball, the ball rolling into the center of the cup, and dropping in at the perfect speed. After visualizing a successful putting sequence, they then took their putt. The third group also was instructed to practice physically putting and to visualize the putt, *but with one twist.* They were instructed to visualize *missing* the putt before putting the ball. This group was instructed to visualize things like the ball going left, going right, stopping before the hole, or just missing the cup. The results were quite eye opening. Group 1 that did the physical practice alone improved in their accuracy after the week by 11%. Group 2 that did the physical practice combined with a visualization sequence of success, improved in accuracy by over 30%. Group 3 that did the physical practice, but visualized missing the putt, declined in accuracy by 21%.[5]

Researchers from Rutgers and Princeton Universities also replicated this study and reported: "Analysis showed that there were significant differences among all groups, with the positive imagery group producing the most improvement, the control condition producing less, and negative imagery results showed performance deterioration."[6]

The psychology department of the University of Central Lancashire in the United Kingdom also studied the effects of outcome imagery in golfer's putting performance. After testing 25 unskilled and 26 skilled golfers, the researchers concluded that the depiction of negative imagery had detrimental effects on putting performance of both types of golfers. They also presented evidence that positive outcome imagery influences performance in a positive way through elevated confidence.[7]

These studies confirm the simple truth of Dr. David Wright –golfers think in pictures and these pictures impact the level of our performance.

Annie Plessinger of Vanderbilt University Psychology Department also echoed these truths in her research on mental imagery and visualization. She reported, "Visual imagery seems to be beneficial to anyone who wants to improve at their sport. Whether you are a recreational athlete or a professional does not matter. The benefits of mental imagery have proven successful at any level." She goes on to say:

> "Virtually all studies show that mental training improves motor skills. More recently, many studies go even further and provide evidence that mental imagery can improve various skills related to sports in actual field context. So if you are a professional looking to break into the top, or an amateur golfer who simply wants to play with his or her friends and win, I recommend incorporating mental imagery along with practice. Not only can mental imagery improve motor skills, it also seems to enhance motivation, mental toughness, and confidence, all of which will help you elevate your level of play."[8]

A 1995 study published in the Journal of Sport and Exercise Psychology also reported similar results as Annie Plessinger's in regards to mental imagery increasing motivation in athletes. The researchers of this study wanted to discover who would spend more time practicing a putting drill. They divided 39 beginner golfers into two groups. The imagery group and the control group. Each group was taught how to putt in 3 sessions. In addition, the imagery group did mental imagery training related to the specific task in their instruction. The results of this study revealed that the imagery group spent significantly more time practicing the putting drill which showed higher levels of intrinsic motivation, or being self-motivated. Plus, the imagery group had more realistic self-expectations, set higher goals to achieve, and continued to do more of the training exercises outside of the experimental setting.[9]

When you take the time to visualize on and off the golf course, these experiences are firing off responses in the body that are the same as actual performance. And according to the above research, visualization is also strengthening the neural pathways in the brain to give you the ability to execute in that same fashion in the future.

This is just a small sample of the hundreds of studies that validate the mind-body connection and prove the effectiveness of mental training techniques such as visualization, mental imagery, mental rehearsal, and others.

Inspirational Insights from the Golf Greats

The greats in the game of golf know the power of the mind-body connection, mental imagery, and visualization. In their own words:

- Byron Nelson said," You can will something to happen, with your body and with your mind. The mind is that strong. You can say, 'I want to get this close to the hole.' **That's when the mind comes in. The mind has to produce positive thinking. All the great players do that."**

- Chi Chi Rodriguez said, "I think good putters see the ball going in, bad putters see the ball staying out."

- Amy Alcott said, "Golf is a spiritual game. It's like Zen; you have to let your mind take over."

- Butch Harmon said, "The biggest strength of Tiger Woods you can't see. It's his mind."

- Ken Venturi said, "After you get the basics down, it's all mental."

- Arnold Palmer said, "Golf is a game of inches. The most important are between the ears."

- Ray Floyd said, "I honestly believe that with a strong mind, you can literally will the ball into the hole."

- David Duval said, "Once you're on the Tour, the mental part of the game is 85-90 percent."

- Lee Trevino said, "I think your mind has a lot to do with the game, even more than practicing. Sure, you've got to practice until you learn all the fundamentals, but if you've been playing golf as long as I have, it's not the practice anymore, and it's the mind."

- Tiger Woods said, "The biggest thing is to have the mind-set and the belief you can win every tournament going on. A lot of guys don't have that; Nicklaus had it. He felt he was going to beat everybody."

For decades, Jack Nicklaus has shared his story about how he would visualize his success. Nicklaus talked about how he would visualize every aspect of his game before stepping on the first tee. He would visualize the entire swing, the trajectory of the ball in flight, and its bounce and roll on the green. According to Nicklaus, 40 percent of his game is the proper set up and proper stance; another 10 percent of his success comes from his swing; and the remaining 50 percent is the psychological and mental side of the game. Nicklaus said that the mental side of his game was like "going to the movies." Jack Nicklaus was also quoted saying:

> "I never hit a shot, not even in practice, without having a very sharp, in-focus picture of it in my head. First, I see the ball where I want it to finish nice and white and sitting up high on the bright green grass. Then the scene quickly changes, and I see the ball going there: its path, trajectory, and shape, even its behavior on landing. Then there is a sort of fade-out, and the next scene shows me making the kind of swing that will turn the previous images into reality."[10]

Some pros also provide insight into the negative power of the mind and mental imagery.

- Sam Snead said, "Of all the hazards, fear is the worst."

- Michelle Wie said, "If you expect a bad lie, even for a second, the gods will know it and give you a bad lie."

- Sergio Garcia said, "If you worry about making bogeys, it makes the game that much more difficult. You put more pressure on yourself without even noticing it."

- Greg Norman once said, "When you golf good, your mind is great. When you golf bad, your mind is terrible."

- Tommy Bolt revealed a powerful truth when he said, "The mind messes up more shots than the body."

- Bobby Locke was quoted saying, "Approaching a putt with doubt in your mind is nearly always fatal."

- Walter Hagen said, "If you worry about the ones you missed, you are going to keep missing them."

- Tom Murphy said "Let's face it, 95 percent of this game is mental. If a guy plays lousy golf he doesn't need a pro, he needs a shrink."

- Norman Von Nida gives great advice in his quote, "Never berate yourself on the golf course. It has disastrous results. Be your best friend out on the fairways. Staying positive can only do great things for your game."

- Dave Stockton Jr. echoed Von Nida's advice when he said, "Never blame yourself. Tour players realize it, and it's why they tamp down imaginary spike marks after missing short putts. Blaming outside agencies for a bad shot is much better for your frame of mind than telling yourself you're a lousy hack."

The True Story of Colonel George Hall

Perhaps the greatest example of the power of the mind and its role in peak performance comes from the true story of United States Air Force Pilot, Colonel George Hall. During a combat mission over North Vietnam, Colonel Hall's aircraft was struck by an enemy missile forcing him to eject from his aircraft. Colonel Hall was captured by the North Vietnamese, thrown into solitary confinement, and forced to endure the horrendous conditions of 'the hole' for 7 years. As a prisoner of war, Colonel Hall experienced regular torture treatments, had to survive off of rotten foods, and almost starved from the meager portions. In addition to all of this, Colonel Hall was beaten so badly that he couldn't straighten his arm for the first 5 years in solitary confinement.

Life under these conditions couldn't get any worse. To survive it all, Colonel Hall used the power of his mind to escape the reality of being a P.O.W. and he would vividly imagine playing golf on his favorite course in California. As he escaped into his mind, Colonel Hall would imagine everything in the greatest detail. He visualized the sights, the sounds, smells, and the feel of being on the golf course. Colonel Hall drove the ball, hit approach shots, he chipped, and putted. He would play every shot and every hole in his mind each day. This visualization of playing golf at his favorite course was Hall's only escape from this dark reality and each day he got more and more into the experience.

Several weeks after his release, weighing in at only 105 pounds and needing two canes to walk around, Colonel Hall insisted on playing golf in a pro-am tournament at his favorite California golf course. During his round, he walked the entire course with both canes and after 7 years of solitary confinement, Colonel Hall finished his round at 3 over par which was one of the best rounds of his life! When asked how he did it, Colonel Hall laughed as he said, "I've played that course over 3,000 times in my head and 3 over par was one of my worst scores."

Now that is the tremendous power of the mind and visualization.

Exercises for You to Experience the Mind-Body Connection

Now that you are more aware of the power of thoughts and mental imagery on the course, let's do some simple exercises so you can have a first-hand experience of the mind-body connection. Every thought that you have affects the body and creates a psychosomatic response.[11]

Chevreul's Pendulum Exercise

One exercise that demonstrates this is called Chevreul's Pendulum Experiment.[12] In order to do this exercise you will need a pendulum and a sheet of paper with a big circle on it with a vertical and a horizontal line intersecting in the middle. (See Appendix I). If you don't have a pendulum then anything on a string will do. To make one, all you will need is a shoe lace, and either a ring, washer, or key. Take the shoe lace, put the ring or washer through it, and you are good to go. You can also do a YouTube search on making a pendulum to discover other ways if this is unsuccessful.

There are four simple steps:

> **Step One:** Place the circular chart from the appendix on a flat surface. Hold the pendulum loosely in your hand, and let it dangle over the center of the circle at the intersection point of the lines. For this exercise to work, simply allow things to happen without helping it or preventing it on your part.

> **Step Two**: Without moving your hand, begin to visualize and imagine with your mind's eye the pendulum moving up and down the vertical line. Imagine as vividly as you can the pendulum moving up and down, up and down, up and down the vertical line. The more you imagine the movement of the pendulum in your mind's eye, the more the pendulum will begin to move up and down along the line. Imagine it going faster and faster and moving further up and down the line, and watch as the pendulum moves all on its own.

> **Step Three**: Bring the pendulum back to rest at the middle of the circle again, and then do the same as before, but this time visualize the pendulum moving left to right along the horizontal line. Visualize that pendulum going left and right, right and left, back and forth along that line. The more you concentrate and visualize the more the pendulum will swing left to right. Imagine the pendulum is extending beyond the circle and notice how much the pendulum moves.

> **Step Four:** Again bring the pendulum back to rest at the middle of the circle, and this time begin to visualize the pendulum swinging around the outer circle. Using the power of your mind, visualize and imagine the pendulum spinning round and round the circle. Just concentrate in your mind on seeing that pendulum spinning and spinning, getting faster and faster going around the circle. The more you concentrate, the more movement the pendulum creates.

This simple experiment, when done correctly, powerfully demonstrates how the mind influences the body. So what makes the pendulum move during this experiment? Is it some mystical force or the power of intention? Not likely. The reason the pendulum moves, seemingly on its own, is due to psychosomatic responses taking place. If you breakdown the word psychosomatic into its root words, you get psyche which is the mind, and soma, which is the body. A psychosomatic response relates to the effects of the mind on the body, and how the thoughts held in the mind create physical responses in the muscle movements of the body. While you imagine the pendulum moving in your mind, this is sending signals through the body, and subtly influences the micro muscles of the body to responding in alignment with the thoughts.

If you are having trouble with this exercise or want to see it in action to help you do it correctly then please visit my YouTube channel at www.youtube.com/thementalcaddie to see a video demonstration of the Chevreul's Pendulum Experiment.

The Lemon Test Exercise

Another exercise that you can do to demonstrate the power of your thoughts on the body is called the "Lemon Test." This exercise works best when your eyes are closed, but can also be done if you really use your imagination as you read these instructions:

> *Take a deep breath in. Now, clear your mind, and relax. As vividly as possible, imagine being in your kitchen and think about all the details of this room. Vividly imagine walking over to your refrigerator now. Imagine what it would feel like to grab the door handle, and open the refrigerator door. Imagine what the refrigerator looks like, feel the cool air coming from the open door, and hear the sound of the hum coming from the refrigerator.*

> *Vividly imagine everything as real as possible. As you look inside the refrigerator, visualize a bright yellow, juicy, ripe, super sour lemon. Imagine picking up the lemon now, taking out a knife, and cutting this juicy, sour lemon in half. As the knife blade cuts into the juicy, sour, ripe, and tart lemon, imagine the sour juices trickling down the knife blade and as it does smell the super sour aroma of the lemon filling the air.*

Now very slowly, take one of the pieces of that sour, juicy lemon and imagine bringing it towards your mouth. This lemon is so ripe, juicy, and sour that you anticipate the feeling of biting into one of the tartest, sourest lemons in the world. As the lemon gets closer to your mouth, you can feel your mouth beginning to water in anticipation of how sour the lemon is.

Now vividly imagine biting into that sour, tart, juicy, ripe lemon. Really experience what it would be like to bite the most sour lemon in the world, and as you do you can feel the sourness tightening your jaws and puckering up your face.

Now imagine taking another big bite of that sour, juicy, tart lemon and your jaws tighten even more and your mouth waters. Take one more big juicy, sour bite and notice what is happening to your body as you do.

If you let yourself get into the last exercise and really imagined biting into a sour lemon, then chances are you felt your mouth watering, your jaws tightening, and your face puckering simply through the thought of eating a lemon.

Everyday Examples

An everyday example that is similar to the Lemon Test described above is when you see flashing red and blue lights in your rearview mirror. Just seeing those lights immediately causes your heart rate to speed up, your muscles to tense, and your breathing to become short and fast. Even if the police car speeds past you, just the thought of getting pulled over created instant changes in your physical body.

The same thing occurs when you go to a restaurant and you are super hungry. Just the sight of the food on the menu causes your mouth to water and the stomach to feel empty. Other examples include waking up from a nightmare and finding yourself breathing fast, covered in sweat, and anxious because of the dream.

One last everyday example of psychosomatic responses is watching a movie. Everybody knows movies are fake. They are scripted, actors play the roles, and it is just images projected on a screen. However, as the lights go down and we get lost into the storyline we forget about the actors and the scripts, and we get actively involved in the story. This causes the body to physically react to the images that are flooding into our minds. Even though we know it's just a movie, the thoughts and images cause us to cry, get excited, anxious, inspired, or even scared, and our physical bodies respond accordingly. After watching a scary movie, many people find their mind playing tricks on them and the slightest sound can bring forth the same anxious, fearful feeling conjured up from the movie they just watched.

These are all examples of how thoughts effect the body, and the same things occur on the golf course. The thoughts you maintain about your swing, your shot, or your results are all influencing your physical body in subtle as well as in very obvious ways during performance.

It is clear from the above research that the mind plays a major role in determining the level of performance all golfers will experience. The information found in this chapter is just the tip of the iceberg into the mind-body connection in golf. With greater emphasis placed all the time on developing the mental side of the game, we can expect an ever increasing level of performance in the game of golf as golfers discover more ways to tap into the true potential of the mind.

TWO

THE TRUTH ABOUT HYPNOSIS

"For this game you need, above all things, to be in a tranquil frame of mind."

-Harry Vardon

Hypnosis is a powerful tool that can help anybody create immediate improvements and long lasting changes in their life more easily and effortlessly than through traditional methods. However, hypnosis is not being utilized nearly enough by most people because it is still one of the most misunderstood subjects in history. In order to make the best use of this extraordinary tool, it is necessary to understand the truth about *what hypnosis really is – and – what it is not.* This chapter is devoted to explaining this truth about hypnosis so that you can understand what it is, how it works, and why it is so beneficial for developing the mental skills of a champion.

In this chapter I reveal the technical side of hypnosis and in the next chapter we will explore how this information relates specifically to golf.

For now, let go of all preconceived notions you may have about hypnosis so you can finally discover the truth and fully appreciate how hypnosis can transform your golf game and your life.

For many decades, Hollywood, the media, and fiction writers have portrayed hypnosis in outlandish and over-exaggerated ways. As a result many people maintain misconceptions about what hypnosis is and how it works.

The easiest way to start a discussion on hypnosis is to begin by saying what it is not.

- Hypnosis is not related to the supernatural, metaphysical, mystical, or magical.

- It has nothing to do with religion, religious practices, or the false superstitions associated with hypnosis.

- Hypnosis is not mind control, brainwashing, or mental manipulation.

- Hypnotized people do not go unconscious, drift off into an alternate universe, or lose touch with their sense of reality.

- Nobody has ever been stuck in hypnosis, nor is it a possibility.

- Hypnosis doesn't make people reveal secrets, it is not a truth serum, and nobody can be made to do things against their will.

Everything that you have seen about hypnosis in the movies, on TV, or read in the strange stories are false. Hypnotists don't have special powers, and they certainly can't control an individual by putting them under some sort of hypnotic spell.

Hypnosis is actually psychology in action, deeply rooted in the science of the human mind, and is a communication process that can help people make the most of the mind's true potential.

The Two Parts of the Mind

To understand how hypnosis works it is necessary to understand the functions of the two parts of your mind: the conscious and subconscious.

<u>The conscious mind</u> is what you are using right now, and the part of the mind you use when you are in a fully alert, waking state of consciousness. Activities of the conscious mind are closely correlated with left hemisphere brain functions which include things like critical thinking, reason, analysis, and logical thinking.

The primary function of the conscious mind is to filter the information you are presented with all day long from yourself and the outside world to determine if it is good or bad, right or wrong, something you like or not, and so on.

This part of the mind is great at helping you to refine your choice in life, assist you in determining what you can do better, what to change or improve, and what is working in your life and what isn't. While it is excellent at pointing out what you should be doing, it doesn't have the power to put it all into action.

The subconscious mind _is your inborn "bio-computer" that runs the show behind the scenes. Perhaps the most important thing to understand about the subconscious mind is it operates exactly like a hard drive of a computer._ A computer accepts information non-critically and simply supports the programs found on the hard drive indiscriminately. If you enter into a computer information like, "the world is flat," "the sky is green and the grass is purple," or any other ludicrous thought like this, the computer will simply accept the information and believe it to be true.

In my opinion, one of the best metaphors for describing the differences between the two primary functions of the conscious and subconscious mind comes from John K. Williams in his book, *The Knack of Using Your Subconscious Mind.* Williams says:

> *"The subconscious mind works creatively upon whatever it is given by the conscious mind. Its nature is set and immutable. In the conscious aspect of personality we have spontaneous choice, volition, and originating action. In the subconscious, because of its nature, we have automatic reaction. The conscious mind is personal, while the subconscious mind is entirely impersonal.*
>
> *Every person who has ever cultivated a garden should understand the two-fold aspect of mind, and the law under which it operates. The conscious mind plants the seed in the soil. It decides what kind of seed it will plant. The soil will, by the law of its being, germinate and nourish whatever is planted -- roses or potatoes.*
>
> *The subconscious mind is the soil, the medium, which by its nature, contains the elements necessary for birth and growth. By the law of it's being,*

the subconscious mind will create and produce anything called for by the conscious mind. It is the nature of the soil to bring forth, but it is not interested in what it brings forth. It does not know if the plant will bear strawberries or tomatoes. The whole economy and the universe would be disturbed and destroyed should the soil not act according to its nature.

The same is true of the subconscious mind. It is a 'doer,' not a 'knower'. It is intelligent without knowing, and conscious only of its purpose and nature, but it is never self-conscious."[1]

Besides operating like a computer hard drive, the subconscious mind has other important functions that help us get through our days with little effort on our part. One of these functions is running the physical body. The subconscious mind is the body's control center where it directs and regulates all bodily functions. It controls things like your heart beat, your breathing, the blood flow through the body, muscle movements, and all internal processes of the organs and bodily systems. Since it is the control center of the body, hypnosis which gives you access to the subconscious, can be used to alter bodily functions, control automatic responses of the body, and even promote self-healing. Learning how to tap into the subconscious mind can be very useful for golfers who wish to control the body in high pressure situations, calm the nerves, and maintain a state of peace in the body during performance.

Another function of the subconscious mind is it is the storehouse of all your memories and contains a detailed memory of all events and experiences in life as well as all the things you have been exposed to. It is like an unlimited filing cabinet between our ears that has all of your experiences stored there, real or imagined. While most of this information is suppressed during the day while you are in your normal waking state, when a person is hypnotized they can access this information easily and without effort.

Hypnotists commonly use a process called "Age Regression" to help their clients discover root causes of their problems and help them overcome their mental blocks impeding their success. While hypnotized and the subconscious mind fully available, the recall ability of clients is truly astonishing. The vast majority are able to relive and re-experience as if it was real again, including events from early childhood that made impressions and shaped their life and possibly their golf game.

You have probably had a natural experience of age regression in your everyday life. One common example is hearing a song come on the radio and it instantly transports you back in time to the experience linked to that familiar song. It might remind you of your wedding, an exciting time with friends, a great travel experience, or even of a negative relationship or event in your life. As you listen to the song, you relive the memories vividly and clearly without any conscious effort on your part. The meaningful song triggered the memory stored in the subconscious and you spontaneously respond in the exact same way you did during the memory. If this occurs with a song, think about what is happening out on the golf course at the subconscious level.

The Subconscious Mind: Habits and Self-Image

The subconscious is not just the storehouse of memories, it also stores all of your habits. There are three types of habits; good ones, bad ones, and utilitarian (which are habits connected with day-to-day living such as how to open doors, start your car, brush your teeth, and so on). The subconscious mind thrives off of habits because the mind is inherently lazy and doesn't want to waste energy trying to figure everything out each day. Imagine how daunting a task it would be if every morning you woke up you had to relearn things like your personality as well as the traits and behaviors that make you who you are. It would take an enormous amount of energy to do this, and in an effort to conserve energy, the subconscious mind forms habits and runs off of them throughout the day.

To reiterate the first point about the subconscious, it will support any habit and doesn't discern the difference between good or bad, or whether the behavior is supportive or destructive. All habits are simply mental programs to the subconscious mind and it can only run on what it has been programmed to know. The conscious mind can analyze your thoughts, emotions, and behaviors to determine if these habits are good or not, but the subconscious just supports the data and works to fulfill what it knows every day. Through hypnosis, you can access your database of habits and strengthen the positive habits as well as delete or modify the negative ones.

The other element of the subconscious mind, which is of great importance, is it maintains the self-image. The self-image is a collection of your memories, traits, behaviors, as well as the things that you have consistently said to yourself and the things you have heard from other people that you believed to be true. All of these things get mixed together to form your self-image or the mental construct of who and what you are. Just like with habits, your subconscious mind will accept any self-image, positive or negative, and will actively work around the clock to support this self-concept to make sure all requirements that define who you are, are achieved each day.

Again, the subconscious can only support what it knows, since it is simply adheres to the data contained in the hard drive. As previously mentioned, it does this to conserve energy so your conscious mind is freed up to be aware of and interact with the people and things that surface in your daily life. If you aren't happy with what you have been producing in life or in the way you feel day-to-day, then the chances are it is a self-image issue. The great thing is you can improve or change the self-image through consistent positive self-talk as well as through hypnosis. By programming the mind to have a new concept of the self, it will work to fulfill these new requirements and actively work to make the new self-image right. When the self-image is corrected then spontaneous changes take place effortlessly due to the new programs in the hard drive and new information for the subconscious mind to support.

In the game of golf, one of the ways the self-image influences performance is through the idea of a handicap. A handicap is the golf version of the self-image which governs performance, and dictates score.

Have you ever wondered why you consistently shoot your handicap on the course? This is due to the subconscious making the image of the self correct. The first step to producing better results on the golf course is to abandon the whole notion of a handicap in efforts to free up your subconscious mind to create a new self-image of the golfer you wish to be. When you do you this, you will release the lid capping your performance, you will cross new thresholds in your game, and you will finally start lowering your score. (See Appendix II for a bonus article on the limitations a handicap puts on performance.)

The great motivator, Zig Ziglar, has said "Change the picture and change your life." He is talking about the self-image and how by changing the picture, your entire life will change.

If it was that easy then why don't more people live the life of their dreams? The reason people struggle to change the picture is because they are using the wrong part of their mind to make the changes.

The typical adult tries to make changes using their conscious mind which is designed to analyze the situation and tell you what you "should" do, but it can't implement these changes long-term. Some people are able to employ their will power for a period of time, but find it only produces temporary results even though it required a tremendous amount of energy, effort, strain, and force. Will power, which is a function of the conscious mind, isn't designed for creating long-term behavioral changes. The reason for this is simple; will power is just like adrenaline. Adrenaline is meant for short bursts of intense physical energy and strength to get through a physically demanding event. However, the power of adrenaline can't be sustained for long periods of time and typically goes away as fast as it comes on. Will power works in the same way, but in mental and emotional energy to get through a difficult mental/emotional situation, like when a person is battling a craving of some sort or has to deal with a high pressure situation on the course. Will power can get you through the moment or the day, but over time, the strength of the will power continuously decreases and eventually evaporates in that particular regard. When this occurs a person feels stuck.

The other reason why will power wasn't meant to change human behavior can be explained by a psychological law:

> *"This law states that when the will and the imagination come into conflict, the imagination will inevitably win."*[2]

> *"The imagination is a function of the subconscious mind which has creative power and it is infinitely more powerful than the will."* [3]

How Hypnosis Works

So how do you change the picture and the mental programs that reside in the subconscious mind? The answer is hypnosis, which isn't a state of mind, but a communication process that gives you access to the super computer between your ears.

Your brain runs off of and emits electrical energy just like other computers, and by slowing down the electrical currents you can access more parts of the mind and maximize the power of your brain to achieve more of your goals. Through the use of an electroencephalography, or EEG, researchers were able to measure these electrical currents in the brain. These electrical currents are measured in Hertz (Hz) or cycles per second. Experts have concluded that the human brain has 4 predominate brainwaves it oscillates or cycles through naturally every day. These brainwaves are called Beta, Alpha, Theta, and Delta.[4]

Beta 13 Hz- 30 Hz (or cycles per second): Beta brainwaves are the dominate brain waves experienced by the mature adult mind. These waves are associated with attentiveness, alertness, selective attention, concentration, and anticipation. Beta waves are related to left hemisphere activity such as critical thinking, reason, logic, analysis, and concentrated mental activities like mathematical problems. If you are fully alert and awake right now, then your mind is operating in Beta brainwaves.

Alpha 7 Hz - 13 Hz: Alpha brainwaves are connected to relaxed attentiveness and wakefulness, as well as daydreaming. In this state of relaxed awareness, the brain-waves slow down and activate more right hemisphere activity such as creative think-ing, inspiration, imagination, and other creative functions. Alpha waves are commonly considered the brainwaves of guided meditation, yoga, and light hypnosis. In sports, alpha waves are associated with the zone and peak performance. While in the zone, the athlete is in a state of relaxed concentration and engrossed in the present moment which gives them the ability to perform in their sport without conscious effort.

Theta 4 Hz- 7 Hz: Theta brainwaves are associated with deep meditation, deep hypnosis, lucid dreaming, and light sleep. Sleep researchers describe the theta state as stage 1 or the twilight stage. In this state, the mind passes through alpha waves and into theta waves which allows the person to lose their sense of lying in bed and their physical surroundings while still being awake. Many great thinkers and artists give credit to this state of mind for bringing about creative solutions and inspiration for their work. While in theta, the subconscious is at the forefront and makes it the ideal state for positive mental programming.

Delta 0.5 Hz - 4 Hz: Delta brainwaves are connected with deep, dreamless sleep. The deeper the sleep the higher the amount of delta waves. In this state, all of your attention is diffused and it is all unconscious mental activity at work in the mind.

Dr. Philip Holt and other researchers from Emory University School of Medicine used EEG's to monitor the electrical brainwave activity through the various stages of mental development. What they found was that the brain of a child, ages 1 month to 6 years old, operates primarily in theta waves when they are fully awake. As the child matures into adolescences, the dominate brainwaves begin to speed up into alpha, which is still a highly suggestible state of mind, and it stays this way until around 19 years old. As the mind matures and becomes fully developed, the dominate brainwave for an adult becomes beta brainwaves which are the fastest in speed but becomes limited to the functions of the conscious mind previously mentioned. Alpha waves typically occur in the adult mind when their eyes are closed and physically relaxed, but it is not as dominate brainwave as in the case of a child's mind when the brain reaches its full maturity.[5] (See Appendix III for more research on brainwave development from Emory University.)

Every day of your life, you experience alterations in your brainwaves a minimum of 7-10 times a day. For example, every morning when you wake up, your brain goes from delta (deep sleep) to theta then to alpha, and finally beta once you fully wake up. The opposite occurs when you are falling asleep: you go from a full waking state of beta and as you relax you enter into alpha waves, then to theta and, finally, delta when you are deep asleep. Other times that you experience a change in your brainwaves and enter into alpha and theta waves include driving your car on autopilot (highway hypnosis), getting lost in a great book, crying during a movie, getting a massage, relaxing by the beach, and so on. Every human being, without exception, experiences these different brainwaves. However, very few people know how to make use of these various states of mind in order to accelerate learning, change behaviors, or make positive improvements in any area of life.

Research using EEG's has shown that the electrical currents (brainwaves) in the mind during hypnosis are the same as meditation, deep prayer states, lucid dreaming, deep relaxation, and so on. All of these mental states are the same in their essence which are alpha and theta brainwaves, but each method achieves these states and makes use of these brainwaves differently. *For example, what separates hypnosis from meditation, is not the state of mind, which is the same, but how the state of mind is achieved and is being used.* Since hypnosis is deliberately using alpha and theta states to elicit changes in behavior and accelerate learning, it is easy to understand that hypnosis is a communication process that takes place while in these naturally occurring brainwaves.

Hypnosis is a Powerful Communication Process

It is important to understand that hypnosis is *not* a state of mind, but a powerful communication process that has three distinct purposes.

- **First**, to deliberately slow down the brainwaves to alpha and theta through suggestions for physical and mental relaxation.

- **Second**, to use suggestions to maintain these brainwave states in order to utilize more mental resources and functions not normally accessible while in a full waking state, or beta brainwaves.

- **Finally**, to communicate positive new suggestions and ideas to the subconscious mind while in this receptive state to accelerate learning.

Why do people struggle to make changes? People struggle to make changes because they are using the wrong part of the mind for long term change and they have lost touch with how they learn. As a result, most people stay stuck acting out old patterns of behavior, thought, and emotion. The majority of our learning takes place during our childhood and includes amazing feats such as language development, and the ability to read and write. During this time as a child, our brains oscillate between alpha and theta brainwaves. These are the super learning states of mind in which our brains are able to learn, process, and assimilate information without conscious effort.

However, as we become adults our primary brainwaves shift from alpha to beta brainwaves which are short, rapid brainwaves that activate left hemisphere activity in the brain like critical thinking. The job of these analytical functions is to judge, analyze, critique, rationalize, justify, etc., all the things we are experiencing internally and externally.

Why people struggle to change is because when they are presented with new information, the adult mind receives it through the conscious mind while in beta brainwaves, or a full waking state. Since the person's brain is operating in beta, the new information is analyzed and filtered, instead of simply being accepted and acted on. A child on the other hand, receives new information while the brain is oscillating between alpha and theta brainwaves. When the child's mind receives information, it goes directly into the creative functions of the subconscious mind, it's absorbed, processed, and acted upon by the subconscious without conscious effort or analysis.

How can we be sure that alpha and theta are the super learning states? We know this because of the major learning accomplishments that occurred in childhood. Language development is perhaps the best example. Many experts believe there is a critical learning period when it comes to learning a second language. Research shows that the younger you learn a second language, the easier it will be to speak it fluently as well as learn additional languages in the future. Why do children learn languages better than adults? One explanation would be the differences in the brainwaves of the child's mind versus the adults. The child, in alpha and theta, learns through experience and absorbing information. They simply take everything in and process it without conscious effort or analysis. The adult on the other hand tries to consciously learn a language through activities like drills, learning vocabulary, trying to make logical connections, etc. This style of learning is slow, tedious, and rarely results in full comprehension, even though a lot of effort can be put into learning the information.

Speech-Language pathologist, Suzanne Evans Morris, Ph.D., reports in *The Facilitation of Learning:*

> "Receptivity for learning is related to specific states of consciousness. Predominate brainwave patterns are associated with different states of consciousness or awareness. For example, beta frequencies ranging from 13-26 Hz are associated with concentration, and alert problem solving; alpha frequencies (8-13 Hz) occur when the eyes are closed and a state of alert relaxation is present; theta (4-7Hz) is associated with deep relaxation with a high receptivity for new experiences and learning."[6]

Other researchers like, Thomas Budzynski, also describe the benefits of alpha and theta states for accelerated learning. Budzynski, who conducted extensive research on learning and the various states, suggests that when people are in theta they able to learn new languages, accept suggestions for changes in behavior and attitudes, or memorize large amounts of information. He says, "We take advantage of the fact that the hypnagogic (theta) state, the twilight state...has the properties of uncritical acceptance of verbal material, or almost any material it can process...a lot of work gets done very quickly."[7,8]

Why hypnosis works: It is a communication process that guides people back into these natural super learning states of mind that everyone experienced as a child. Hypnotists don't actually "do" anything to their clients. They can't force a person to change or possess the power to bestow people with special abilities they didn't have before. In other words, it won't turn you into Tiger Woods overnight.

Hypnotists are Teachers and Guides

The way that hypnotists help people is by serving two important roles: a teacher and a guide.

Hypnotists are teaching people how to re-access the super learning states within them through agreed-upon suggestions in a deeply relaxed and "learning" state of mind. All hypnosis is self-hypnosis, which means that even when guided by a hypnotist, it is still a process of self-improvement that is generated from within the person and not from an outside source. Hypnotists teach people how they can use their minds more productively to create positive solutions in their life.

Hypnotists also act as **guides** *in this self-improvement process. This is priceless because having a skilled guide to assist with the communication, allows the client to simply absorb information instead of having to consciously provide it to themselves, which could change the brainwaves and take a person out of the super learning states. A guide enables a person to learn through absorption like a child does, which gives the person the ability to once again experience accelerated learning without conscious effort.*

When people get hypnotized, they aren't entering into a mystical place or an alternate reality where magical things happen and their life suddenly improves. What is really occurring when a person is hypnotized is they have relaxed their mind and body, and slowed down the electrical currents occurring in the brain. When the electrical currents are slowed and the brain is experiencing alpha and theta brainwaves, then more of their brain is active and in use as modern research suggests. As the brainwaves reduce speed through the acceptance of suggestions for relaxation, left hemisphere mental activity like critical thinking and analysis decreases while right hemisphere mental activity such as creative thinking/problem solving and imagination increases. This allows a person to make use of their subconscious mind and apply more mental energy to the achievement of one specific goal.

Suzanne Evans Morris echoes these points in her work and reports:

> "The presence of theta patterns (4-7Hz) in the brain has been associated with states of increased receptivity for learning and reduced filtering of information by the left hemisphere. [Theta patterns] create a state of coherence in the brain. Right and left hemispheres as well as subcortical areas become activated in harmony, reflected by equal frequency and amplitude of EEG patterns from both hemispheres. This creates an internal physiological environment for learning which involves the whole brain. The linear, sequential style of problem solving preferred by the left hemisphere is brought into balance with the global, intuitive style of the right hemisphere and limbic system (subcortex). This allows the learner to have greater access to internal and external knowledge and provides a milieu for expanding intuition in problem solving...the ability to reduce 'mind chatter' and focus the attention which is critical for efficient learning."[9]

It is no longer a question of "if" hypnosis works, we know that it does as confirmed by scientific research. Tom Silver and legendary hypnotist, Ormond McGill, in their book, *Hypnotism*, say:

> "It is important to realize that there is indeed a way of monitoring levels of hypnosis using scientific medical devices such as the EEG machine. This type of monitoring levels of hypnosis is factual science and validates the true reality of hypnosis. EEG will be the physical tool to help cross hypnosis into full acceptance and usage in combination with all other mental and medical methods of healing."[10]

Chapter Review

Let's summarize the information from this chapter.

1. Hypnosis is not supernatural or a mystical phenomenon. It is psychology in action, based in the science of the human mind, and something that every person can utilize for success, empowerment, and improvement.

2. Hypnosis is a communication process that slows down the electrical currents in the brain in order to give you access to the subconscious mind and the super learning states you experienced as a child.

3. Hypnosis is a communication process and not a state of mind. Two common terms that you will hear in discussions on hypnosis and that will appear throughout the remainder of this book are "Hypnotic State" or "State of Hypnosis." What these two terms are referring to is not an exclusive mental state designated as hypnosis. These terms imply how the alpha and theta brainwaves were achieved and how they are being used. This is the same as "meditative states" which refer to alpha and theta brainwaves achieved through meditation.

4. All hypnosis is self-hypnosis which means it is a self-improvement process. In order to be hypnotized all one has to do is follow simple step by step instructions for relaxation and then absorb the positive suggestions presented to the mind. The only people who can't be hypnotized are those who reject the instructions for relaxation or those that don't want to participate. However, everyone has the ability to be hypnotized and make use of this incredible communication process for accelerated learning and application of the new ideas.

5. There are no dangers that can occur when a person is hypnotized and the worst thing that can happen is the person falls asleep which shuts down the ability to learn.

6. One great thing about hypnosis is it *does* produce positive side effects such as a reduction of daily stress, physical rejuvenation, more restful sleep, and a more positive mental attitude to name a few.

7. A person never gives up control when hypnotized and it is a way to regain control of areas of your life that got out of control.

In a nutshell, all the portrayals of hypnosis in Hollywood and fiction books are false.

The truth is everybody can positively benefit from making self-hypnosis a part of their daily life. It is the best known way to operate the greatest computer in the world and maximize your brain's power to achieve all of your goals faster and easier.

THREE

HOW YOUR MIND FUNCTIONS ON THE GOLF COURSE

"Success in this game depends less on strength of body than strength of mind and character."

- Arnold Palmer

Now that you have an understanding about how the process of hypnosis works and the different functions of the conscious and subconscious minds, it is time to explain how this information applies specifically to your golf game.

Just like in life, the two parts of your mind have completely different functions to fulfill in order to bring out peak performance on the golf course. By understanding these different functions and how to make the most out of each part of your mind, it increases your ability to execute at a higher level, get the most out of each shot, and most especially, lower your score. In this chapter, you will discover how the mind functions on the golf course as well as how hypnosis can dramatically enhance the positive benefits of the mental training techniques that are commonly used in golf.

On the Course: The Conscious Mind is the "Thinking Part"

Let's start this chapter by discussing the various roles of the two parts of your mind so you can understand how to use your *total mind* to play your best on the course.

The conscious mind in golf can be thought of as the "thinking part" and its primary responsibility on the course is to help you assess situations you are faced with in order to make the best decisions.

This "thinking part" of your mind uses left hemisphere brain functions, such as analysis, critical thinking, logic, as well as other functions to assist in your decision making so you can determine the best actions to take in any given situation. The "thinking part" of your mind has the ability to calculate mathematics and numbers which naturally makes the conscious mind very skilled at determining distances of the shot and taking into account other variables such as wind, the slope of the course, elevations, the distance to carry a hazard, the type of lie, and so on to determine the correct yardage of every shot. Because of its ability to process information in this way, it is the part of the mind that is best used for club and shot selection. In addition, the conscious mind also helps in decision making by analyzing the risk versus reward of a shot in a given situation. This "thinking part" of the mind is highly effective at determining the pros and cons of taking a particular action and helping you to refine your choices through analysis and logic to figure out the right shot, or action to take while on the golf course.

Another important function of the conscious mind is monitoring your self-talk and your thoughts on the golf course. The thoughts and self-talk that you have about a shot will determine the types of pictures your mind is creating. These pictures in turn direct your subconscious and body on how to perform on the shot at hand. It is very important that your use conscious mind to maintain positive thoughts because the type of thinking you have on the course plays a critical part in determining your level of performance. This topic will be discussed in length in the next chapter.

In addition to decision-making on the course as well as monitoring and directing your thoughts, the conscious mind is also excellent at analyzing your performance to determine what you did right or wrong. The conscious mind, using its processes of analysis, is quick to point out areas of improvement that you need to develop for better performance as well as the logical steps to achieve it. However, as mentioned in the previous chapter, it can point out all the things you need to do or should do, but lacks the ability to implement these changes in your game.

<u>On the Course: The Subconscious Mind is the "Performance Part"</u>

If the conscious mind is the "thinking part" then that means the subconscious mind is the "performance part" on the golf course. The subconscious mind is the "doer" and its primary role on the course is to execute the golf swing that you practiced, developed, and grooved.

Another primary function of the subconscious mind is to take the thoughts and self-talk generated from your conscious mind and use them to activate your imagination for shot performance. It is important to know that your subconscious can't determine the difference between real or vividly imagined events. When thoughts are directed to the mind, the imagination turns these thoughts into mental movies of the ideas taking place, and these mental movies direct the body on how it's to perform the shot. These mental movies can be either good or bad, but the subconscious doesn't make this distinction. It simply begins to create the thoughts that are held in the mind and works to make it a reality. Herein lies the power of visualization.

Visualization is your subconscious mind's method of turning your thoughts, and imagination into reality. When you visualize your mind is creating the neural pathways necessary for swing execution. The visualizations you have about a shot are your subconscious mind's instructions on how it is to perform and how it is to direct the body to execute the shot.

Let's focus now on the first fundamental principle of peak performance which is understanding the conscious mind is the "Thinking Part" and the subconscious mind is the "Performance Part". This is an important fact that must be internalized if you want to achieve the ultimate goal in peak performance which is to be able to "perform without conscious effort."

The legendary golfer, Bobby Jones, echoed this truth when he said, "We swing our best when we have the fewest things to think about." The overwhelming majority of golfers think way too much while addressing the ball and, as a result, end up using the thinking part of their minds while trying to execute the shot instead of using the performance part, the subconscious. Conscious effort over the ball always leads to mediocre or negative results because performance using the conscious mind is never as fluid or natural as when you get out of our way and allow the subconscious to execute the swing you developed. The reality is, every golfer has swung a golf club so many times that very little conscious thought is required to actually execute your best swing. It is the conscious thoughts about the swing that inhibit your best performance from being consistently released.

For example, when you first learned to ride a bike there were a lot of things that you had to consciously think about in order to ride the bike successfully. At first, you had to be conscious of your balance, steering the handle bars, pushing down on the pedals, proper weight distribution, and more, in order to stay on the bike and keep it moving. Once you internalized these basic skills, you then simply hopped on the bike and went speeding off, and no conscious thought was needed to ride the bike. Assuming that you haven't ridden a bike for a long period of time, chances are that if you wanted to take a bike ride, you could just get on it and go, as if no time had passed. You trust that your subconscious mind has remembered how to ride a bike and as a result you hop on and ride perfectly without conscious effort on your part. Well, if this is true about riding a bike, then it is also true about other things you have learned to do, like your golf swing. Chances are great that you have swung your golf clubs and hit balls many more than times you have ridden your bike. This means your subconscious mind has already formed a habit and knows exactly what to do to execute your best swing – and you can do it without effort or thought. When you are playing golf in "the zone" you are putting your subconscious learned behavior into action and your performance, when it comes to taking the shot, is "without conscious effort". This state of relaxed concentration gives you the ability to make the most out of your talents simply by keeping yourself out of your own way. When you become too mechanical, or entertain too many thoughts while addressing the ball, you will always fail to perform at your highest level.

The Signature Test Exercise

Here is a simple yet incredibly powerful exercise that you can do right now to drive this first principle about peak performance into your mind. The exercise is called the signature test and here is how it is done. Take out a piece of paper and sign your name as you normally do. Now underneath that first signature, consciously try to duplicate the same signature and try to match the same pen strokes as before but using your conscious mind and effort. Once you have done that, compare the two.

What you will find is when you simply signed your name using the performance part of your mind, the subconscious, the pen flowed and your signature came out normal. However, when you consciously tried to mimic the same signature, performance was slow, choppy, mechanical, and rough. Consequently, you were able to produce a signature, but it wasn't as easy to do, it took more effort, and the appearance of the second signature is probably mediocre at best. This is the exact same thing that is occurring during most golfers swing. *They are trying to consciously perform the swing instead of allowing the subconscious mind to perform what it has been trained to do.* When you learn how to use both parts of your minds, you can make the best decisions and direct your mind to success through conscious thought ***and*** when it comes to performance produce better results by allowing your subconscious mind to execute your best swing more effortlessly.

The Four Levels of Learning

The Signature Test Exercise provides an example of how the conscious mind is limited in its ability to perform compared to the subconscious mind. This can also be explained by the levels of learning we go through when learning any new skill, regardless of what it is.

When you set out to learn anything, including how to swing a club and execute a new skill on the course, you go through 4 different levels of learning to reach a state of mastery.[1] These levels include:

> **Level 1**: Unconscious Incompetence
>
> **Level 2**: Conscious Incompetence
>
> **Level 3**: Conscious Competence
>
> **Level 4**: Unconscious Competence

Level 1, unconscious incompetence, is when you don't know what you don't know. For example, before you took up golf, you didn't know anything about the game, how to swing a club, or what to do to execute a golf shot.

As you take more interest in the game, you start moving into **Level 2** which is conscious incompetence. In this level of learning you become aware of the game, the rules, the golf swing, etc, but you still don't know what to do or how to do it.

When you begin picking up the clubs, learning to swing, and taking lessons, then you begin to progress to **Level 3,** which is conscious competence. In this level of learning, you are aware of what to do and how to swing a club, but it requires lots of conscious effort to do it. For example, a beginner golfer needs to think about a number of different things in order to execute their swing. They have to consciously think about the proper grip, set up over the ball, the backswing, the release of the swing through the impact zone, and finishing the swing. In this stage of learning, the golf swing can be executed but it requires constant conscious thought to do so and the results are like the second signature in the exercise, the swing is mechanical, choppy, and slow.

Once we have practiced the mechanics of the swing over time, we eventually move into learning **Level 4**, unconscious competence. In this stage of learning, habits have been established in the subconscious mind and we are able to perform the actions without having to consciously think about them. We simply do it without a lot of effort as in the case with riding a bike, driving a car, signing your name, and so on.

Many golfers, due to the amount of practice and number of repetitions of their golf swing, have actually achieved **Level 4** in the learning process and can simply pick up a club and execute a beautiful golf swing without effort. This is often the case when a golfer is at the driving range. There is no pressure on performance and so they simply swing without conscious effort and produce great results.

However, because the vast majority do not understand the different functions of their mind, they end up falling back into **Level 3** when they are in a performance situation and, as a result, underperform on the golf course due to trying to consciously execute their swing. *When a golfer is thinking too much while addressing the ball, they are ac-tually regressing in their level of mastery and basically taking a step back in their prog-ress. When you think over the ball, you are using your conscious mind "the thinking part" and as a result performance is done with too much conscious effort and inhibits the natural flow and movements of the body, just like in the signature test.* You must train yourself to use your subconscious mind to execute the swing you have grooved and practiced in order to consistently bring out your best on each and every shot.

How to Swing and Not Think

A common question that typically surfaces at this point is: "How do I develop mechanics of a swing if I'm not supposed to think about my swing?" At first, to develop your swing mechanics you need a combination of both parts of the mind – the "Thinking Part" and "Performance Part" -- in order to learn. When learning any new skill there will be a period in which you have to work through learning **Level 3** to develop proper mechanics. You will have to be conscious of certain things at first in order to do the new moves correctly and this is where the thinking part really helps. It will point out if you are positioned properly, doing the right take away, and finishing your swing for example. However, the goal is to integrate the new behavior so it becomes a habit, and little or no thought is required to execute. In other words, mastery is reached when you can perform your swing without thinking, which is the ultimate in subconscious performance, or the state known as the zone.

Besides doing self-hypnosis to train your mind to execute without conscious effort, which you will learn about in subsequent chapters, there is an awesome drill that you can do at the driving range to train yourself to get out of your own way and allow the subconscious to take over its role of performing your perfect swing. This drill takes into consideration the conscious part of learning and teaches you how to shift out of it to perform with the subconscious mind. In essence, it teaches you how to take your swing from practice mode to performance mode.

Practice Mode to Performance Mode Driving Range Drill: Next time you are at the driving range, take 15 golf balls and divide them into three groups of 5. You are going to hit the first group of golf balls in practice mode. Practice mode is when you use your conscious mind, or 'Thinking Part' to execute the swing. While in practice mode, it is appropriate and acceptable to be thinking about mechanical aspects of your swing while over the ball. For these first 5 balls, take every shot being fully conscious of your swing and making sure you are doing the proper mechanics for the move you are learning. After you hit the first 5 balls, hit the second group in semi-performance mode. Semi-performance mode is when you limit your swing thought down to one key aspect that you are working on such as your backswing, release, finish, and so on. The goal of these shots is to limit your thinking over the ball so you can begin to perform what you are working on with less conscious thought and more with the subconscious mind. Fight the temptation to entertain too many thoughts and keep your conscious mind focused on just one aspect about your swing. Once you hit the second group of balls, you are going to take the last shots in pure performance mode. Performance mode is when you simulate real performance on the golf course. While taking these shots, consciously select your target, do your pre-shot routine, and take the shot as if you were competing. The goal of this last group of balls, is practicing your full shot routine and developing the mental skill of quieting the mental chatter during swing performance.

As you address the ball in performance mode, quiet your mind as much as possible, mentally focus on an image of your target, and take the shot without thinking about swing mechanics. Work on freeing your mind and allowing your subconscious mind to execute what it was practicing. For many golfers this is something easier said than done. If you need help clearing your mind and can't seem to quiet the mind enough to get out of your way, then a helpful tip is to think about something positive and unrelated to golf while addressing the ball. Examples include holding onto thoughts about things you are grateful for, positive memories of the past, people you love, or anything else that makes you feel good outside of the game of golf. The reason this is effective is because these thoughts will occupy your conscious mind which frees up your subconscious, "the performance part", to execute the swing. It might feel awkward at first, but you will quickly discover that your subconscious can perform and produce amazing results without any help from the thinking part of your mind.

Another simple tip is to focus your attention solely on your target and practice holding a mental image of it in mind while addressing the ball. Many of the great ball strikers have revealed that the mental image of their target is often so vivid in their mind that the ball appears to be a blur and seems to just get in the way of their swing. Whether you use these helpful hints or not is unimportant. What is important, is taking time to practice getting into your performance mode and learning how to quiet your mind over the ball so the subconscious can perform your best swing.

This drill is a very effective way to speed up the learning process on the range so you can train yourself to perform at a higher level on the course. Put it to the test. You will love the results.

The Most Powerful Habit: The Pre-Shot Routine

The next key principle about the mind and performance is to understand that the subconscious mind thrives off of habits. As mentioned in the previous chapter, the subconscious is the part of the mind that stores your habits, triggers you into action, and oftentimes it can seem like you are running on autopilot. Just as in life, golfers have all sorts of habits that are influencing their performance at a subconscious level some of these are good while others are bad and inhibit our best. You will learn later in this book how to change habits through self-hypnosis so you can program your mind for success. Right now, let's explore the most powerful habit to establish for peak performance on the golf course.

One of the most important habits for every golfer to develop is a solid pre-shot routine. Having a consistent pre-shot routine is one of the quickest ways to elevate your play on the course. A pre-shot routine helps you get into the present moment so that you can give your full focus to the shot at hand, it relaxes the mind and body, and gets you prepared by programming your mind and body on how to execute. The goal of developing a consistent pre-shot routine is the same as the goal of developing your swing – to do it so many times that it becomes second nature and becomes a positive habit on the course that is done with minimal effort.

Davis Love Jr. once said, *"A routine isn't a routine if you have to think about it."* Besides increasing focus, enhancing the visualization of the shot, and having a relaxation effect, why is having a routine so important for success in golf? It is important because the routine itself activates the performance part of the mind, the subconscious. When your routine becomes a habit, it relaxes your brainwaves into alpha since little thought is required to execute habits. When your brain slows down into alpha, it easier to visualize the shot more vividly, your mind focuses more powerfully on a single idea, and it's easier to execute your swing. As the routine becomes an ingrained habit, it naturally increases course confidence and becomes a significant competitive edge because *the situation may change, but the routine always stays the same.*

Research supports why the pre-shot routine is one of the most important habits to develop to improve performance. In 2012, a study was published in the International Journal of Golf Science showing the effects of a pre-shot routine on 3 elite European Tour golfers with a minimum of 6 years' experience on the tour. Among the participants, two were waiting for their first victories on the tour, and one was very successful with 4 European Tour victories and Ryder Cup experience. Prior to the study, none of the golfers worked with a sport psychologist or any type of mental coach.

The results of the study revealed some impressive results and indicated that incorporating a pre-shot routine created an immediate improvement in performance. All golfers lowered their scoring average as well as increased intensity of the flow experience (as measured by the Flow State Scale). Participant 1 lowered his scoring average from 71.8 to 69.6 and reported that the pre-shot routine enabled him to focus his attention away from swing mechanics as well as reduced his fear of poor performance. Participant 2 reduced his scoring average from 70.8 to 68.7 and said the pre-shot routine helped him relax, focus his attention appropriately, and kept him from incessantly thinking about his swing during the round. This reduced his worry about underperforming on the course. Finally, Participant 3, lowered his scoring average from 71.5 to 68.5 and reported that, imagining his best shots he ever had in his pre-shot routine increased his confidence and made him feel like he was going to hit a great shot every time he picked up the club.[2]

Now let's discuss how to use your total mind in your pre-shot routine so that you can establish good habits of performance. Lynn Marriott and Pia Nilsson from Vision 54 introduced a concept of the "think box" and the "play box".[3] In the "think box", they instruct golfers to do all their thinking about the shot using the conscious mind. Some of the activities in the "think box" include determining yardages, club selection, the type of shot, and so on. Then they have the golfers imagine crossing over an imaginary line and enter into the "play box". In the "play box", the golfer is instructed to quiet their mind and let their swing rip. This is certainly one way to approach your pre-shot routine in order to utilize both parts of your mind on each shot.

I would like to expand on this concept, and add one other key element that makes a pre-shot routine even more effective. In my opinion, the best pre-shot routines are designed to take you from thinking or using your conscious mind and bridge the gap into using your subconscious mind for performance. To achieve this, a process like the 15 ball drill that takes you from practice mode to semi-performance mode to performance mode needs to be established for on the course.

The pre-shot routine I recommend has three zones, each with distinct purposes. **These are the thinking zone, programming zone, and performance zone**. Let's go over these zones now so you know exactly what to do to establish the most effective pre-shot routine for getting in the zone before each shot.

The thinking zone takes place when you are by your bag making decisions about the shot at hand. While in the thinking zone, you use your conscious mind to evaluate the wind, elevation, yardage, slope, lie, etc to determine the course of action you are going to take, i.e., club and shot selection.

Let's go over two simple strategies you can use in the thinking zone to assist you in making smart decisions on the course and the shot at hand.

The first decision making strategy is called **L.D.T**. which stands for Lie, Distance, Trajectory.[4]

L.D.T. is an easy to remember strategy that will keep you focused on the most important elements prior to all shots: The lie of the ball, the distance to your selected target, and the trajectory needed to get the ball there. According to researchers Owens and Bunker, when golfers focus on this simple sequence and apply it in their game, it has shown to help them make better mental decisions and control anxiety on the course.[5]

The second decision-making strategy is called the "Problem-Solving Model" and is based on Personality Type. There are 4 aspects of your personality that are hard-wired from birth. Your Personality Type determines your natural inborn preferences in 4 different categories:

1. How you manage your energy: Extroversion or Introversion.

2. How you gather information: Sensing or iNtuiting.

3. How you make decisions: Thinking or Feeling.

4. How you prioritize your life: Judging or Perceiving.

Each person has 4 preferences, so there are a total of 16 different Personality Types. Knowing your Personality Type helps you increase your awareness of your individual way of managing your energy, gathering information, making decisions, and prioritizing your time with others, which promotes greater understanding of yourself and other people.

In the "Problem-Solving Model", the focus is on how you gather information and how you make decisions. In their book, *FROM STRESSED TO BEST: A Proven Program for Reducing Everyday Stress,* authors Ruth Schneider and David Prudhomme, write[6] :

"There is a way to ensure you make the best decisions, personal or professional. The best decisions take into account all four Modes of Operating:

- ✓ **Both** modes of gathering information: **Sensing (S)** and **iNtuition (N).**

- ✓ **Both** modes of making decisions: **Thinking (T)** and **Feeling (F).**

Use the following Problem Solving model and notice how much confidence you gain when making decisions – knowing you have looked at things from all angles."

PROBLEM Solving Model

Let's go over this decision-making strategy for you now in a golf context so you *know* exactly how to implement this strategy on the golf course.

When faced with a decision on the course, especially if you are in between clubs, ask yourself the following questions to make the best decision in the moment:

1. What are the facts and details about the shot at hand? (Sensing)

2. What are all the possibilities (club and shot options) that I have? (iNtuition)

3. What are the pros and cons of taking a particular action? (Thinking)

4. What feels right or what shot makes me feel the most comfortable? (Feeling)

This strategy for decision-making is highly effective because it gives you the ability to evaluate the situation from all angles to choose the best action to take to produce the desired result.

Confident decisions lead to confident performance. Bernhard Langer was quoted saying, "Be decisive. A wrong decision is generally less disastrous than indecision." Use these two strategies to make decisions on the course that you can trust.

After you have determined the best club and shot for the situation in the thinking zone, it is now time to get behind the ball and enter into the **programming zone**. The **programming zone** is the element of the pre-shot routine left out of the "think box" and "play box" model. When you are behind the ball preparing for your shot, it isn't time to make decisions which should already be done at this point, it is time to program your subconscious mind and your body to execute what you want. *The purpose of this step in the pre-shot routine is to get your mind moving away from conscious thought and begin bridging the gap to the subconscious for performance by getting the creative part of the mind involved.*

During this step of the routine there are 3 primary things you want to achieve.

1. First, you want to use your conscious mind and affirm with your self-talk what you want to achieve on the shot at hand. Do this in a positive way, such as "I am ripping this drive straight down the middle of the fairway," or "I am stuffing this approach shot tight to the flagstick." More on using affirmations will be discussed in the next chapter.

2. Next, you want to visualize the shot and create a mental movie of your affirmation coming to life. This step begins to activate the subconscious mind because imagination is required in order to visualize the shot. You can think of visualization as the instructions to the subconscious mind and body on the way it is to perform. ***The golden rule is: the more vivid the visualization of the shot is, the better the performance will be.***

3. Finally, you want to connect with the shot in your body by getting the right feel for the swing you are about to execute. While visualizing your shot, begin to feel the thoughts transferring to your body. Let the pictures in your mind guide your body in getting the right feel. Here you are connecting the

mind and body, and preparing yourself for peak performance by calibrating your swing with visualizations of a successful shot.

The goal of the programming zone is to tell your brain what you want to do through an affirmation, show your brain what you are expecting it to execute by visualizing the shot and activating the imagination, and finally conditioning the body through body rehearsal to execute what you have practiced.

After you programmed your mind, it is time to cross the imaginary commitment line and address the ball in the **performance zone**. When you follow this routine, there is nothing left to think about over the ball. You have already said what you wanted to do, you visualized it, and connected to it by getting the feel of the swing, so what is left to think about? Nothing. It is now time to let the subconscious mind and muscle memory take over to execute what you just programmed yourself to do. While over the ball, the best thought to maintain is the outcome image of the shot you visualized. By focusing on the outcome image or a target image, the mind will follow through and execute the mental images you are holding in mind. Remember the mind's job is to produce perfectly and the subconscious can only perform what it knows and has been instructed to do. This pre-shot routine involves your total mind to increase the likelihood of a successful outcome. In addition, it is designed to train you over time to easily transition between using your conscious and subconscious mind on each shot. When you are able to execute without conscious effort over the ball then you will have mastered a true performance mode on the course.

Just like all aspects of your game, this pre-shot routine takes practice in order to master it. It is important that you take time to practice this at the range so that it is easier to execute during performance on the course. Always keep this in mind, *what you do at the range, you will do on the course.* Make the commitment to practicing this recommended pre-shot routine each time out on the range and simulate your performance so you too can start experiencing the benefits of a well-established pre-shot routine in your golf game. More on this later.

Your Brainwaves and How They Influence Performance

In the last chapter, we went over the various brainwaves that every human being experiences each day. Understanding these brainwaves can be highly beneficial to all golfers who wish to take their golf game to a higher level. Since the goal in performance is to be able to execute without conscious effort and use your subconscious mind to perform the swing it is important to know which brainwaves activate the subconscious mind in the most powerful way. In this section, we are going to discuss the brainwaves of "the zone", why alpha brainwaves are more valuable than beta brainwaves in performance, and how to get your mind into alpha brainwaves to enhance all aspects of your golf game. (In later chapters, I will explain how self-hypnosis techniques are also effective in getting your mind into alpha brainwaves.)

A Quick Review: Beta brainwaves occur in the brain when you are wide awake, alert, and fully aware. These are the brainwaves commonly associated with the mental activities of the conscious mind and the thinking functions. Alpha brainwaves are the ones the brain experiences when you are in a state of relaxed concentration such as when daydreaming, taking a stroll through a garden, sitting by the beach, getting lost in a great book, driving on auto-pilot, and so on. While in this relaxed state, the subconscious mind shifts to the forefront and its creative functions begin to take over the majority of our thinking. It gives you the ability to perform complex tasks like driving, without the requirement of any conscious thought because of the habit.

What is commonly referred to as "the zone" is when you are performing while your brain is in a state of relaxed attentiveness or relaxed concentration which are alpha brainwaves. When you are grinding on the course and exhibiting lots of effort to execute, your brain is operating with beta brainwaves which are the ones commonly associated with left hemisphere mental activity such as critical thinking, critiquing, and analyzing. Just knowing this indicates that one of the goals to be able to consistently play golf in the zone is the developing the mental skill to keep the mind relaxed and operating in alpha waves. It is possible to train your mind to get into, maintain, and perform in alpha brainwaves on command through self-hypnosis and other state management methods on the golf course. By the end of this book, you will know exactly how to do it.

For now, let's discuss some simple ways besides self-hypnosis to get your brainwaves into alpha so that you can immediately start playing golf more with your subconscious mind and access the zone more often. The first method is perhaps the simplest way to achieve alpha waves, but be sure not to overlook it because of its simplicity. Research shows the adult brain typically experiences alpha waves when they are relaxed with their eyes closed. Closing your eyes and doing some deep breathing will cause the mind and body to relax and the brainwaves to begin to slow down.

However, there is an easy technique you can do that will naturally cause the mind to get into alpha brainwaves much quicker. In his research, Jose Silva, creator of the well-known program Silva Mind Control, reported that when a person closes their eyes and looks up at a 20-30 degree angle as if looking through one's forehead, it caused the brainwaves to slow down into alpha waves.[7] The reason this occurs is eye movements stimulate electrical activity in the brain, and when you sleep at night, the eyeball's roll back and point straight up. When the eyes are closed and at a 20-30 degree angle, it triggers the mind to begin relaxing in the same way as when you get ready for bed.

So the simplest way to get your brain in alpha brainwaves or the mental state of "the zone" before a round of golf is to close your eyes for a few moments, imagine looking through your forehead with your eyes at about a 30 degree angle, and do some deep breathing while you visualize yourself playing your best. This is perhaps the simplest method of doing self-hypnosis and very effective since it naturally slows down your brainwaves and programs the mind for success. Spend five minutes before each round of golf doing this simple exercise and step on the first tee in a relaxed performance mode.

Another interesting way to achieve alpha brainwaves before stepping up on the first tee box is to simply slow down your activities and actions prior to a round of golf. One example of this comes from the 4-time U.S. Open Champion, Ben Hogan. Hogan was observed during the mornings before tournament rounds of golf intentionally doing everything extra slow. He would reduce the speed of all his morning activities such as brushing his teeth, combing his hair, driving to the course, warming up and so on in order to be mentally and physically relaxed in the tournament.

Perhaps, it was just coincidence that Ben Hogan did this or maybe he was way ahead of his time because by reducing the pace of his activities and doing things with relaxed awareness he was actually slowing down his brainwaves into alpha, or "the zone" state. Hogan wasn't the only one who reportedly did this. Johnny

Miller said numerous times on television that before a competitive round he would take 20 minutes to shave. In 1945, Byron Nelson was said to have driven to the course 10 mph slower than normal. John Jacobs was observed taking 5-10 minutes to put on his shoes.[8] All of these activities promote present moment awareness, relaxed concentration, and mindfulness – three qualities of mind that can help any golfer play better and enjoy the game more.

Follow these simple suggestions for relaxed awareness and you too can effortlessly slow down your brainwaves. So when it comes time to tee off, your mind is already in the zone. This method was obviously very successful for Hogan and the others, so perhaps it's time to give it a shot in your game.

Slowing down on the golf course in between shots is also a great way to maintain the zone state, or alpha brainwaves during the round, as well as increase your ability to perform. After a poor shot or when you aren't performing to your standards, the natural tendency is to speed things up. In a state of stress or frustration, most golfers make hasty decisions that aren't always well thought out, they rush through or abandon their pre-shot routine, and worst of all, speed up the tempo of their swing. If this sounds like you, then the best thing you can do in these situations is learn to slow yourself down. To do this, start by deliberately changing your breathing by taking some deep breaths, walk a little slower to the ball, take your time making decisions, and get back to the basics. This slower pace in doing things will naturally cause the mind and body to relax so you can get back to playing golf rather than stressing out. Trying to play golf in a stressed state shuts down the subconscious mind, speeds up brainwave activity which will make you more critical, and keeps you out of the zone state. If you find yourself stressed then it's important to remind yourself, "Slow it down, refocus on my routine, and I will perform better".

Hypnosis Is Already a Part of Golf

With an ever increasing emphasis on the mental side of golf, mental training techniques such as visualization, mental rehearsal, guided meditation, and mental imagery have become common terms in the golf world and referred to frequently by commentators on television.

While many are aware of these mental training techniques, most are unaware that the key ingredient that supercharges these techniques is actually hypnosis. The point most commonly left out of the majority of golf psychology books and in discussions about these training techniques is the relaxed state the elite golfers get into *before* mentally going through these processes. These mental training methods will produce good results when done with the conscious mind in beta brainwaves. However, when using hypnosis to achieve alpha and theta brainwaves, the subconscious mind takes over and the imagination turns these methods into lifelike experiences that make major impressions on the inner mind.

Hypnosis is the missing link and the secret to getting the true benefits of these techniques.

Just like mental imagery and visualization, hypnosis is rooted in science and has proven to be effective in a vast number of research studies.

Researchers have shown that when martial artists combined mental imagery techniques with relaxation training into one process, which resembled hypnosis, it was significantly superior in boosting performance compared to just imagery training or relaxation training by itself.[9] An additional study confirmed these findings and found that when relaxation and imagery where combined with goal setting, energy control, and self-monitoring techniques, it produced positive performance effects on a golf putting task.[10]

John Pates of the University of Derby in the United Kingdom studied the effects of hypnosis on an elite Senior European Tour Golfer. The participant in the study was a 52 year old male, with 2 years of Senior European Tour playing experience, but with no tour event wins and no previous mental training by a qualified practitioner. The golfer met with the hypnotist once a week for a live session and was given an audio session to listen to each day in between sessions. This was done each week and over the course of 11 tournaments.

The results of the study showed that the hypnosis sessions significantly effected performance in a positive way and lowered the golfer's scoring average from a mean score of 72.8 to a mean score of 68.6, which for a golfer at this elite of a level is a tremendous difference. The results also showed that the hypnosis sessions consistently improved golf performance and intensity of the flow state during real competitions from a mean flow score of 119.3 to a mean flow score of 151.6 (as measured by the Flow State Scale).[11, 12] In addition, the results of the hypnosis intervention increased the participant's prize money and, after just 3 weeks into the study, the participant won his first Senior European Tour event.

Pates reports:

> "The qualitative data also revealed some interesting findings. First, the data showed that hypnosis may increase positive emotions such as confidence and fun. Second, it also appeared hypnosis elevates the feeling of mental relaxation resulting in feelings of calm. Third, the intervention appeared to improve a player's ability to focus his attention on task-relevant information and to help the player cope with distractions. Fourth, the intervention appeared to augment positive thinking by suppressing cognitions such as judging, monitoring, and censoring, and fifth, the technique seemed to alter the golfer's perception and feelings of control. Taken together, these findings are consistent with the outcomes of a number of clinical experiments wherein hypnosis positively controlled emotions, thoughts, feelings, and perceptions."

Pates continues, "The results of the study indicate that a hypnotic intervention may be an effective way of preparing professional golfers for significant competitions."

This study confirmed a similar one conducted by John Pates, and fellow researchers Rachael Oliver, and Ian Maynard from Sheffield Hallam University involving novice golfers. Again, hypnosis proved to be successful at consistently improving golf putting performance and accuracy as well as increased intensity of flow experience. [13]

Other interesting research reveals that hypnotic states are almost identical to peak performance states, and they share many of the same qualities including: changes in thinking (less paralysis by analysis); memory (amnesia); perception (slow motion and enlargement of objects); dissociation (pain detachment); and information process (parallel processing).[14, 15] Other shared aspects of the two states are: dissociation/detachment from one's surroundings, absorption, feelings of control, and perceptual distortions such as altered perceptions of time.[16] Because of the overwhelming similarities between flow and hypnotic state, researchers suggest that utilizing hypnosis in mental training may increase personal control of the flow experience and accessing the zone on the course.[17]

In the chapters to come, you will discover how to elicit the relaxed mental state the elite golfers utilize to enhance the power of these techniques as well as learn specifically how to incorporate all these training techniques into your self-hypnosis sessions to improve your golf game.

Let's conclude this chapter with two powerful examples of major winners who have utilized hypnosis to succeed on the golf course. The first one is South Africa's Louie Oosthuizen who won the 2010 British Open by incorporating a post-hypnotic suggestion to trigger focus enhancement, to stay present on the course, and keep himself relaxed. The trigger Oosthuizen used was a red dot on his golf glove.[18] Before each shot, Oosthuizen was seen taking a deep breath and focusing all of his attention on the red dot for 5 seconds. This action was designed to slow his brainwaves down and activate hypnotic suggestions to achieve a state of relaxed focus and concentration. You can watch his post-game interview where he discussed the red dot trigger –and, of course, he leaves out the secret key to making it work, hypnosis. Here is a link to his interview or you can do a simple YouTube search to find it yourself. The video link: http://www.youtube.com/watch?v=ndqDfAZrurU.

The second example comes from, arguably one of the most polarizing golfers of all time, Tiger Woods. There are many reports of Tiger Woods getting hypnotized since the age of 10 and everyday throughout his amateur career, by his father's friend and Navy psychologist Jay Brunza. Brunza, in an interview about Woods said, "Tiger's genius is his ability to use his creative imagination." In my opinion, there is no doubt that Tiger knows the power of the subconscious mind for peak performance, unbreakable focus, and championship level golf. On YouTube you will find a video titled "Tiger Zone" which is an interview with Tiger and Brunza discussing the mental side of the game.[19] At one point, Tiger mentions that they do these "sessions" to harness the power of his subconscious and creative mind. The sessions he is referring to are hypnosis sessions, which is what professional hypnotists call their time working with their clients. Here is the link to the video so you can see it for yourself: http://www.youtube.com/watch?v=QEaWv0SBp3A.

Let's finish with one other quote from Tiger, "My mother's a Buddhist. In Buddhism, if you want to achieve enlightenment, you have to do it through mediation and self-improvement through the mind. That's something she passed on to me; to be able to calm myself down and use my mind as my main asset."

Chapter Review

1. The **"Thinking Mind's"** primary functions on the golf course:

   ➢ Decision Making

      • Club Selection

      • Shot Selection

      • Calculating Yardage

   ➢ Risk vs Reward Analysis

   ➢ Determining what can be improved upon, corrected, and plans of action to get better

2. The **"Performance Mind's"** primary functions on the on the course:

   ➢ Swing Execution

   ➢ Visualization

   ➢ Imagination

   ➢ Source of habits - The most important habit on the course is a solid and consistent pre-shot routine

3. **Three Zones: An Effective Pre-Shot Routi**ne Using Your Total Mind

   ➢ **The Thinking Zone** - Where decisions are made

   ➢ **The Programming Zone** - Where you direct your mind and body how to perform

   ➢ **The Performance Zone** - Where you turn your thoughts into reality

4. **Alpha Brainwaves are "The Zone" Brainwaves**

   ➢ Alpha Brainwaves occur when the mind is in a state of relaxed awareness

   ➢ Alpha Brainwaves can be achieved through:

      • Self-Hypnosis.

- Closing your eyes, putting your eyes at a 30 degree angle (like looking through your forehead), and deep breathing for a few minutes.

- Slowing down your movements, activities, and behaviors before a round of golf.

5. **Hypnosis is Already a Part of Golf**

➢ It is the secret ingredient that enhances mental training techniques like mental rehearsal, visualization, and mental imagery. The elite golfers get maximum benefit from these well-known mental training techniques.

FOUR

SELF-TALK, AFFIRMATIONS AND AUTOSUGGESTION

"Stay true to yourself and listen to your inner voice.
It will lead you to your dream."

-James Ross

The starting point to developing the mind of a champion is to actively take back control of your mind and begin directing it towards your goals and dreams through the power of positive self-talk, affirmations, and autosuggestion. The way you communicate with yourself plays a pivotal role in your ability to produce success in golf and life. There is no such thing as a random thought and every thought that you have has tremendous creative power moving you in a direction of success or failure. In order to produce the best results on the golf course it is important to understand the various aspects of self-communication and how these elements intertwine to create a mind that is on a one track path to your goals and success.

In this chapter, these elements of self-communication will be explained so that you can effectively use your thoughts to enhance your performance on the golf course. Also, you will discover negative programming words to eliminate from your vocabulary that inhibit and prevent success. You will learn how to get your mind off of auto-pilot and reclaim control so you can direct it towards your goals every day. Finally, I will reveal the missing piece left out of most discussions on self-communication: the best times of the day to use these strategies for positive mental programming and success enhancement.

What is Self-Talk and How Does It Influence Us?

Self-talk is the inner dialogue going on inside of your mind and the way you talk to yourself throughout the day. For most people, this inner dialogue seems to never stop and thoughts seem to flow randomly and unceasingly through the mind. The National Science Foundation (NSF) estimates that the human brain produces 12,000-50,000 thoughts per day and the number of thoughts depend on how 'deep of a thinker' the person is.[1] Other institutions such as UCLA's Laboratory of Neuro Imaging (LONI) suggest that the human brain produces 70,000 thoughts per day. What is unfortunate is the fact that the experts conclude that of these 50,000+ thoughts a day, 65-80% of these thoughts are negative in nature.[2] This tremendous amount of negative thinking is one of the main reasons why many people feel stuck in life, imprisoned by their mind, and unable to reach their goals. The negative nature of self-talk occurs because the majority of people are not aware of their self-talk or monitor the activity of their thoughts. As a result, their minds are operating on auto-pilot and they simply allow any thought positive or negative to be entertained in their mind.

It is important that you become aware of your self-talk since the way you talk to yourself will influence your level of motivation, the actions you take, and the way you feel throughout the day.

Everything you do in life starts with a thought and all thoughts have power. The way you communicate with yourself through self-talk is a major determiner of the results that will be produced in any endeavor, including your golf swing, performance on the course, and scorecard.

One of the easiest ways to explain how a seemingly simple thought can have the power to influence performance can be explained using the acronym **T.F.A.R.**, which stands for **T**houghts, **F**eelings, **A**ctions, and **R**esults. **T.F.A.R.** is like an equation that reveals the chain reaction of how thoughts manifest in reality. The thoughts you hold in your mind are the catalyst that sets everything else in motion;

thoughts produce your results. When you have a thought, it immediately begins processing in your mind and as the thought processes, it generates a feeling or an emotion inside of you. These feelings created by the thought will determine the type of action you are going to take, and the type of action you take will determine the results you experience.

Let's use two simple examples to demonstrate this point. Imagine that you are on a tee box and you want to stripe it down the middle of the fairway. Let's assume that you are holding the thought "I can do this" in your mind. This positive thought immediately begins to create pictures and images in the mind's eye of you succeeding in this situation. These positive images generate and fuel confident feelings in your body. When you feel confident, positive, and relaxed, you tend to take positive actions. Positive action typically leads to positive results. On the flip side, if you start this chain reaction with a thought like "I can't do this" then the mind forms negative mental pictures, which create feelings of doubt and negative emotions. When you experience doubt, insecurity, and stress you tend to take wrong actions, like speeding up your routine prior to a shot, and consequently, produce a poor result.

Obviously, there are times when you have a positive mental attitude and you still don't produce a successful result. I think Dr. Bob Rotella addressed this point best when he said, "The correlation between thinking well and making successful shots is not 100 percent. But the correlation between bad thinking and unsuccessful shots is much higher." *Every thought you have creates energy and sets into motion this chain reaction in either a positive or negative direction.*

Now that you are beginning to understand that each thought you have paves the way for either success or failure, it would appropriate at this time to discuss two major misconceptions people have about their mind. These misconceptions keep so many people trapped in patterns of negative thinking and producing results less than what they are capable of.

Your Mind is Your Servant, Not Your Master

The first misconception held by many people is the idea that their mind is their master, when in fact it is their servant. Most people have an untrained mind and as a result they believe their minds are in charge, operate randomly, and have control over them directing them to do certain things. In a way they are right, not because the mind is a dictator, but because they have voluntarily given it control over their life. For example, have you ever seen a very spoiled child throw a temper tantrum in a store in order to get their way? Technically, the parents are the ones in control, but who is really running the show? The answer is obvious, it's the undisciplined child.

This same concept is at work in most people's minds. For many, the mind is an untamed wild child who is used to doing whatever it wants. The mind is out of control and as a result, any type of thought, positive or negative, has permission to flow through the mind unfiltered. This is one of the reasons why so many people struggle in life as well as on the golf course, and why it seems as if their minds are working against them. Begin to take back control of your mind by recognizing that you are the boss and the mind is your servant. *When you take* **complete respon- sibility** *for the thoughts you allow in your mind, it marks the beginning of a great leap forward in harnessing the mind's true power to achieve your goals.*

Direct Your Mind to What You Want to Achieve

The second big misconception that needs to be overcome is the belief the mind doesn't need to be consistently directed towards what you want to achieve. Unfortunately, most people are uninformed when it comes to directing their minds towards success and, as a result, they produce mediocre results. It is important to understand your subconscious mind is always moving in the direction of your most prevalent, consistent thoughts and the subconscious is always striving to make these dominant thoughts correct and a reality.

Whether you are actively directing your mind down a path of your choosing or simply leaving it to chance, the subconscious mind is always at work seeking out a direction to move towards each day. For most people, who have an untrained or undisciplined mind, they aren't actively directing their minds towards their dreams and, as a result, they are more susceptible to be influenced by the media, market- ers, and other negative influences everyone is bombarded with on a daily basis. So instead of taking control of their thoughts, they choose to do nothing, thinking that thoughts are random and have no power, and consequently are led by other sources. This is one of the reasons why so many people are frustrated, stressed, producing less than adequate results, and primarily negative in nature.

Negative Self-Talk Affects Performance

Negative self-talk can have detrimental effects on your performance in several ways. First, as discussed earlier, every golfer thinks in pictures and these pictures direct the body on what to do and how to execute. A golden rule to understand is **what you picture in your mind, you produce**. Negative self-talk creates images and pictures in the mind of negative results occurring, and because the body always produces the pictures, the mind believes that the negative outcome is the desired result. This results in a greater likelihood of achieving the negative picture, not because it is what you really desired to do, but because it is what your mind was focused on. Whatever your mind focuses on, expands.

Second, negative thoughts create varying levels of stress in golfers. Stress producing thoughts fire off the fight/flight stress response in the body and the hormone cortisol is released. This cortisol release creates physical tension in the body which will inhibit the natural flow of body movements to execute your swing and consequently it hurts your overall performance. In addition to tension, when the stress hormone cortisol is released in the brain, it shuts off access to neocortex part of your brain, or higher brain functions. In an interview on the Golf Club Radio Show, with host Danielle Tucker, Lynn Marriott of Vision 54 described what the neocortex is responsible for in golf performance. Marriott said "What resides in the neocortex is fine motor skills, perception, better decision making, coordination, and sometimes people transition at the top of their swing get off because they are in a too high of a state of cortisol."[3] Negative thinking goes way beyond simply creating tension – it is literally shutting down the part of your brain needed to make the right decisions, have the proper perception of the situation, and execute your best swing.

Third, negative thinking takes a golfer out of the present moment and keeps the mind focused on either the past or the future, which are both negative states on the golf course. When I had my clinical hypnosis practice I have observed that people that primarily focused on the past tended to be depressed and those primarily focused on the future experienced anxiety. The same thing holds true in the game of golf. For some, they step up to the tee and hit a poor shot. This bad outcome starts the process of negative thinking. The golfer then gets inside their head and analyzes everything that went wrong, whether or not they did things right, and other negative thoughts enter into the mind about the shot that just happened. They then drag all this negativity with them to their next shot, and instead of being in the present moment, their minds are still rehashing all the things that went wrong on the last one. When it's time for them to take their shot, they are not focused on the shot at hand, tend to abandon parts of their routine, and take their shot without truly focusing. The result in this situation is very predictable. The tension created by the critical thoughts, the lack of focus due to holding onto the past, and the negative pictures in the mind, all work together and produce another poor shot.

A similar process occurs when the mind is focused on the future. Let's assume a golfer is off to a great start and is on pace to post one of their best scores. The tendency most golfers have in this position is to get ahead of themselves and start anticipating the future. When this occurs, it brings forth negative thinking and anxiety, even if at first glance it appears that it is positive because it is focused on a successful future outcome. Future thinking is negative because it takes the golfer out of the present moment, which results in a lack of focus on the shot at hand. In addition, these thoughts tend to be anxiety producing, which results in physical tension and cortisol release in the brain. When golfers become future oriented, they tend to get tight and start trying to steer the ball to their target instead of just executing their routine and swing, like they did to get to this point. Score becomes the main focus in the mind instead of execution of the process, and as a result most golfers underperform and fail to post their low score like the start of the round indicated.

A golden rule to remember is: ***If you are thinking of the past or future, then it is negative thinking on the golf course.***

Fourth, negative self-talk prevents all golfers from fully enjoying their round of golf. Negative self-talk stems from a paradigm of perfectionism which is solely focused on outcomes. There is a lot more to golf than just the final number and enjoyment comes from the process, not just the end result. The paradox is the more focused you are on the score, the less likely they are to achieve that score. Results come from enjoying the game and focusing on the aspects of the game that you can control. If you control these elements and put your focus on their execution, then the results naturally happen. *Focusing purely on score is a form of negative thinking and one way to destroy all hope of a good score and an enjoyable round of golf.*

If you want to enjoy golf more and overcome negative thoughts follow the advice of Bobby Jones who said, "The real way to enjoy playing golf is to take pleasure not in the score, but in the execution of strokes."

How to Overcome Negative Self-talk and Take Back Control

As you can tell from the above information, positive self-talk isn't a luxury. It is a necessary requirement if you want to bring out your best consistently on the golf course. Just like it has taken time to develop the muscle memory to execute your golf swing, it takes time to build your mind muscles to develop the core beliefs and positive mental attitude to achieve your dreams. Let's go over the steps to correcting your self-talk now.

The first step to improving the quality of your self-talk is to take ownership of your mind and claim responsibility for your thoughts. To the championship golfer, there is no such thing as a random thought. Sergio Garcia said, "I always think under par. You have to believe in yourself." All thoughts are powerful and must be positive in order to produce the best results. The best golfers understand the importance of positive thinking and actively monitor their thoughts to make sure they are moving them in the direction of success and their choosing. This all starts with making the decision to take complete ownership of your mind.

Mentally say to yourself right now, *"I am the boss of my mind. The mind is my servant and I direct it. I am responsible for my mind and the thoughts that I entertain. I make the commitment now to overcoming my old negative thinking, maintaining only positive thoughts and thinking like a champion."*

Now that you made this decision to improve your self-talk, there are certain words that you will want to eliminate from your vocabulary that are negative programming words to your subconscious mind. Inadvertently, many people program their mind for failure by using certain words. The subconscious mind doesn't always respond to the words themselves, but the images the words convey in your mind's eye. By eliminating these words and making these simple shifts in your self-talk, you can make an immediate difference in your performance, because it will create different pictures for the subconscious mind to act upon.

The first word that you want to eliminate is the word "Don't". The word "don't" can have devastating effects on your performance and can actually increase the likelihood of executing the thing you "don't" want to do. The reason this occurs is simple. The subconscious mind does not understand negative connotations in language and to the subconscious mind, do and don't, are the exact same thing. I will prove that to you right now. Whatever you do *"Don't think of a pink gorilla playing golf."* When you read that, what did you immediately think about? Of course, the pink gorilla playing golf. Here are other examples: "Don't think about hitting this in the water."; "Don't put this one in the trees."; "Don't hook this tee shot." Simply by reading these words, your subconscious mind immediately creates pictures and thoughts of doing exactly what you want to avoid. If you are completely honest with yourself, then you will realize that every time you told yourself "don't do this" while on the course, you ended up doing it. *Your mind produces what you picture.*

Remember the Brain Imaging Center in San Antonio reported that when you visualize, you create 80% of the neural pathways needed to execute the task. So if you are saying things like "Don't do this..." then it creates the picture of it in your mind and you are 80% of the way to executing that negative idea.

To overcome this, you must monitor your thoughts and become aware when you are using this negative programming word before your shots. Once you become aware, cancel the thought, and replace it with a positive thought that affirms what you DO want. For example, instead of saying "Don't hit this in the water" replace that thought with "This is going right to my target" or "This one is on the green." When you affirm what you *do want*, your mind will create positive pictures and you are 80% of the way to the positive goal.

The second word that you want to eliminate is the word "Try". The word "try" can have an equally devastating effect on your swing performance as the word "don't". The reason "try" is a negative programming word is because there is no state of "trying" and it is a direct program to the subconscious mind to fail. I will prove this to you right now. Find an object that is around you and *try to pick it up*. Chances are you just picked up the object, so put it back down because the instructions were *"Try* to pick it up." Now you are probably not picking up the object, but I said *"Try* to pick it up." The lesson behind this example is you either do something or you don't, but there is no such thing as trying.

"Trying" is a negative programming word that sets the mind up to fail and gives a person a hook or way out. A golfer might say "I will try and practice tomorrow." More often than not, tomorrow comes and goes and the golfer says, "Sorry I tried, but just couldn't make it." Since there is no state of "trying", the subconscious mind immediately defaults into the path of least resistance, which is no action. The first step to eliminating this negative programming word out of your vocabulary is to again become aware of when you think or say this word. Next, cancel the thought and immediately replace it with a positive affirmations that again declares what you actually want to achieve. For example, instead of saying "I will try and get this on the green" cancel that thought and replace it with "I will put this on the green" or "I can do it." Make the decision to never be satisfied with "just trying" from now on. Either do it or don't do it. By doing so you will have less stress, and better results on a more consistent basis.

The third word that you want to eliminate is the word "Hope". To play golf at your highest level, confidence is a must. An easy way of creating greater confidence through your self-talk is by eliminating the word "hope" from your vocabulary. "Hope" is a weak word and a word that implies doubts in the mind. I will give you a few examples outside of golf to explain my point. Imagine that you are at the doctor's office and the doctor says to you, "I just learned how to conduct this operation, *I hope I get it right*." Here is another example. Let's assume you took your car to get new brakes and the mechanic says, "I never installed brakes on this model of car before, I *hope* I installed them correctly." In both examples, I am positive that nobody would feel confident in those situations. If you were at the doctor's you would want to "KNOW" they knew what to do and can do it. If you just picked up your car then I know you don't want to "hope" you are going to stop at the stop sign and you would want to "KNOW" you will. There is a major difference between hoping and knowing.

Repeat the following affirmations and notice what makes you feel more confident, positive, and empowered.

- "I hope I will play well today" versus "I *know* I will play well today."

- "I hope I can get this in the fairway" versus "I *know* this is one is in the fairway."

- "I hope I make this putt." versus "I *know* this putt is in."

This simple shift in language can make profound differences in the level of confidence that you feel inside. Eliminate the word "hope" from your vocabulary and replace it with "know." This is one of the easiest ways to quickly eliminate doubts from the mind and redirect your mind to greater success on each shot and every round of golf.

The fourth word that you want to eliminate is the word "If". You already know that when you play golf with doubts, it opens the door to poor execution of shots and rounds of golf that you must grind through. "If" is a super wimpy and weak word that like "hope" projects doubt into your mind.

Let's go through some examples to prove how weak the word "If" is. "If I play my best today, I will do well." "If I focus on each shot, then I hit the ball well." "If I can hit greens in regulation then I might have a chance." As you can see, none of these thoughts produce much confidence. What you want to do to *immediately* make a shift and keep your mind moving in the positive direction towards your goals, is to replace the word "if" with "when". Notice the difference in your confidence when you use the following affirmations instead of the first series.

- *When* I play my best today, I will achieve my goals.

- *When* I focus on each shot, I always hit the ball well.

- *When* I hit the greens in regulation, then I will score well.

- *When* I achieve my goals, I will feel the pride of accomplishment.

Self-talk with the word "when" creates much more confidence and a sense of knowing it will happen rather than the weak word "if".

A saying I like to use with my golfers is, "It isn't a question of "if" you are going to succeed, but "how and when" you will do it." Eliminate the word "if" and replace it with "when". When you do this, you will experience much more confidence while pursuing your goals and dreams, and a higher level of performance on the golf course.

The fifth word that you want to eliminate is the word "Can't". When a person says "can't", it means one of two things. First, the person doesn't know how to do something, or the person doesn't want to do something. One way to eliminate "can't" from your vocabulary and all the stress it produces, is when you catch yourself saying "can't", immediately ask yourself, "Is it that I don't know how to do this or is it that I don't want to do it?" This question is an immediate state changer back in a positive direction and removes all negative feelings connected with the limiting idea that comes from the word "can't". First, if you don't know how to do something then you can learn and second if you don't want to do it then you can release all stress attached to it. *The reality is you can do anything, so eliminate the word "can't" and create more success.*

The sixth and last negative programming word that you want to eliminate is the word "Need". Do you ever like to do things that you "need" to do? For example, "You need to pay the bills." "You need to take out the trash" "You need to do go to work." Of course these are things that have to be done, but how motivated are you to do things that you need to do? On the course many golfers say things like, "I need to hit this fairway."; "I need to keep this out of the water."; "I need to make birdie here". Ben Crenshaw said, "A 'must make' attitude puts too much pressure on your stroke." The word "need" brings with it an idea of force and pressure which can inhibit performance. It is better to say "I want to do this,"; "I want to hit the fairway,"; "I want to make birdie here,"; "I want to drain this putt." This is a much better way of communicating with yourself and evokes empowerment inside the mind, instead of the feelings of force and pressure. The word "need" brings forth tension, "want" brings forth peace, excitement, and confidence.

In 2012, the International Research Journal of Applied and Basic Sciences published a study which aimed to discover the effectiveness of instructional and motivational self-talk on basketball shooting performance. Researchers randomly assigned 57 participants, age 20-26 years old, into 3 groups: a motivational self-talk group, an instructional self-talk group, and a control group. The motivational self-talk group was instructed to use the phrase "I can" before shooting tasks and the instructional self-talk group was instructed to use an instructional phrase like "wrist, center." The control group did the tasks without self-talk instructions. The results showed that both motivational and instructional self-talk groups outperformed the control group in shooting tasks. In addition, the motivational self-talk group outperformed the instructional self-talk group.[4]

Another study published in the same journal revealed similar findings with dart throwing. Results showed that participants who combined positive imagery with positive self-talk had the best performance of the 5 groups. The researchers go on to say, "The findings suggest combination of positive mental imagery and self-talk is a potential technique to improve performance, the combination of negative mental imagery and self-talk can hamper performance where as positive self-talk can remove negative effects of mental imagery."[5]

The words you use, may seem insignificant, but do in fact have tremendous power. As you start changing the words you use, you will change your results.

Quick Review of Self-Talk

➤ Eliminate the word "Don't" out of your vocabulary and instead focus on what you "Do" want to achieve.

➤ Eliminate the word "Try" because there is no state of trying and it sets your mind up to fail. Replace it with "I will do it," "I can do it," or "I will do my best to...".

➤ Eliminate the word "Hope" and replace it with "Know". When you "know" you can achieve something it is much more powerful than just "hoping" you can accomplish your goals.

➤ Eliminate the word "If" and replace it with "When." It is not a question "if" you can, but "how and when". Say to yourself, "When I achieve my goals..." "When I execute on the course..." "When I focus today..." "If" implies doubts, but "when" builds confidence.

➤ Eliminate the word "Can't" from your vocabulary and if you catch yourself saying this word immediately ask yourself, "Is it that I don't know how to do this or I don't want to do it?" This gives you the ability to apply your energy to learning the new skill or to releasing stress about doing it.

➤ Eliminate the word "Need" or the phrase "I need to do this..." and replace it with the word "want". Wanting to do something invokes excitement and positive energy. Needing to do something drains energy and makes the action forced.

Action Steps to Take When You Encounter Negative Self-Talk

Now that you are aware of negative programming words to eliminate from your vocabulary and the words you can use to shift your self-talk back to a positive direction, the next step in taking control of your mind is actively monitoring your thoughts. Awareness is key in the correction process. Without awareness, our mind's operate on auto-pilot. With awareness, you can then train yourself to cancel the negative thoughts and replace them with positive ones that will fuel your mind and body to achieve the desired goal.

1. Become aware and acknowledge the negative thought that surfaced. Awareness of your negative self-talk is important because if you aren't aware, you cannot shift. This is the starting point in the correction process.

2. Cancel the negative thought. Once you are aware of the negative thought simply say to yourself "Cancel" or "Cancel That", in order to break the negative flow of the thoughts. This simple action can make a big difference in interrupting the old pattern of thoughts and temporarily opens the mind to accepting a new idea. (If you are unable to break the flow of negative thoughts by mentally saying cancel, then please refer to the trouble shooting chapter to find out how to do a pattern interruption).

3. Correct your self-talk by replacing it with a positive thought that is directed towards your goals.

4. Repeat if needed.

Here is a simple example to demonstrate this process. Let's say you had the thought on the tee box, "Don't hit this in the water." The moment you recognize the negative self-talk, say to yourself or out loud, "Cancel that", and replace it with what you want to achieve such as "I'm putting this shot right on my target straight down the middle of the fairway." Another quick example would be, "I really need to make this putt." Once you are aware of the negative language which in this case is "need", a word that provokes stress and pressure, mentally say to yourself "Cancel" and replace with a positive such as "I want to roll this in and I will."

Changes in your self-talk won't happen overnight because the habitual, negative thoughts have had lots of reinforcement which will need to be chiseled away one thought after another. Think of the untrained mind like a spoiled child who is used to doing whatever it wants. It will take time to discipline the child and correct the behavior due to what was allowed and reinforced in the past. As you begin this process of correcting negative self-talk, at first it may seem like an internal battle going on inside your mind. This is a great sign that you are making improvements and heading in the right direction. It is a great sign of progress because that means you are becoming aware of the negative thoughts coming to mind that used to be on auto-pilot and were subconsciously hurting your performance on the course. It also indicates that you are no longer accepting the old negative programming and your self-image is improving.

At first it may be a lot of work as you become aware of how much negative think- ing is actually occurring in your mind. *However, your mind is worth the effort of correcting this and each time you actively cancel the negative and replace it with a positive, this process will get easier to do and your mind will become increasingly more positive.* After a few weeks of doing this, your self-talk will be completely transformed. You will notice that you have a more positive mental attitude and that your thoughts are primarily positive in nature and supportive of what you want to accomplish. In addition, you will notice that negative thinking occurs less often and when it does, it is much more noticeable and correctable right away, since it is incongruent with your new positive outlook.

Here is a great metaphor to keep in mind when beginning this process of correcting the self-talk. Think about a rocket getting ready to blast off to outer space. In order for that rocket to get off the ground, it takes a considerable amount of energy and power to lift it in the air. It also requires a tremendous amount of power to push through the gravitational pull of the Earth before it breaks into outer space. But, once the rocket breaks through the force of gravity, little effort is required to move the rocket through space at high speeds and covering great distances.

A golden rule to put into practice when correcting your self-talk is: Gradually Leads to Sudden.

Remember at first it may seem like a battle because of all the negative thoughts that come to mind. Embrace it, since it means progress. The only way you can improve things is to be aware of things. Acknowledge that the negative thought is there, mentally cancel it, and correct it. Each time you do the easier it will get and the more positive you become. Over time, this consistent positive self-talk will form new belief systems that will support you in your pursuit of your goals.

A very important thing to keep in mind when you begin correcting your self-talk and training your mind to be more positive is to refrain from beating yourself up for having a negative thought come to mind. Negative thinking is a habit of most people and it's important to realize that you can't break this habit with more negativity, criticism, and put downs. Being hard on yourself is another form of negative thinking that adds resistance to the change and strengthens the old ways.

The way to defeat the negativity is with kindness and optimism – it can't be done any other way. It is necessary to embrace an attitude of patience, love, and forgiveness with yourself. Have faith in the fact that each time you cancel and replace the negative thoughts, it gets easier each time. The more you combat the negativity with positive energy, the easier it will be to establish a habit of optimism.

The Power of Affirmations

One way to increase the power of your self-talk is to make use of positive affirmations. Affirmations are a form of deliberate self-talk that are specific positive suggestions intended to move you towards your goals, dreams, and desires. Many people are familiar with affirmations. However, key pieces of information are often left out of the explanation which prevents people from experiencing maximum benefits from affirmations. When you know how to use affirmations effectively, you will find it much easier to notice great results from this form of self-talk.

In this section, you will discover how to effectively use affirmations and how to employ the will power from your conscious mind to accelerate the development of a positive mental attitude, achieve your goals, and have greater success on the golf course.

Both self-talk and affirmations are forms of self-communication that use the conscious mind and its functions to direct the subconscious mind in a specific direction. Remember that the conscious mind's primary function is to judge, evaluate, and critique the information you are being exposed to. Through self-talk and affirmations we make use of the conscious mind's resources to help us refine our choices so we are focusing our minds on a positive direction as well as using our will power to reinforce the goals we have selected.

The difference between self-talk and affirmations: *self-talk is an inner dialogue that is occurring in the conscious mind and affirmations are deliberately using your self-talk in a specific way.*

When correcting your self-talk to improve your mental attitude, it requires you to monitor the activity that comes and goes in the mind, and make shifts in the moment to redirect your mind in a positive way. When using affirmations to create a more positive mental attitude, it requires that you set aside a few minutes each day to deliberately direct your mind with specific positive suggestions.

Now that you know the differences between self-talk and affirmations, let's go over the rules to successfully using affirmations.

The first rule of successful affirmations is they must be presented in a positive way. This may seem basic; however, as you can see from the list of negative programming words, this is something that is often overlooked. It is important that all your affirmations refrain from the negative programming words mentioned in the previous section and that all affirmations are positive in nature.

The second rule is affirmations must be stated in a present tense. Instead of saying that "I will be confident", a more powerful way of declaring the affirmation is stating, "I am confident." By stating the affirmation in the present tense it sends direct messages to the subconscious mind to be that now. Otherwise, what occurs when using a future tense is the mind asks the question, "When will this happen?"

It is important that when you say affirmations to keep them in present tense and maintain an assumptive attitude that it will be this way. You may not experience the affirmation happening in the moment, but over time this shift will occur and you will begin to experience the impact of the affirmation. However, you can't program the mind with this tool using future oriented thinking. It's all about "now" to the subconscious mind.

The third rule is affirmations must be specific and the more specific they are, the better. Remember affirmations make use of the conscious mind and one of its jobs is to refine choices to get us moving in the right direction. It is important to take this into consideration when using affirmations so you can make them as specific as possible for goal achievement. Instead of saying "I want to be more accurate on the course" it is better to say an affirmation like, "I am precise and accurate off the tee and I put every tee shot right in the middle of the fairway."

The fourth rule is that affirmations must be believable – what you are suggesting to yourself must be achievable. For example, a golfer who consistently shoots in the 90's would benefit more from an affirmation such as "Every day it gets easier and easier for me to score in the 80's" instead of using an affirmation like, "I am a scratch golfer who consistently shoots even par or better." Of course this golfer could reduce their score eventually to become a scratch golfer in time; however, in their current position, this idea is less believable than scoring in the 80's. The more believable the affirmations are, the more impact they will have on the mind and the quicker you will get to your goals. A general rule of thumb is your affirmations should expand your mind on what's possible while still keeping it realistic enough to be achievable.

Now that you know some of the rules to follow when creating your affirmations, let's shift gears slightly and discuss the correct way to deliver affirmations to yourself. It is important to remember that when using affirmations, you are employing your conscious mind's will power to elicit the changes in your thoughts and to influence the subconscious mind.

In order to use affirmations effectively follow these simple rules:

1. First, affirmations are best done when you are standing in front of a mirror and looking yourself directly in the eyes.

2. Second, it is important that you stand in a way that projects supreme confidence and authority. So stand tall, put your shoulders back, and maintain a look in your eyes of the confident person you are becoming or wish to be.

3. Third, when repeating your affirmations, say them in a confident, strong tone of voice, even if you don't feel that confident when first starting out. *Follow the timeless advice for accelerating learning which is – "fake it till you make it".*

Why are these important rules to follow when declaring affirmations? It's important because for these thoughts to make an impact on the subconscious mind, your body language, tone of voice, and the message all need to be congruent in order to be effective.

The last point worth mentioning here in regards to affirmations is: *consistency counts and the more you repeat the same affirmations, the greater the impact it has on your subconscious mind*. When using your conscious mind and will power, it is important to know that it can take a period of 21-30+ days of consistent program-ming for it to bypass the critical factor of the mind and register in the subconscious mind as a new mental program.

In addition, *consistency activates the law of compounding which simply states that the more the idea is presented to the mind the greater the impact due to reinforcement.* What is great about the law of compounding is each time the same suggestion is repeated, it reinforces and strengthens all the other affir-mations previously presented to the mind. In just a short period of time, the power of the affirmation grows considerably with each repetition. Remember, for the mind to have a clear direction to move toward, it must be told consis-tently, until it gets ingrained and naturally moves towards it with little thought or effort.

Quick Review on Affirmations:

> ➤ Affirmations are deliberate use of self-talk that are specific towards what you desire to achieve.

> ➤ Affirmations must be said in a positive way to create pictures in the mind of success and what you want to achieve.

> ➤ Affirmations must be said in the present tense to direct the mind to cre-ate the changes now, even though it might take some time to accept it as a mental program.

> ➤ Affirmations must be specific and clearly identify what you want to achieve.

> ➤ Affirmations must be believable to the mind; they should stretch you, but not so far that it is unrealistic.

> ➤ Deliver affirmations to yourself in front of a mirror with positive, con-fident body language and tone of voice. When you believe it, you will achieve it, so be sure to say your affirmations as if they are a reality right now.

> ➤ Consistency counts. The more you repeat the same affirmations, the stronger they will become.

At the end of this chapter, you will discover how to create an affirmation script, the best times of the day to do your affirmations, as well as a simple program that you can do to make use of the natural self-hypnotic states we experience every day to speed up the acceptance of these new mental programs.

Autosuggestion: The Bridge to the Imagination

Now I would like to explain autosuggestion, the other form of self-communication and how it can be used to stimulate the subconscious mind and the imagination to train your mind for better results.

The process of autosuggestion came into existence in 1884 from a French physician name Emile Coué who came to the realization that many of the problems and illnesses his clients experienced were actually created by their mind. He came to the conclusion that if the mind created many of the common ills people experienced then it could also be the cure of them. During his research and experimentation, Coué identified an important truth in regards to the power of the subconscious mind: imagination is infinitely more powerful than the will.[6] This truth was later echoed by perhaps one of the greatest thinkers of all time, Albert Einstein when he said, "Imagination is more important than knowledge. For knowledge is limited to all we know and understand, while imagination embraces the entire world, and all there will be to know and understand."

Coué realized imagination has tremendous power and creative energy that can be used to heal, if directed in the right way. In addition, he understood that the subconscious mind knows infinitely more than what we do consciously. The subconscious mind is aware of the goals you have, the things you want to improve or strengthen, and the things needed to change in order to achieve the results you desire. So he came up with a very different approach to wellness for his patients: *his approach was autosuggestion.*

Coué was so successful with his autosuggestion approach to wellness that he quickly became very popular in France and throughout Europe because of the simplicity and effectiveness of his method. His method of autosuggestion didn't cost anything, was simple enough that anybody could do, and required no effort on the part of his patients except saying a few words. This approach was so successful that his patients were overcoming major illnesses and diseases of the time and it got him such notoriety, eventually he even worked with many of the French Royalty and the elite using his simple remedy.

So what was Coué's method? Instead of giving his patients a pharmaceutical prescription, Coué gave his patients a mental prescription that consisted of repeating a 12 word autosuggestion as often as possible throughout the day and a minimum of 3 times every hour.

This autosuggestion is so effective and applies to every area of life that it is the only one that you will ever need to remember. It is the ultimate suggestion and one that needs to become everybody's master mental program if you desire to have a healthy, happy, and success filled life.

The ultimate autosuggestion is:

"Every day and in every way I am getting better and better."[7]

The autosuggestion created by Emile Coué is a perfect suggestion. Write this down, put it in places in your home and office that you will see often, and commit this to memory because this seemingly simple suggestion has the power to completely transform your life and your golf game.

What makes this autosuggestion so powerful? The answer is simple. Your mind cannot reject this thought because every day in some way you are making improvements. Since the conscious mind can't reject this suggestion, it goes directly into the subconscious mind and activates the imagination and the innate higher intelligence of the subconscious for creative problem solving.

This autosuggestion overcomes the problem most people typically experience when first using positive self-talk and affirmations. Before the mind gets trained to have a consistent positive mental attitude, people using affirmations can encounter resistance in their mind. Resistance emerges in the untrained mind due to the specific nature of the affirmation. For example, a golfer might say to themselves, "I am confident on the tee box" and the critical nature of the conscious mind might kick in and say "That's not true, you just hit three balls in the woods." This is why your will power is needed when using affirmations until your mind gets trained to persist past the resistance and overcome the critical factor mechanism of the mind.

However, will power and force are not required when doing autosuggestion. Due to the general nature of this autosuggestion, the conscious mind cannot reject it and the thought goes directly to the subconscious mind where it is acted upon. Unlike affirmations, autosuggestions are most effective when they are general in nature, done in a relaxed state of mind, and allow the subconscious to create whatever it feels is needed in the situation without force or effort.

Emile Coué's autosuggestion "Every day and in every way I am getting better and better" is a perfect suggestion that doesn't require any variation. Refrain from deviating too much from this original suggestion and making it more specific. The more specific it becomes, the less effective it is. If you want to make this suggestion slightly more specific, simply attach one or two words at the end of the autosuggestion. For example, "Every day and in every way I am getting better and better *at golf*" or "Every day and in every way I am getting better and better *at putting*." Variations like this are acceptable, but it is recommended to stick to the original autosuggestion since your subconscious already knows your intentions for using it.

Autosuggestion is a form of self-communication that is intended to bridge the gap between the conscious and subconscious mind without using self-hypnosis. Turn this autosuggestion into a mantra and repeat it as often as possible throughout the day. This will continually activate your imagination and keep your subconscious mind moving you in a positive direction and improving things in your golf game without conscious awareness. Make this autosuggestion a part of your daily routine and you will notice that in just a short period of time it will transform your life in many positive and wonderful ways.

Quick Review of Autosuggestion:

➢ Autosuggestion is a general suggestion that activates the higher intelligence of the subconscious mind and stimulates the imagination to help you create success.

➢ The imagination is more powerful than your conscious will, and can be used to accelerate the learning process.

➢ Autosuggestion is best done when you are in a relaxed state mentally and physically.

➤ Autosuggestion doesn't require will or force for it to be effective. The less effort, the more effective the autosuggestion will be.

➤ General is always better than specifics when doing autosuggestion. The general nature of the autosuggestion gives the subconscious mind freedom to create whatever is necessary for improvement. Trust the power of your subconscious mind to do all the work.

➤ When doing autosuggestion, it is best to repeat it 10-20 times to compound the suggestion in your mind.

How to Make the Best Use of These Three Forms of Positive Mental Programming

All three of these forms of self-communication – self-talk, affirmations and autosuggestions – need to be developed in order to train the mind to create a consistent positive mental attitude in life and for peak performance on the golf course. Developing these aspects of communication will help you make use of your total mind and use it in more effective ways. This section is devoted to teaching you how to take this information and put it into action.

Perhaps the most important thing to know about using affirmations and autosuggestion to maximize their impact on the mind is knowing the critical times of day to do deliberate positive mental programming. While it is true that many golfers have heard about affirmations and some may even have heard of autosuggestion, the point most commonly left out of explanations is the time frame your mind is most receptive to this type of communication and new information. These critical times of the day are the first 20 minutes after waking up and the last 20 minutes before going to bed.

During these two periods of time, the mind is in a natural hypnotic state and highly receptive to new information due to the natural changes that occur in your brainwaves. When a person is getting ready to wake up in the morning, the brain naturally cycles through the various brainwaves to take you from delta brainwaves (or unconscious sleep state) into beta (or fully alert and awake). What is occurring during this process is a steady increase in brainwave activity. Here is the cycle of the brainwaves that occurs in everybody's mind when waking up. At first you are in delta brainwaves while you are deep asleep and as the brain speeds up the activity you eventually transition into theta brainwaves. As you become more aware of your surroundings and prepare to open your eyes, your mind transitions into alpha brainwaves. When your eyes open up, you remain in alpha brainwaves for 20 minutes before your brainwaves achieve beta brainwaves or full alertness. At night the opposite occurs. The brain goes from being fully awake in a state of beta brainwaves and as you begin preparing for bed, the brainwaves begin to slow down and shift into alpha brainwaves, or a state of relaxed awareness. Then as you are lying in bed, the brainwaves slow down even more and you begin losing sense of your environment, like lying in bed, and you slip into theta. Eventually, the brainwaves slow down even more and you achieve delta brainwaves when you enter into deep sleep or a state of unconsciousness.

Now that you are familiar with the different brainwaves, you know that alpha brainwaves are a state in which our minds are highly receptivity and open to new information. During these two critical times of the day, you can utilize these natural alpha waves to condition your mind for success through affirmations and autosuggestion. Think of these times of the day as your naturally occurring self-hypnosis time and make the commitment to utilizing these times to move you closer to your goals.

To make the best use of these times, I highly recommend creating a positive affirmation script that is specific to your goals and what you want to achieve. Writing up a positive affirmation script is fun to do and very effective for conditioning the mind during these receptive time frames. A written script is important for two reasons. First, it requires very little thought to read them in the mornings and night when you are in a relaxed state. The script eliminates having to think about what to say, you simply read it in a confident tone of voice. Second, remember consistency counts and the more the same suggestions are repeated the more it gets compounded in your mind which strengthens and reinforces the new thoughts. Your affirmation script doesn't have to be long and it is recommended that it is only a paragraph or two that takes 2-3 minutes to read. Shorter is always better because if it is too long you won't do it or have time to do it. Keep your script positive, specific to your goals, and motivating.

Here are some ways to create an affirmation script for mental programming. Get out a piece of paper or bring up your word processor on your computer, and devote a few minutes to developing your script. One way to get started is to create a list of positive affirmations about your golf game and what you would like your golf game to be like.

For example, here is a short sample list:

1. I am a confident golfer.

2. I trust my swing and make a confident swing on every shot.

3. I am fearless on the greens and believe I can make every putt.

4. I am calm, cool, and relaxed under pressure and perform at the highest level.

5. I hit my approach shots tight to the flagstick.

6. I love making birdies and make them all the time.

7. Confidence flows through my body when my driver is in my hands.

Obviously, this list can go on and on. If you refer to Appendix IV, you will find a list of 100 affirmations you can use for your affirmation script and to help you generate ideas.

If you are having trouble coming up with positive affirmations or ways to describe what you want your experience to be on the golf course then ask yourself questions like the ones found below to help you generate some thoughts. Write down your answers because they can be used in the creation of your affirmation script.

Question 1: "What do I do well when I play in the zone?"

Question 2: "In what ways do I want to improve my golf game?"

Question 3: "How do I want to think and feel on the golf course?"

Question 4: "If I was a championship caliber golfer how would I perform on the course?"

Asking yourself questions like these will give you lots of great ideas for affirmations to include in your script and things that will get you excited about your golf game. When writing your script, you are designing the mental programs for your mind and how you want to perform on the course. Make sure it is something that will inspire you, motivate you, and keep you excited about developing your game as you move towards your dreams.

Now that you have a bunch of written affirmations about your game that describe the way you want to perform on the golf course, it is time to combine these affirmations into a motivating script. Here is an example of a completed affirmation script:

> *I am an outstanding golfer who has a determined spirit and the focused mind of a champion. I am confident in my golf game and trust fully in my talents and abilities. Every time I step foot on the golf course I enter the zone. I am focused, confident, relaxed, and empowered. From tee to green I have the power to dominate on the golf course.*

> *I play golf with a fearless attitude and always maintain a positive mental outlook. I believe in my game and make every swing with confidence and precision. I have a consistent pre-shot routine that gives me the power to release my perfect swing into every shot I take. My pre-shot routine focuses my mind, I visualize the shot, and execute my swing perfectly and accurately. I am accurate from anywhere on the course, I am precise with all approach shots, and I love sticking my shots tight to the flag.*

> *I play golf consistently in the zone because I am focused on every shot and execute at the highest level. I am confident, empowered, and unstoppable. I believe in my talents and love showing off my skills on every shot I take. I am an outstanding putter and a birdie-making machine. I love rolling in putts and do so consistently on every green I face. I easily read it, visualize the line, and sink it.*

> *Every day and in every way all aspects of my game are improving. I am a champion, a winner, and victorious on the golf course. Every time I play golf I gain more and more confidence and succeed in all situations. I am the best and getting better all the time.*

Besides creating an affirmation script to program your mind with the qualities and traits of a champion golfer, you can also write affirmation scripts about specific aspects of your game. For example, you could create a script just for increasing focus, the ability to be calm under pressure, or to simply stay in the present moment on the course. Another type of script could be created about your specific keys to victory and peak performance. You can also create scripts that act as a mental review of swing mechanics to accelerate the learning curve and drive into your mind key swing thoughts. This can be done for swing mechanics for your driver, your short game, putting performance, and so on.

Here is another example of an affirmation script to increase your ability to play golf in the present moment.

> *I am an incredible golfer who has the power to play golf completely in the present moment. I make the full commitment to focusing my mind fully on every shot I take because when I am present with the shot my best swing is released. The only shot that matters to me on the course is the shot I am taking. The shot I am taking is the most important shot in the round and is worthy of my full focus and concentration.*
>
> *I love every shot I take on the course and each swing causes me to become more and more enthralled in the present moment. All that matters to me is the shot I am taking and making a confident swing on that shot. Nothing else comes to mind while playing golf except the shot at hand.*
>
> *I have the mind of a champion and all champion golfers focus fully in the moment. Every shot is important to me and gets my best. This power to play golf in the present moment causes my score to get lower and lower and lower."*

Take some time to create an affirmation script that will get you closer to your goals and program your mind with the most important information for success in your game. Your script doesn't have to be perfect. You can always refine your script, add new elements to it, or simply create a series of scripts to use. What is most important is that you take action and write one or immediately start using one of the examples found in this chapter or in Appendix V.

Bringing It All Together

Now that you have your affirmation script and know the ultimate autosuggestion, let's go over bringing it all together for successful A.M. and P.M. mental programming sessions.

Here are the steps to follow in the morning:

1. Before getting out of bed in the morning and while in a very relaxed state, begin to repeat your autosuggestion to yourself 10-20 times. Because the subconscious mind is fully available when you first wake up, stimulate your imagination by letting the autosuggestion roll around in your mind "Every day and in every way I am getting better and better." Remember that no effort is needed for autosuggestion, except repeating the words, and this time of day is the perfect time for autosuggestion.

2. Once you get out of bed after repeating your autosuggestion, go in front of the mirror stand tall and confident, and say your affirmation script in a confident tone of voice.

3. Go about your day with a positive mental attitude and one that is directed towards success, your goals, and dreams.

At night the process is going to be flipped:

1. As you are getting ready for bed, stand in front of your mirror in a confident posture, look yourself in the eyes, and read your affirmation script in a positive tone of voice.

2. When you get into bed, let yourself begin to relax and allow the autosuggestion to go through your mind 10-20 times to activate the subconscious mind before sleeping.

3. Enjoy a restful night of sleep knowing your subconscious is actively working for you through the night and getting you closer to your goals.

Consistently making use of these two times in the day to do positive mental programming is perhaps the easiest way to train your mind to produce better results in all aspects of life including your golf game. This process is simple and highly effective in transforming your mental attitude and accelerating the process of goal achievement. Remember, your mind will be doing this anyway, so why leave it to chance. Instead, take advantage of this natural hypnotic state of mind to motivate and program yourself to achieve your dreams and goals in golf. Commit to this process for 30 days and you will find it makes such a difference in your performance and your life that you will do it forever.

Self-talk, affirmations, and autosuggestion are the foundational building blocks to creating an empowered mind.

Harness the power of your self-communication and you will notice a natural shift in your ability to perform on the course, an increase in your motivation, and a positive mind that enables you to reach and achieve your goals. Follow the advice in this chapter and you will be on your way to developing the mind of a champion on the golf course.

FIVE

RELAXATION TRAINING

"You don't play golf to relax, you relax to play golf."

- Dr. Joseph Parent

A prerequisite for self-hypnosis as well as high level swing performance on the golf course is relaxation training. As Bobby Jones has said, "The enemy in golf is tension." Well, if tension is the enemy of performance, then relaxation is the solution that gives you the power to tap into more of your potential on the course and perform your best.

In this chapter, you will discover simple and effective ways to relax your body and manage physical tension on and off the golf course. The purpose of this chapter is two-fold.

1. First, learning how to relax the physical body is a necessary step to get the most benefits out of your self-hypnosis sessions. When you learn to deeply relax the body then it becomes infinitely easier to relax the mind in order to be receptive for self-hypnosis.

2. Second, learning how to release tension from the body will dramatically improve the quality of your current swing without making changes in your mechanics. When the body is relaxed during your swing then it

becomes much easier to execute your most natural swing with a fluid, smooth, and rhythmic motion.

Relaxation is a required skill to develop in order to achieve mental mastery through self-hypnosis as well as peak performance on the golf course, and this chapter will explain effective ways to achieve these goals.

This idea of relaxation as a key to success in golf is not a new concept in anyway. In fact, it has been known since the late 1800s as revealed in this Samuel Mure Fergusson quote, "Golf is eminently a game of relaxation of mind, if not of body." However, in my experience as a mental golf coach I have found that it is something that is intellectually understood by golfers, but it is not consistently applied in most golfer's game, especially on the course. I believe there are two main reasons for this. First, golfers are told they need to relax, but most actually don't know how to do this. Second, many golfers are actually unaware of how tense their bodies are while taking their shot. This lack of awareness causes golfers to harbor tension in their bodies that consequently causes poor swing performance. When this occurs on the golf course, many amateurs are quick to assume it was a mechanical issue that created the bad swing and completely overlook the fact that it was more likely the tension in the body, and not a mechanical flaw, that threw off their swing.

One of the easiest ways to fix your current golf swing and give yourself the best ability to perform is by incorporating relaxation training into your daily routine.

Learning How to Breathe Properly

The first foundational step in relaxation training is learning how to breathe properly. Now I know what you are thinking – "Proper breathing"? Don't I already know how to do that?" Believe it or not, most people aren't realizing the full benefits of proper, deep breathing because society has drilled into them the mentality to "stand tall, chest out, and stomach in." While it is true that this approach may help you look your best, it is preventing most people from experiencing the relaxation response that comes from proper breathing. As you go about your day and carry out your daily tasks, your breathing is typically short, and shallow with a more rapid pace. When you are breathing in this way, it is mostly done by your chest and ribs that expand and contract instead of your lungs, diaphragm, and abdomen.

One of the best teachers of proper breathing are sleeping babies. If you observe a baby sleeping then you will notice that their belly rises and falls with every breath. Proper diaphragmatic breathing comes from the abdomen and diaphragm, and not from the chest. When you breathe properly, you should notice and feel your abdomen moving outward as you inhale which gives your lungs the ability to fully expand and fill up with oxygen, and notice your abdomen falling as you exhale and release all the air out.

Deep Diaphragmatic Breathing

Here is an exercise you can do right now to teach yourself how to breathe properly from your diaphragm. All you will need for this exercise is a book, a floor, and yourself. First, lie flat on the floor and put the soles of your feet on the ground with your knees pointing to the ceiling. Next, put the book on your abdomen covering your naval. The goal of this exercise is to breathe with your abdomen and diaphragm which will cause the book to rise and fall with your breathing. Begin by slowly inhaling through your nose, and allow the abdomen to expand as your lungs fill up with air causing the book to rise. Now exhale slowly through your mouth, release all the air from your lungs, and feel your abdomen lowering the book back to the starting position. Continue breathing like this for a few minutes and focus on making the book rise and fall with every inhalation and exhalation. After just a few minutes of proper breathing like this, you will naturally feel more relaxed physically and mentally.

Now that you know the proper way to do deep diaphragmatic breathing, let's discuss how you can increase the relaxation response by controlling the breath. An important point to know about deep breathing is that it is a two part cycle. Brian Alman, Ph.D. and Peter Lambrou, Ph.D., in their book *Self-Hypnosis: The Complete Manual for Health and Self-Change,* said:

> *"Breathing is a cycle that has both an activating part and a relaxing part. A deep satisfying inhaled breath is activating; oxygen stimulates the brain and feeds the cells throughout the body. Exhaling is the let-go; tension is released, carbon dioxide is expelled and the muscles tend to relax during this part of the cycle."*[1]

Because the calming effect of the breath comes from the exhalation it is important that this part of the breath cycle is slow, and controlled. If you think about how you breathe when you are stressed, it is easy to notice that you either hold your breath and restrict oxygen to the brain and body or you have short, fast breaths from the chest and not the diaphragm which causes more stress and tension. In both situations, the two things that are neglected are breathing deeply from the abdomen and, most importantly, a long, slow, controlled exhale. During times of stress on the golf course, if you deliberately breathe with your diaphragm, hold the breath for a few seconds, do a slow, controlled exhale, and repeat this several times you will find a great reduction in the level of stress you are experiencing. In addition, it will create a feeling of control in the situation as well as relaxation in the mind and body which enables you to make the best decisions and perform at a better level on the next shot.

Let's go over another breathing exercise that you can use during times of stress to relax the mind and body so you can perform your best. One of my favorite breathing techniques that I recommend to my golfers is what I call the 3-6 method. The 3-6 method is simple to remember and easy to do. Here are the steps:

- Begin by inhaling through your nose using your abdomen and diaphragm for 3 seconds.

- Hold your breath for another 3 seconds.

- Next, do a slow, controlled exhale through your mouth for 6 seconds (double the time of the inhale) and then pause for 3 seconds in between breaths.

- Then repeat for 10 breaths or as much as needed.

This is an excellent method for keeping your cool on the course and it is recommended that you use this method before shots, in-between shots, or while waiting for your turn. It will keep your mind and body relaxed and keep you in the present moment. By focusing your mind on this technique, it will distract you away from stressors and give you the ability to manage stress in a more effective way on the course.

Here are some things to remember about this style of breathing. First, as you become more proficient at deep breathing, you can expand the number of seconds for the inhale, pause, and exhale of the breath. Instead of doing a 3 second inhale, you may prefer to increase it to 4 or 5 seconds with an exhale of 8-10 seconds. This breathing cycle doesn't have to be rigid and after a little practice you will be able to discover what works the best for you.

Just remember the golden rule to activate the relaxation response: For every 1 second of inhalation, do 2 seconds of exhalation.

Since the exhale is the relaxation part of the breath cycle it is important to always double the time of the inhale and make it a slowed deliberate exhale. Next, when inhaling, it is recommended to do this through your nose in order to avoid getting a sore throat from this style of breathing, and exhale through your mouth because it is easier to regulate and control the air releasing from your lungs. Another key point to remember is the pause between the inhale and exhale as well as between breaths. This is important because as you learn to breathe with your abdomen and diaphragm, you will be flooding your brain with more oxygen than it is used to. More than 1/3 of the oxygen goes straight to your brain and can cause a feeling of lightheadedness due to the amount of oxygen the brain receives. By pausing after a deep inhale, it prevents this feeling from occurring. If you notice yourself becoming dizzy from this breathing cycle, stop immediately, and return to your normal breathing until the feeling is gone.

It is also recommended that you breathe like this as often as possible on the course. Make it a goal to take a few breaths like this before taking your shot, and throughout the round. It will keep you focused, relaxed, and centered in a state of confidence while playing golf. Finally, it is recommended to do 3-5 breaths like this before starting your process of self-hypnosis and the relaxation processes you are going to learn in this chapter. This is a great way to get your mind and body prepared for deep relaxation and successful self-hypnosis sessions.

Mindfulness Breathing

Besides deep diaphragmatic breathing, there are other ways to use your breathing to relax your mind and body. One of these methods is called Mindfulness Breathing and it is the foundational lesson when beginning to learn Insight Meditation or Vipassana.

Mindfulness breathing is a method taught by Buddhist monks as a way to quiet and still the mind as well as enter into a relaxed, meditative state. This style of breathing has nothing to with trying to control the breath, in fact, just the opposite.

Mindfulness breathing is focused on being aware of the natural inhalation and ex-halation of the breath. The practice of mindfulness breathing is simple and basic, but don't let that fool you because it can take considerable work to master it. The goal of mindfulness breathing is to be in the present moment and simply acknowl-edge the inhale and the exhale of each breath as it naturally occurs.

The basic practice of mindfulness breathing is to clear your mind of all thoughts and focus your attention solely on your breathing. Every time you inhale you men-tally say to yourself, "I am aware I am breathing in" and as you exhale you men-tally say to yourself, "I am aware I am breathing out." Many people who practice mindfulness breathing simplify the acknowledgement of the breath to mentally saying "In" on the inhale and "Out" on the exhale. In-between breaths, the goal is to maintain a quiet, still mind without any excess thoughts, and wait for the next breath to emerge. As the next breath emerges, simply acknowledge the inhale and the exhale, and keep repeating this same process.[2]

When you first begin practicing mindfulness breathing, you will more than likely experience your mind wandering, filled with thoughts, and have a difficult time focusing completely on your breathing. If you notice this happening, simply and lovingly acknowledge that your mind has wandered from your breath and gently reconnect with your breathing by returning to the practice of being only aware of the inhale and exhale. With practice you will notice a great reduction in mental ac-tivity and mind chatter as well as an increased ability to be in the present moment by connecting with your breathing in this way.

There are many important benefits to a golfer who practices mindfulness breathing on and off the golf course. Mindfulness breathing is a method of guiding yourself into alpha and theta brainwaves which are the same brainwaves associated with self-hypnosis. With a few minutes of daily practice, this style of breathing will teach you how to quiet your conscious mind, or the thinking part, to eliminate the constant flow of mindless mental chatter and the barrage of thoughts that so often flood the mind. Both of these benefits can help you tremendously on the golf course. For starters, by training yourself to be able to elicit alpha brainwaves, you will improve your ability to enter into the zone on the course, because alpha brainwaves are the ones you experience when you are in a state of peak perfor-mance or the flow state. In addition, by learning how to quiet the conscious mind, you can learn to take every shot with mental clarity, focus, and confidence when addressing the ball in a competitive setting and achieve the ultimate goal, performance without conscious effort.

Mindfulness breathing keeps you centered in the present moment which is crucial to lowering your score and a high level of performance on the course. When you learn to stay "in the present" on the course, it will help you avoid the common pitfalls golfers experience during a round of golf. These include the downside of getting ahead of yourself on the course, becoming too caught up in the score, or worrying about future outcomes. It also gets your mind out of being stuck in the past, helps you to move on after a poor shot, and eliminates excessive frustration and tension that can come from a few bad swings. Paul Azinger said, "Staying in the present is the key to any golfer's game. Once you start thinking about a shot you just messed up or what you have to do on the next nine to catch somebody, you've lost." Mindfulness breathing helps you avoid these pitfalls, allows you to maintain control of your mind, and focuses your mental energy on the only shot that matters...the one you are taking in the present moment.

In addition, mindfulness breathing on the course is an effective way to keep your body relaxed and loose, as well as keep your mind calm and quiet. By focusing your attention solely on the inhale and exhale of your breath, it slows down mental activity and gives you the ability to use your total mind on the shot. When the mind is calm, you are accessing more brain power so you can make the best decisions in the moment as well as execute your swing with your subconscious, instead of the thinking part of the mind. This style of breathing also keeps your mind focused on something positive versus getting distracted from all the outside influences on the course like other golfers, tournament activities, spectators, and so on.

Mindfulness breathing is a powerful way to keep you in your inner zone, centered in positive energy, and at peace in any given situation. If all of this wasn't enough, you also get the benefits that come from proper diaphragmatic breathing and the relaxation response it provides to the body.

An excellent way to transform mindfulness breathing into positive mental programming is to follow the teachings of the famous Vietnamese Zen master, Thich Nhat Hanh. He instructs his students of meditation to attach words to the breath to conjure up transformational images from nature that represent their desired outcome. For example, if a person desires to be more flexible in life and their interactions with people, rather than using the words "In" and "Out" they might use the words "Swaying" on the inhale and "Tree" on the exhale. These words when connected to the mindful breathing invoke thoughts of a tree being rooted in the Earth and flexible enough to bend with the elements as they come and go. This simple meditation not only keeps you in the present moment and connected to your breath, it also creates mental imagery in the subconscious mind to help internalize the desired change. If a person desires to be a calmer, stronger person in life, they might connect the words, "Mountain" and "Solid" to their breath in order to create an image of immovable strength in the mind. Perhaps a person wishes to have a more quiet mind, they might attach the words "Still" and "Lake" to their breath to create an idea of perfectly calm water and associate it to their mental state.[3] There are endless ways to apply this lesson to enhance the practice of mindfulness breathing, and limitless possibilities of words choices to connect to your breathing that create a positive mental attitude and integrate new learning.

The words you attach to your breathing don't have to be just images from nature. To enhance the experience and do positive mental programming, you can also use words that relate to your performance on the course, your keys to victory, swing thoughts, outcomes, and so on.

Here are just a few practical examples of how you can apply this practice specifically to your golf game to improve performance on the course.

Inhale ⟹	Exhale
Effortless	Power
Pure	Swing
Solid	Contact
Precise	Accurate
Let's	Do It
Let	Go
Relaxed	Focus
Unbreakable	Focus

Slow	Down
Visualize	Execute
Peak	Performance
Pure	Roll
Roll It In	The Cup
I Can	Do It
Anything is	Possible
Birdie	Machine
Total	Commitment
Full	Focus
Confidence	Now
Power	Now
Commit	Now
Relax	Now
Focus	Now
Success	Now

Obviously, this list can go on forever and I am sure you are already thinking about the most powerful combination of words for you to use. Experiment with various combinations and use different words to create success in whatever situation emerges on the course.

When you create a mantra like this on the course, it has a powerful effect on your performance due to the consistent positive mental programming and the calming effect your breathing has on your mind and body.

Perhaps, the two most powerful words that you can attach to your breath on and off the golf course are the words "Thank" and "You." These two power packed words will increase your vibration and positive energy by putting you into an attitude of gratitude. The law of attraction states that "you get back what you send out." When you are constantly sending out gratitude to the world through this simple meditation, then the law of attraction takes over and you will begin to receive more things to be grateful and thankful for.

Whether you agree with the law of attraction or not, the fact remains, anytime you are on the golf course there is something to be grateful for because any day on the golf course is better than a day stuck in the office. The words "Thank You" attached to your breath will cause your mind to actively seek out things that make you feel grateful on the course. Whether that is being out in nature and enjoying a beautiful day, the way you are striping the ball, being with friends, or simply time away from work.

It is impossible to feel negative while in a state of gratitude, and this mental attitude has the power to keep you positive, patient, calm, and completely enthralled in the present moment on the course. Put this practice to the test for three weeks as often as possible throughout your day and while playing golf. I guarantee it will change your attitude in life and increase your level of enjoyment you experience during every round of golf.

Doing deep diaphragmatic breathing as well as mindfulness breathing on the course is an effective way to play golf in the present, keep your mind and body relaxed, and give you the ability to get more enjoyment from each swing. Off the course, it will reduce daily stress and practicing these breathing exercises will make it easier to achieve positive results with the process of self-hypnosis as you will learn soon.

The Tension-Release Technique

Now that you know the proper way to breathe to induce relaxation for managing your mental and emotional state on and off the golf course, it is time to take this section on relaxation training to the next level by learning how to release the harbored tension in your body. As mentioned previously, most golfers are unaware of the amount of tension that is actually in their body during their swing. The next step in relaxation training for peak performance is increasing your body awareness so that you can recognize when your body is relaxed and ready to perform versus when you are tense and tight.

The Progressive Muscular Relaxation technique will help to achieve this goal of increased body awareness by teaching you firsthand the difference in your body when it's completely relaxed versus tense. This technique uses a series of muscle contractions/sensations to increase levels of self-awareness and relaxation. It is a method that has been proven by researchers to decrease anxiety for optimal psychological states of performance.[4] I like to call this technique the Tension-Release Technique to make it easier for everyone to remember.

This relaxation method is an active process that will teach you the difference between when the body is tense versus relaxed so that you can identify when the body is starting to store up tension in the muscles that can inhibit your swing and how to quickly relax it away in seconds for peak swing performance.

Here are the steps to the extended version of the Tension-Release Technique for use when doing relaxation and mental training off the golf course:

Step 1: Find a quiet place where you can sit back and relax undisturbed for a few minutes.

Step 2: Close your eyes and block out distractions from the outside world. Then begin the process of relaxation by doing some deep diaphragmatic breathing as described earlier. Breathe in through your nose for a count of 3, hold it for 3 seconds, and slowly exhale through your mouth for 6 seconds. Pause and repeat for a few moments.

Step 3: Starting with your feet and moving up, imagine your body is divided into 10 regions or muscle groups.

- Region 1: Feet and Ankles
- Region 2: Lower Legs
- Region 3: Upper Legs
- Region 4: Hips and Buttocks
- Region 5: Abdomen and Lower Back
- Region 6: Chest Muscles
- Region 7 Upper Back

- Region 8: Shoulders and Arms

- Region 9: Neck

- Region 10: Head and Face

Step 4: Beginning with region 1, focus all of your attention on the muscles in your feet and ankles. Take a deep breath in and as you do tense all the muscles of your feet as tight as possible. Hold your breath and squeeze the tension in your feet for 5 seconds. Next, exhale through your mouth, instantly let go of all the tension, and let all the muscles of the region go completely loose, limp, and relaxed.

Step 5: Now move up the body to muscle region 2. Focus all of your attention on muscles of the lower legs. Breathe in deeply through your nose while simultaneously tensing all the muscles found in this region. Hold your breath for 5 seconds while continuing to tense the muscles tighter and tighter. Exhale your breath, and let all muscles instantly go loose, limp, and relaxed as you release the tension.

Step 6: Continue moving up the body and repeat this tension/release cycle for the remaining 8 muscle regions.

Step 7: Once you finish tensing and releasing all the muscle groups you will have a feeling of deep relaxation and will be in a state of physical and mental well-being that is free of all tension.

At this point you have a choice to either emerge yourself or do positive mental programming. If you decide you want to simply emerge out of the state of relaxation and continue on with your day then start by taking some deep breaths to re-energize yourself, begin reorienting to your surroundings by becoming aware of the chair you are sitting in, and then simply open your eyes feeling refreshed and revitalized. If you choose to take advantage of this state of deep physical and mental relaxation to do positive mental programming, simply begin repeating a positive suggestion to yourself 10-15 times, like a mantra, and then follow the same steps as were described above.

It is recommended to do this exercise at least once a day for a few weeks to improve your ability to relax as well as recognize and release harbored tension in the body. Commit 5 minutes of your day to doing this exercise. The more you do it, the more relaxed you will get each time. In addition, regular practice of this relaxation technique will dramatically reduce your level of daily stress, refresh your body, and keep your mind positive and calm.

Taking the Tension-Release Technique to the Course

After practicing at home, you can apply the Tension-Release Technique on the course to instantly relax your body before every shot. Remember, the enemy in golf is tension and this technique can be used to wipe it out of your game so you can execute your best swing freely, naturally, and more consistently.

I call it the 15 Second Golf Swing Cure. Instead of breaking down the body into 10 small regions, condense the process down to 3 major regions of the body; The Lower Region (Feet, Calves, Thighs, Buttocks and Hips), The Mid Region (Abdomen, Chest Muscles, Lower and Upper Back), and The Upper Region (Arms, Shoulders, Neck, Face, Head).

Here is what to do:

1. Take a deep breath in through your nose and as you breathe in, tense all the muscles in the lower region. Hold your breath for 5 seconds and squeeze the muscles as tight as possible. After the 5 seconds, exhale through your mouth and let all the muscles go completely loose, limp, and relaxed.

2. Then breathe in deeply again while tensing as much as possible the muscles of the mid region. Hold your breath for 5 seconds, keep tensing the muscles, then exhale and relax the muscles completely by letting them go loose and relaxed.

3. Finally, do the same process for the upper region. Breath in deeply, squeeze all the muscles of this region tight for 5 seconds, exhale and let the muscles become limp, loose, and totally relaxed.

1-2-3-NOW – you have eliminated all the tension in your entire body, step up and execute your shot, calm and focused – you are ready to perform your most natural swing.

Apply this technique when you are in your golf cart, while you are waiting for your turn on the tee box or green, and especially after poor shots. It can work wonders in your game and one that needs to be in every golfer's mental toolbox to execute at a high level. You never know when you are going to need it.

Why is this skill so valuable to develop? Because it helps you overcome a common pitfall most amateur golfers make on the course which is messing with their swing after a poor shot or two.

Many golfers have a hard time accepting a poor shot on the course and it causes them to question what they did wrong, look for advice from playing partners which usually is wrong, and make tweaks to a swing that doesn't need it. When this happens on the course, it can be disastrous for the golfers confidence, score-card, and enjoyment of their round. If you are ever struggling on the course, before messing with your swing, do the tension release technique as a first response to see if it is tension that creating the poor swing. More often than not, it's pent up tension that's causing the swing challenges and not a mechanical issue creating the problem.

A golden principle to follow in times of struggle on the course is: Eliminate tension before tweaking mechanics.

Apply this principle in your game and you will be amazed at how effective it is for getting your swing back on track. Certainly, if you use the tension-release technique several times throughout the round and your swing doesn't improve that day, then it would be appropriate to look at what errors in your mechanics are causing the problem. But remember, during scoring rounds it's always best to avoid swing changes, do the best with what you have that day, and work on eliminating tension so you can swing more relaxed and naturally. As Walter Hagen once said, "You don't have the game you played last year or last week. You only have today's game. It may be far from your best, but that's all you've got. Harden your heart and make the best of it." So save the tweaks for the range, and use the 15 second golf swing cure to find your best swing during your round.

During a workshop at the National Guild of Hypnotists Annual Convention, I shared this technique with the students in the audience. The next day, a man walked up to me and said he wanted to shake my hand and thank me personally. I asked him what for because I never seen him before in my life. He said his wife was in my lecture and when she came home she shared this technique with him. That morning he was playing golf with some of his friends and he decided to apply this technique on the course. He said he did it before every shot and it helped him to take 8 strokes off his score. His friends couldn't figure out what was making him play so well and were badgering him about getting lessons and that he was a ringer. He was thrilled with the result and made a special trip to the hotel to thank me for sharing it with his wife.

Practice using the 15 Second Golf Swing Cure at the range and apply it in your game while out on the course. It just might surprise you with how effective it is in giving you the ability to execute your best, most natural swing more effortlessly and consistently.

Another version of the Tension-Release Technique can be applied to the releasing of mental and emotional tension. If you just hit a poor shot or are dealing with frustrations on the course, you can use a version of this technique to overcome these tensions, instead of venting on the course or having an emotional outburst. Here is what you do:

- First, focus your mind on all the frustrations you are experiencing and make a fist.

- Next, breathe in deeply and as you do, mentally direct all your frustrations and negative thoughts into your fist, and clench it as tight as you possibly can.

- Then, hold your breath for 5 seconds and keep squeezing all the frustration into your fist making it get tighter and tighter. Exhale your breath, completely relax your hand so it is loose and limp, and let the frustration leave with the tension.

While you will experience immediate relief, sometimes it can be short- lived depending on your level of frustration and negativity. If you are really frustrated, just keep repeating the process as much as needed until you regain your composure and a sense of control. This is a much better way of dealing with things instead of putting all that hostility, frustration, and negativity into your next shot or carrying it over to the next hole.

If you want to do this exercise more covertly so nobody can see what you are doing, simply put your hand in your pocket. I heard that Tom Watson, in times of intense frustration during a tournament and still needing to maintain composure, at least in the eyes of the viewing public, would deal with this negativity by putting his hand in his pocket and squeezing his thigh muscle sometimes to the point of bruising. I find that using your fist is a much better approach to achieve the same objective, but whatever works.

The Passive Progressive Relaxation

Now that you are familiar and have probably done some practice with an active form of the progressive relaxation, let's go over how you can do a passive version of this exercise. The passive style of the progressive relaxation follows a similar principle as the tension-release technique, but instead of actively tensing and releasing the muscles you use suggestions and thoughts to direct the muscles into relaxation.

Here is an example of how to do the passive style of progressive relaxation. A sample script is also included in Appendix VI.

Find a quiet place where you can sit back, and relax without outside distractions. Turn your phone off, dim the lighting in the room, and turn on some soothing ambient music to enhance the experience if possible.

Step 1: Start by doing a few minutes of deep, diaphragmatic breathing to trigger the relaxation response in your body. After a couple of breaths close your eyes, and let your mind and body relax deeper. Mentally say to yourself:

It is time to relax now. I give my mind and body full permission to enjoy this time of deep relaxation. From this point forward every breath that I take calms and relaxes me more and more on every level. I am happy to have this time to relax and I value this time away from the world that is all for me. The deeper I relax the better I feel and the better I feel the easier it is to relax completely and totally"

Step 2: Now focus your full attention on the muscles of your feet and imagine relaxing, calming energy circulating through your feet and relaxing all the muscles. As you do this, mentally say to yourself suggestions for relaxation, such as:

As I focus my attention on my feet, all muscles begin to relax, deeply and completely. All muscles in my feet are relaxing and going loose, limp, and relaxed.

My feet have supported me all day long, and I give all muscles permission to let go now and enjoy the feeling of deep, soothing relaxation. The muscles of my feet are now relaxing and letting go. With every breath I take it increases the sensations of deep relaxation in my feet. All the muscles in my feet are now completely relaxed.

Step 3: Continue moving up the body and focus your attention on the muscles in your lower legs. Breathe in deeply and imagine the warm relaxation spreading up from the feet and into your calves, shins, and all the little muscles in the lower half of your legs. As you focus on the warm relaxation moving through this area mentally say to yourself:

The relaxation is now moving into my lower legs and circulating through all the muscles, tendons, and fibers in my calves. Every breath I breathe causes my muscles to relax more and more. The warmth of this deep relaxing energy is melting away all tension and stress in my lower legs and causes my legs to feel completely at peace. The muscles in my lower legs are letting go completely. They are completely relaxed now.

Step 4: Focus your attention now on your upper legs which include the quads, hamstrings, and knees. Breathe in deeply and imagine the warmth of the relaxation spiraling up and circulating through the upper legs. Mentally say to yourself:

My legs are beginning to relax completely. All tension is unlocking and melting away in my upper legs. The warmth of the relaxation washes through every muscle, tendon, fiber, and cell of my legs. My legs are completely letting go. I can feel my legs relaxing deeply now. All tension is gone and my legs are loose, limp, and completely relaxed.

Step 5: Keep moving up the body and focus on the relaxation entering into your hips and buttocks. As you concentrate on this muscle region, mentally say to yourself:

My hips and buttocks are now releasing all tension as the relaxation swirls through this area. All the muscles are releasing, letting go, and becoming free of all tensions. I can feel the warmth of the relaxation calming and soothing all the muscles. My hips and buttocks are completely relaxed now and all parts of my body continue to relax deeper with every breath I take.

Step 6: Progress up the body and place your full concentration on relaxing your abdomen and lower back. Breathe in deeply and imagine the warm relaxation moving into these muscles and mentally say to yourself:

As the relaxation moves into my abdomen and lower back, it instantly and automatically begins to release all tension and fills this region of my body with peace, comfort, and relaxation. The warmth of this deep relaxation is unlocking all the muscles and all muscles let go completely into total comfort. My abdomen and lower back are relaxing so completely. These muscles are completely relaxed now and becoming more and more relaxed with every breath I take.

Step 7: Now begin to focus your attention on the relaxation spiraling up into your chest and upper back. Breathe in deeply and direct the warm soothing relaxation into these muscles and mentally say to yourself:

My chest and upper back are being consumed by the relaxation and all muscles are letting go so completely now. Every breath I take invokes greater and greater levels of relaxation in this part of my body. The relaxing energy is swirling through all the muscles, organs, tendons, fibers, and cells of my chest and upper back. The relaxation moves up my spinal column releasing all tensions and flooding my body with total comfort and complete relaxation. All muscles are letting go into relaxation so quickly and deeply now. All parts of my chest and upper back are completely relaxed now and feel peaceful, warm, and comfortable.

Step 8: Focus your attention now on the relaxation moving into your shoulders and throughout your arms and hands. Breathe in deeply and imagine the warm relaxation flowing through these parts of your body and mentally say to yourself:

The relaxation is now spreading through my shoulders, down my arms, and to my fingertips. All remaining tension in the body is being pushed out now through the tips of my fingers as the relaxation takes over completely. All stored tension is leaving now going out and away, out and away, out and away through my fingertips. Relaxation is now spreading through every inch of my arms and shoulders, calming and relaxing me deeply. All tension is now gone and replaced by peace, comfort, and relaxing energy. My shoulders and arms are now completely relaxed and peaceful.

Step 9: Keep progressing upwards through the body and direct all of your energy on your neck muscles. Breathe in deeply and imagine the warm relaxation spreading throughout all the little muscles of your neck and mentally say to yourself:

The relaxation is now working its magic on all the muscles of my neck, loosening and relaxing all muscles completely. My neck has done an excellent job supporting my head and it now has permission to completely relax and enjoy time off. It feels as if my neck is being massaged and all the muscles of my neck are going loose and relaxed. My neck muscles are relaxing now and peace is flowing into these muscles. The warm relaxation is soothing away all tensions now. My neck muscles are now completely relaxed and relaxing more and more with every breath I take.

Step 10: Finally focus your attention on the muscles of your face, head, and scalp. Visualize the relaxation spreading it's warmth into this part of your body and mentally say to yourself:

The warm relaxation is now moving into my head, face, and scalp smoothing out all the muscles. My jaws are relaxing and loosening causing my mouth to separate as the peace settles in. My facial muscles are unlocking now and returning to a state of pure relaxation. All the muscles in my head and face are releasing all tension and melting into the comforting relaxation that has taken over. My face, scalp, and head muscles are now completely and totally relaxed. I am in a state of perfect relaxation."

You can increase the level of overall relaxation by mentally saying to yourself:

My entire body is now completely blanketed in deep, soothing relaxation. Every breath I breathe keeps increasing the state of relaxation I am now feeling. My entire body is now at peace. Each and every time I have the intention of relaxing it gets easier and easier to enter into deeper and deeper levels of relaxation. The next time I relax in this way I will quickly and easily relax this completely and continue to relax deeper every time. I enjoy these feeling of deep relaxation and my body feels rejuvenated, restored, and back in a perfect state of peace.

To emerge from this state of deep relaxation, mentally say to yourself:

> *In a moment I will count from 1 to5 and at the count of 5, I will open my eyes feeling refreshed and revitalized. When my eyes open, this relaxed state will stay with me and I will feel great in every way. As my eyes open I feel centered, grounded, and peaceful.*
>
> *1... I am returning to the world completely relaxed, yet energized.*
>
> *2... I am becoming aware of my surroundings now and I feel great.*
>
> *3... As I breathe in deeply I feel energy returning into my body as if I am coming up from a refreshing nap.*
>
> *4... I feel great in every way and on the next count my eyes will open and I feel even better.*
>
> *5... My eyes are opening now, I am energized, and ready to go about my day in a positive way."*

Here are a couple of important things to know when doing this type of relaxation exercise. At first, this relaxation exercise should take you about 15-20 minutes to complete. As you get better at relaxing your mind and body you will be able to achieve deeper states of relaxation much faster and easier. However, be sure to give yourself adequate time at first to get into this type of relaxation experience so that you can get maximum benefit from the exercise.

Next, there is a tremendous amount of flexibility in the type of mental suggestions you give yourself for relaxation. There is no need to memorize the above or the script for this exercise found in the appendix. These are just ideas to get you started and as you do the exercise you will discover what thoughts and suggestions work best for you and create the deepest states of relaxation.

Finally, it is important to know that when doing any sort of progressive relaxation you always want to start at your feet and work up the body, and not from the head down. Many hypnotists and psychologists who utilize a progressive relaxation technique, regardless if it is an active one like the Tension-Release technique or a passive version which we just covered, make the common mistake of starting with the head and neck, and then progress down the body. The best place to start is at the bottom of the feet and work up the body because the feet are the easiest muscles to relax and the neck muscles are the hardest. Since the neck's responsibility is to support and stabilize the head and brain, they are last muscles to relax and can take the longest to do so. Naturally, it would be best to start with the easiest muscles and progress up to the most difficult so they have more time to loosen up, let go, and relax completely.

Once you have practiced and achieved success using the passive relaxation method, there are adaptions you can do that take less time for use on the golf course, just like the various versions of the Tension-Release Technique.

The Body Scan

The shortened version of the passive progressive relaxation technique is called a Body Scan.

A body scan is doing a mental scan of your body to assess the level of relaxation or tension in the body. To do this, take a deep breath in and close your eyes. Imagine your body as a 3 dimensional grid system with green indicating relaxation and red indicating tension. Using your imagination in this way will give your mind's eye a visual representation of stress and relaxation in the body. Starting at your feet and moving up your body, scan the muscles of your body to determine if there are any areas of the body that are tense, tight, or stiff. If you notice any tension in any part of the body or you visualize a red section then do this simple breathing exercise to eliminate it. Focus your mind on the areas of the body that are tense. Breathe in deeply and imagine drawing in relaxation into your body and as you exhale imagine this relaxing energy flowing into this part of your body transforming the muscles from red to green. Do this for all muscles that are tight and tense, or the parts of the body the mind indicates are red. Once you do this, do another quick assessment of your body to determine if all parts are green which will let you know it's "go time" and the body is a relaxed state ready for performance.

Another version of this exercise can be done by closing your eyes and again doing a quick mental scan of your body. If you notice any tension then breathe in deeply and as you exhale imagine waves of warm relaxation washing down through the body from the top of your head to the tips of your toes. As you exhale each breath, focus on relaxation flowing through all muscles, tendons, fibers, and cells of the body releasing all tension through the tips of your fingers and toes. Do this at least 3 times and then do another quick scan of the body to make sure all muscles are loose, relaxed, and ready to perform your shot.

After doing one of these body scan exercises, it is a good practice to follow it up by physically doing a quick stretch, loosen up the muscles with a quick shake or waggle, or simply let the muscles go loose and limp like a handful of rubber bands. Pay particular attention to your neck, shoulders, and arms while doing this to ensure the tension is released totally in these parts because these are the most common places golfers hold onto tension. A quick body scan followed by a physical loosening of these muscles will get your body in a prime state for performance and execution of your shot.

Chapter Review

This chapter revealed some of the most effective relaxation training methods for use on and off the golf course as well as for enhancing your ability to relax the physical body for self-hypnosis. You now know how to do proper diaphragmatic breathing for relaxation, how to elicit the relaxation response using your breath, and ways to do mindfulness breathing. We covered long versions of active and passive progressive relaxation and shortened versions for use on the golf course to give you the ability to quickly relax your body for peak performance as well as manage your emotional states while playing golf.

It is important to practice these techniques so that they become second nature and come to mind while performing to keep you at your best. The more you practice these techniques the more effective they will become.

1. Bobby Jones said, "The enemy in golf is tension" and by learning to eliminate tension it is one of the easiest ways to boost performance.

2. Relaxation Training has two main purposes:

   ➢ It will help you learn how to relax and get the most of your self-hypnosis sessions.

   ➢ It will help you increase your level of performance by improving your ability to swing with a relaxed and loose body, as well as handle adversity better on the course.

3. Proper breathing to trigger the relaxation response is deep diaphragmatic breathing, or belly/abdominal breathing.

4. The two parts of the breathing cycle:

    ➢ The activating part which occurs when you breathe in deeply and oxygen stimulates the brain and feeds the cells throughout the body.

    ➢ The relaxing part which occurs when you slowly exhale the breath and release the carbon dioxide from the body.

5. The 3-6 Method is the recommended breathing method to trigger the relaxation response:

    ➢ Breathe in through your nose for 3 seconds using your diaphragm and abdomen.

    ➢ Hold your breath for 3 seconds.

    ➢ Exhale slowly and controlled through your mouth for 6 seconds.

    ➢ Pause for 3 seconds and repeat.

6. Mindfulness Breathing: Having a clear mind and being mindful of the inhale and exhale of your breathing.

    ➢ When you notice yourself breathing in, mentally say to yourself, "In" and as you become aware of the exhale mentally say to yourself, "Out."

    ➢ You can use other words to attach to your breathing to focus your mind such as "Relaxed - Focus," "Confidence - Now," or "Peak - Performance".

7. The Tension-Release Technique:

    ➢ Start by doing deep diaphragmatic breathing and closing your eyes.

    ➢ Take a deep breath in and tense all the muscles of your feet, hold your breath while tightening the muscles for 5 seconds, exhale slowly and instantly let the muscles let go and relax.

    ➢ Progress up the body repeating this process for the remaining 9 regions of the body: Lower Legs, Upper Legs, Hips and Buttocks, Abdomen and Lower Back, Chest Muscles, Upper Back, Shoulders and Arms, Neck, Head and Face.

➢ Finish with positive mental programming or simply open your eyes.

8. 15 Second Golf Swing Cure (Tension-Release on course application):

➢ Use the same process as described in the Tension-Release Technique but instead of 10 muscles regions condense it down to the 3 major regions:

• Lower Region Muscles: Feet, Calves, Thighs, Buttocks, and Hips.

• Mid Region: Abdomen, Chest Muscles, Lower and Upper Back.

• Upper Region: Arms, Shoulders, Neck, Face, and Head.

➢ Use this technique before performance to relax the body in 15 seconds and after a poor shot to eliminate harbored tension in your body.

9. The Passive Progressive Relaxation:

➢ The passive style of the progressive relaxation follows the same basic principle as the tension-release technique, but instead of actively tensing and releasing the muscles you use mental suggestions and thoughts to direct the muscles into relaxation.

➢ For example, focus on the muscles of your feet and mentally suggest to yourself, *"My feet are relaxing and letting go. All tension is leaving as I focus on the muscles of my feet loosening and relaxing. The muscles are totally relaxed now."*

➢ Progress up the body from your feet to the top of your head. The process should take you 15-20 minutes to complete.

➢ Finish with positive mental programming or simply open your eyes.

10. Body Scan:

➢ This is a shortened version of the progressive relaxation for doing quick mental scans of the body to determine your level of relaxation or tension in the body.

➤ Take a deep breath in, close your eyes, and imagine the body as a grid system.

➤ Green indicates relaxation and Red indicates tension.

➤ If you notice areas of tension then eliminate it by doing this simple breathing exercise: Breathe in deeply and imagine drawing relaxation into your body and as you exhale imagine this relaxing energy flowing into this part of your body transforming the muscles from red to green.

SIX

STEPS TO SELF-HYPNOSIS

"I've learned to trust the subconscious. My instincts have never lied to me."

-- Tiger Woods

Now that you have some of the foundational steps for controlling your mind through self-communication and have practiced the relaxation training techniques, it is time to begin learning how to do self-hypnosis. In this chapter, you will learn the ins and outs of one of the most effective methods of self-hypnosis available so that you can use this incredible tool to take your golf game to the next level.

The easiest and most effective way to learn how to do self-hypnosis is to first get hypnotized by a trained professional. Getting hypnotized by a trained professional gives you the opportunity to be guided through the experience without having to think about what to do or delivering suggestions to yourself. This can be very helpful at first so you can become familiar with how it feels to be deeply relaxed and how simple it is to learn through just absorbing the positive messages. After being hypnotized by a professional it is easier to get yourself back into the relaxed state of concentration on your own since you will have had a firsthand experience.

As an alternative to seeking out a professional hypnotist, I put together a free self-hypnosis starter audio that will guide you into alpha and theta waves and give you an experience of getting into self-hypnosis. This audio is a training tool that teaches you, step- by-step, how to practice self-hypnosis and become familiar with the process. To succeed with the audio, all you have to do is follow the instructions for physical and mental relaxation and you will be on your way to mastering the steps of self-hypnosis. You can access this free bonus audio by going to www.golfersguidetomentalfitness. com. Also, you can access another free audio and receive an entire golf hypnosis session to increase your course confidence by going to www.mentalcaddie.com and signing up for the newsletter. These two resources will definitely help you accelerate your learning curve and get you on your way to mastering self-hypnosis for your golf game.

Let's start with an overview of a self-hypnosis session. Each self-hypnosis session is going to have 3 basic parts; beginning, middle, and end. Every hypnosis session is going to start with what is called a hypnotic induction. This is the process of relaxing the body and the mind to get into the receptive states of alpha (light hypnosis) and theta (deep hypnosis). After the induction, the middle portion of the self-hypnosis session is the programming phase. In the programming phase, you will be delivering to yourself positive suggestions about what you want to achieve or going through exercises like mental rehearsal or visualization for improvement on the course. Finally, each self-hypnosis session will be ended with what is called the count out. The count out is giving yourself suggestions for emerging from the relaxed state with energy and rejuvenation, a trigger for getting back into self-hypnosis easier and faster, as well as suggestions for integrating the learning. Every self-hypnosis session will follow this basic format of inducing the relaxation, providing suggestions for your improvement, and then a count out for emerging from your session.

Key Pointers for Getting the Greatest Benefits from Self-Hypnosis

As you prepare to start your practice of self-hypnosis there are some key pointers that will help you achieve better results and faster with this process.

First, the experience of self-hypnosis is subjective in nature and the experience will always be unique to the individual. Hypnosis is not a one size fits all phenomena and there is no right or wrong way to do self-hypnosis or experience it.

Second, hypnosis is a natural experience and should feel very comfortable and normal. Remember, hypnosis is not what is portrayed in the movies. You will never enter into alternative realities, be levitating around the room, or go off to some mystical place. It is a process that makes use of naturally occurring brainwaves of the human mind which means you will always be conscious, maintain a level of awareness of your surroundings, and feel similar to times when you were deeply relaxed or lying in bed after a restful night of sleep.

A great way to describe the state of self-hypnosis is to think back to times when you were at the beach. When you first arrive at the beach, you are aware of all the people running around, the noises of the people talking and music playing on the radios, and all the activity going on around you. However, after you settled into your spot and begin to unwind, several minutes later you find yourself so relaxed that all you can seem to hear are the ocean waves and nothing else bothers you. This is what it will feel like as you get into self-hypnosis. At first, you may be aware of activity or sounds around you, but as you begin to relax your mind and body everything will become peaceful and nothing will disturb you. You will notice that all that matters while in this state of deep relaxation are the suggestions you are experiencing and the moment. Self-hypnosis can be easily described as a state of peacefulness intended to enhance learning.

The third important point is self-hypnosis is a mental skill that takes time to develop fully. Just like learning any new skill, developing your ability to do self-hypnosis will take practice, patience, and persistence. You can't learn self-hypnosis simply by reading this book, it must be practiced in order to become proficient with it. *Think of your mind as a muscle and, just like other muscles, it requires exercise to get strong. **Self-hypnosis is mental fitness for your mind**.* Everybody will have varying ability of how deeply they get into self-hypnosis. Some people are very skilled at self-hypnosis right away, while others will need more practice to get into very deep states of relaxation. Regardless of how quickly you progress, understand that self-hypnosis is a skill everybody can learn how to do and with each session you will get better and better at getting into this state of deep relaxation.

The final important point I want to highlight is that is self-hypnosis can't be achieved through force. Sometimes the thing that holds people back from getting into self-hypnosis is wanting it too much or trying too hard to get into this state of mind. A great example of this is trying to fall asleep a night. When you are tossing and turning at night and try to force yourself to sleep, it becomes counterproductive and results in your becoming more and more awake. The harder you try to fall asleep the less likely it is to happen. This is called the Law of Reverse Effect.[1] Only when you relax and let the natural processes take over, do you finally drift off to sleep. The same thing holds true for doing self-hypnosis. Force and conscious effort will inhibit your ability to successfully enter into alpha and theta brainwaves and experience the benefits of these states. The greatest thing about self-hypnosis is the fact that the less you do the better.

Besides force or trying to get into self-hypnosis, the other thing that prevents people from experiencing the full benefits of self-hypnosis is thinking too much or analyzing what is going on. Both of these mental activities involve your conscious mind, and the part of the mind you are wanting to bypass to get access to the subconscious mind, your bio-computer. When you are using the conscious mind to question if you are doing things right, trying to force yourself into self-hypnosis, or thinking too much, it is causing your brainwaves to speed up and stay in beta. It is important that you give yourself permission to turn this part of your mind off, take a break from its non-stop flow of inner dialogue, and simply get into the experience of relaxation, as you naturally do each night before bed. To be successful with self-hypnosis, you don't need to think or try, just simply experience the peacefulness that this process provides.

Remember all self-hypnosis is subjective in nature and there is no right or wrong way of doing things, so trust that you are doing things that are right for you and understand that each time you do self-hypnosis it will get better and better. Keep these important points in mind when beginning your practice of self-hypnosis so that you can get maximum benefits from the process right away.

The Steps of Self-Hypnosis

Step I: Hypnotic Induction

What is the hypnotic induction? The hypnotic induction is the communication process that is designed to elicit a state of deep physical and mental relaxation through suggestions for relaxation. By accepting suggestions for relaxation, it slows down the brainwaves so that your subconscious mind becomes fully available and increases your mind's receptivity for accepting positive suggestions. If you practiced some of the exercises from the relaxation training chapter then you already have some experience in relaxing the physical body. Physical relaxation is the first step in self-hypnosis because when the body is relaxed, it makes it much easier to re-lax mentally since physical relaxation begins the process of slowing down your brainwaves.

However, the goal in self-hypnosis is to achieve a deep state of mental relaxation so that information is received while the mind is in a state of heightened suggest-ibility, which simply means in a state of learning and receptivity. Effective self-hypnosis inductions will include instructions first for physical relaxation followed by mental relaxation which you will learn how to do shortly.

The Elman Induction Method

In more than a decade of working as a board certified hypnotist and helping people achieve success in their lives through hypnosis, one of the most effective induc-tion methods I have ever come across is called the Elman Induction. The Elman Induction was created by Dave Elman, author of *Hypnotherapy*, which is a col-lection of lectures and trainings he gave to medical professionals including doc-tors, psychiatrists, and dentists teaching them how to hypnotize their patients.[2] What makes the Elman Induction so effective is its systematic approach to helping people relax their body and mind in a clear and easy way. Also, since it was the method taught to doctors who had little time with their patients, this induction method only takes a few minutes – typically between 2-5 minutes to get into a deep state of self-hypnosis versus the 15-20 minutes it can take using a progressive relaxation method described in the previous chapter.

The self-hypnosis starter audio that I created is a version of the Elman Induction. It is recommended that you use this audio to help you learn the steps of self-hyp-nosis. This audio will guide you through the process and once you internalize these steps, you will be able to repeat it anytime you wish. So go my website right now, www.golfersguidetomentalfitness.com, download this free audio, and go through your first experience of self-hypnosis.

Let's go over my self-hypnosis version of the Elman Induction process now so that you understand how and why this systematic approach is so effective.

Step 1: Begin by finding a place where you won't be disturbed and a place where you can relax and let go. Dim the lights, turn on some soothing ambient music, and create an environment of relaxation. Once you found this place, make yourself comfortable and put your body in a relaxed position. This can either be done in a seated position or lying down whatever is most comfortable for you. If you decide to remain seated, place your feet flat on the floor, and let your arms relax comfortably at your sides or in your lap. If you decide to lay down, then uncross your legs and rest your arms along your sides without touching the body. **A golden rule to follow is if you are feeling tired or it is late in the day then the seated position is better so that you don't fall asleep.** The only time hypnosis is ineffective is if you fall asleep, because all of your concentration gets diffused making it impossible to learn.

Step 2: Now that you are in this relaxed position, the next step is to find a spot on the ceiling to focus on to initiate the process. It is best to find a spot that is slightly elevated so that your eyes are gazing at the spot at a 30 degree angle. Remember when the eyes are in this position it causes the brain to naturally begin slowing down your brainwaves into alpha. This preliminary step is simple, but be sure to do it because it is an effective success booster. Once you find a spot to focus on, simply gaze at that spot with relaxed concentration. Use your imagination and imagine looking through that spot on the wall or ceiling as if you were gazing at a nice, relaxed scene like being at the beach, taking a stroll through a park, or whatever is a relaxing scene for you. As you gaze at that spot in an effortless way, begin doing some deep diaphragmatic breathing, as explained earlier to begin the process of physical relaxation. After you take a few deep breaths, mentally suggest to yourself that your eyelids are getting heavy, relaxed, and wanting to close. As you give yourself this suggestion, don't fight it or resist it, instead use your imagination and let this thought take over in the mind. Imagine it happening and you will begin to experience it. Within a few seconds, you will notice your eyelids feeling heavy, relaxed, and wanting to close, and as you feel this, let the eyelids relax and close down.

Step 3: When your eyes close, keep looking through your forehead as if you were still staring at that spot on the wall and continue doing your deep breathing. Now you are going to begin the process of physical relaxation. To do this, the first step is to focus on how great it feels to have your eyes closed and these few minutes away from the world and the stresses of life. Next, begin relaxing all the muscles around your eyes, your eyelids, and eye brows. Focus your attention on relaxing the muscles around your eyes so much that they just won't work. Let them relax so completely and totally that all the muscles just won't work and once you are satisfied that you have done that hold onto that deep relaxation and test your eyelids to make sure they won't work. This simple test is a measure of the relaxation you permitted in your eyes and it only needs to be one or two attempts to open the eyes. The goal here is to relax your eyelids so much that even though you might manage to move your eye brows, your eyes remain closed and completely relaxed. Once you have achieved this relaxation in your eyes, stop testing, and imagine the relaxation is flowing from the top of your head and all the way down to the tips of your toes. Imagine the relaxation as a warm, golden wave that washes down through every muscle, tendon, fiber, and cell of your body relaxing all parts of you and deepening the state of relaxation you are experiencing.

Step 4: Next, you are going to deepen the relaxation by doing a process hypnotist's call fractionation. This process simply means you are going to open and close your eyes three times to enhance the state of relaxation. Here is what you are going to do. Mentally suggest to yourself something like this:

In a moment I will open and close my eyes. The moment I close my eyes this feeling of relaxation I now have will become twice as deep. When I close my eyes, it is my mind's cue to double the relaxation flowing in my body.

Once you suggest this to yourself, open your eyes for just a second and then close them. The moment you close them, imagine that warm wave of relaxation washing down through your body doubling the relaxation in every part of you. Then you are going to repeat this a second time. Mentally say to yourself:

In a moment I will open and close my eyes again. This time when I close my eyes the feelings of relaxation will become 10 times deeper. The moment my eyes close, is my mind's cue to enhance this relaxation and it becomes 10 times deeper throughout my body.

Again, let your eyes open slightly for a second then close them and imagine that warm wave of relaxation flowing from the top of your head to your toes making the relaxation 10 times deeper. Repeat this step one more time by mentally saying to yourself:

In a moment I will open and close my eyes one more time. The moment I do this feeling of relaxation will become deeper than ever before. When my eyes close it is my mind's signal and cue to let go into relaxation deeper than ever before.

One last time, gently open your eyes for a second, close them, and imagine the warm wave of relaxation taking you deeper into relaxation than ever before.

Step 5: After doing this step, you should be experiencing pleasant sensations of relaxation in your entire physical body and all the muscles becoming loose, limp, and relaxed. Now just like you did with your eyes to start the process, you are going to focus your attention on a larger muscle such as your arms and begin relaxing all the muscles in your arms so they become so relaxed they just don't want to move or work. Mentally say to yourself something like this:

My entire body is completely and totally relaxed. All the muscles in my arms are so relaxed and at peace that even if I tried to move them I find I cannot. They are so wonderfully relaxed, so heavy, and peaceful that they are impossible to move. Even if I try to lift my arm I cannot, the harder I try the more relaxed, heavy, and peaceful my arms become.

Once you have done this and you are satisfied that you relaxed your arm muscles so much that they just won't work, give them a quick test, make sure they won't work, and continue to relax deeper by imagining that relaxation you let into your arms is washing down through your entire body. Just like the first relaxation test in your eyes, you only need to test the relaxation in your arms for a second or two. After you are successful, feel free to slightly adjust your body if and when needed for greatest comfort.

At this point in time, you will be in a state of complete physical relaxation, which is the first phase of self-hypnosis. Many people begin to notice wonderful and pleasant changes occurring in the body. Just about everybody will notice that their breathing has slowed down and become steady and rhythmic. Most are aware that their heart rate has also slowed and become relaxed. Some people, as they let go, experience a comfortable feeling of heaviness in their body as if they are sinking or melting into the chair. While others when they relax, feel lighter and oftentimes report feelings of being so light it feels as if they are gently floating. You may be aware of the flickering and fluttering of your eyes lids from time to time as well as the need to swallow more because the salivary glands work differently in hypnosis. Both of these are wonderful signs of letting go. People often report feelings of tingling in parts of their body, like the pins and needles feeling you get when a muscle falls asleep and some people let go so completely that they report a feeling of comfortable numbness in parts or the entire body. These are just a few of the sensations commonly experienced during a hypnotic induction and throughout the session. (A complete list of these will be included at the end of the chapter). It is important to remember that hypnosis is a subjective experience, meaning everybody will experience something unique. Experiencing just one of these signs or sensations is your mind's indication that you are immersing yourself in the process and beginning to enter into alpha and theta brainwaves. As you practice self-hypnosis, you will notice these familiar signs coming over you as well as deeper and deeper experiences of them each time.

Step 6: Getting back to the steps of self-hypnosis, now that you have achieved a state of physical relaxation, it is time to relax your mind and there is a simple process to follow to achieve this. The goal of mental relaxation is to have a quiet and clear mind in order to bring the subconscious to the forefront so your imagination and creative functions of mind can take over. Here is how mental relaxation is achieved using this method. Mentally say to yourself:

Now that I have complete and total physical relaxation it is time to relax my mind. In a moment I will begin counting backwards, silently in my mind, starting with the number 100. With each number I say, it doubles my mental relaxation. With each number I say it causes my mind to become more and more peaceful, relaxed, and quiet. After I say just a couple numbers, my mind will become so completely relaxed that all the numbers will simply disappear, vanish, and be gone indicating that my mind is in a state of complete relaxation."

Once you have given yourself this suggestion, let it sink in for a moment, imagine this happening, and begin the process of letting the numbers disappear. To do this, when you inhale say to yourself the number, as you gently exhale say to yourself "deeper relaxed". For example, wait for your natural inhale to occur and as it does mentally say to yourself "100" and as you exhale say to yourself "deeper relaxed". Wait for your next natural inhale and say to yourself "99" and as you exhale gently say to yourself "deeper relaxed." Again wait for your next natural inhale and as it occurs say to yourself "98" and as you exhale say to yourself "deeper relaxed". Repeat this process of mental relaxation until your mind becomes so relaxed that the numbers disappear and fadeout of your mind. Once the numbers have disappeared, your mind will be in a state of mental relaxation and is now open and receptive to accepting new ideas about yourself and your golf game.

The goal of this mental relaxation exercise is to release the numbers as soon as possible. In my former hypnosis practice and after working with thousands of individuals, the majority of clients were able to relax away the numbers after just a few, and oftentimes before the number 98. For clients who have a more difficult time mentally relaxing it can take them a little longer but everybody is able to relax the mind in this fashion. The only difference is the amount of time it takes to achieve this goal.

Here are a couple quick helpful hints to assist you in this process of mental relaxation. First, no force or effort is required to relax your mind. Again, force and effort increase brainwave activity which will slow down the process or make it difficult to relax away the numbers. Allow the numbers to surface in your mind and then relax them away through suggestions for mental relaxation. Second, you can use mental imagery to assist in this process. For example, you can imagine the numbers as wispy clouds in the sky that are breaking apart as the sky becomes clear and blue. Mental imagery like this is an easy way to stimulate the imagination, allow the conscious mind to wander, and have a visual image of the numbers disappearing from view. Third, refrain from analyzing what you are doing and trust that your mind will relax and cause the numbers to disappear. With practice, you will find this to become increasingly easier and easier to do, and after a while, the mind will become so used to this type of relaxation that it will happen almost automatically. Finally, even though the goal is to let the numbers go as close to 100 as possible, let yourself relax mentally at a speed that is right for you. There is no difference if you let the numbers go at, let's say 99, or in the 80's or even later, because the same state of mind will be achieved regardless of when. All it indicates is the length of time it took you to completely relax your mind. You can use this number as a benchmark to track your improvements in the development of this mental skill and your progression in using self-hypnosis.

Once the numbers have disappeared, you have successfully achieved a state of physical and mental relaxation through self-hypnosis which means you are now in alpha or theta brainwaves, and a state of heightened suggestibility. There is nothing more to it.

Quick Review of the Elman Induction for Self-Hypnosis:

1. Find a comfortable place to relax where you won't be disturbed.

2. Fix your gaze on a spot high up on the wall or ceiling, and stare at the spot in a relaxed way. Use your imagination and pretend you are looking through the wall and at a relaxed scene.

3. Do some deep breathing to start the process of physical relaxation.

4. Close your eyes and imagine looking through your forehead at the spot of the wall.

   a. Focus on your eyelids and how good they feel to be closed. Start by relaxing all the muscles around your eyes, your eye lids, and your eye brows. Relax them so much that the muscles just won't work. Once you are satisfied that you have done that, test them and make sure they won't work.

   b. Send that relaxation you allowed in your eyes to the rest of your body. Imagine a warm wave of that relaxation washing down through your body from the top of your head to the tips of your toes and relaxing every muscle in its path.

5. Next, do the fractionation exercise, which is the opening and closing of your eyes, three times. Each time you open and close your eyes, increase the feelings of relaxation in your entire body. Follow the instructions from the description above or the ones on the audio from the self-hypnosis starter.

6. Focus on relaxing a large muscle such as your arms the same way you did with your eyes. Relax the muscles so completely that they become so loose, limp, and relaxed they are impossible to move. Relax them so much that even the thought of moving them is too much effort. Once you are satisfied that you have done that, test them and make sure they won't work. This completes the process of physical relaxation.

7. Now it's time to relax the mind which is very easy to do after physical relaxation. To do this you will begin mentally counting backwards from 100 in this way. When you notice yourself breathing in, mentally say to yourself "100" and as you exhale mentally say to yourself "deeper relaxed." Repeat this process in a gentle and peaceful way until all numbers have disappeared. Don't try to hold onto the numbers, the goal is to let them drift out of your mind as a way to indicate mental relaxation.

8. When the numbers have disappeared, you are in a state of physical and mental relaxation, and ready to begin the process of positive mental programming through hypnotic suggestion.

Why the Elman Induction Method is Effective

Now that we have gone over the steps of the Elman Induction method, let's go over the reasons behind these steps so that you can understand why they are effective at guiding you into self-hypnosis.

The very first instruction in this process is to find an elevated spot to gaze at and imagine you are looking at a peaceful, relaxed scene. This simple step prepares the mind in two ways. First, the position of your eyes looking upwards naturally begins to slow the brainwaves to alpha. This occurs because this mimics the movement of your eyes when going to sleep at night. When you relax and drift asleep, your eyes gently roll back into the sockets and point upwards. This is a way of triggering the mental relaxation to begin, but without going to bed. The second purpose of this step is to get the mind to begin to daydream. When you daydream, your imagination comes to the forefront of your mind giving access to the creative subconscious while simultaneously allowing the conscious mind to wander. This is effective because your goal is to lessen the analysis and thinking of the conscious mind and mentally engaging in serene mental imagery is one way to do this. As the subconscious mind begins to take over, left hemisphere mental activity begins to reduce as the mind wanders into a daydream like state. This is another simple way to begin the process of mental relaxation. Even though these instructions may seem basic, they are actually the beginning of the transition from beta brainwaves to alpha and eventually theta.

Next, you are instructed to focus on the muscles around your eyes and relax them to the point they won't work. Once you achieved this deeply relaxed state in your eye muscles, you are instructed to test them to make sure they won't work, and then send that relaxation down through the body. This is a powerful step in the process for several reasons. First, this step is designed to create a model of relaxation for your entire body. The reason you start with a small muscle like the eye muscles is because it is easier to control and manipulate the small muscles before moving on to larger ones. By creating a model for relaxation like this, the subconscious mind begins to create the same response through the rest of the body. Second, doing this step successfully, believe it or not, is already an indication that you are in a light level of hypnosis. Hypnotists commonly refer to the Aron's Depth Scale for measuring the depth of hypnosis a client reaches. Aron's Depth Scale has 6 stages of depth and each has a simple test to indicate the depth level.[3] When you relax your eyes to the point they won't work, test them, and they remained locked and closed, you have achieved Stage 1 on the Aron's Depth Scale, indicated by the eye catalepsy. Catalepsy simply means either extreme relaxation where the muscles are so relaxed they are completely loose and limp like a rag doll, or extreme rigidity where the muscles are so rigid that they are impossible to move. So just by relaxing your eyes to the point they won't work and with a successful test that means you are already in a light stage of hypnosis. Finally, this step is powerful because it validates that your mind is responding to your suggestions and the self-hypnosis process is underway.

The next step in the process is fractionation and involves the opening and closing of your eyes three times. When Dave Elman, the creator of this induction process, was learning about hypnosis, he read that each time a person gets hypnotized they will go deeper into the state of relaxation and they will do so easier and faster with every experience. Elman questioned why a person would have to wait for 3-4 visits to a hypnotist's office to be able to get into deeply relaxed states associated with hypnosis. He thought why not hypnotize the person, send them to the waiting room, and then hypnotize them again, and do this throughout the day. Then a person would be able to get proficient at getting into hypnosis, deeply and easily. But, he didn't stop there and came up with another idea of hypnotizing a person, then emerging them, and doing this several times within a few minutes in order to cut down the time it takes to achieve the benefits of this deeply relaxed state. The process of fractionation is designed to achieve this goal in a short period of time.

What you are actually doing when you open and close your eyes, is re-inducing self-hypnosis in yourself several times, making it increasingly easier to double the state of relaxation throughout the mind and body.

After fractionation you will naturally be in deeper level of hypnosis which makes it easier to achieve the next set of instructions in the process of self-hypnosis. This step of the process has you focus on a larger set of muscles like your arms and relax these muscles to the point they won't work just like you did with the muscles around your eyes. Since you have provided a model for relaxation with your eyes to the subconscious mind, it is will be easier to achieve the same success with larger muscles. When using hypnosis, small successes lead to big successes because each step builds on the previous success. This part of the process is called arm catalepsy and it indicates Stage 2 on Aron's Depth Scale of hypnosis. The arm test, like the one with your eyes provides a measurable way of determining your progress in relaxing and letting go into the process of self-hypnosis. When you are successful with this step, it indicates that you have achieved complete physical relaxation in the body and that you are in a good, workable state of self-hypnosis and receptive to new ideas and suggestions.

As you can see from this explanation, this induction process is systematic and designed to make self-hypnosis an easy thing to do. After you achieved physical relaxation, the final step is mental relaxation. The process described earlier is one of the simplest ways to achieve mental relaxation and dramatically increase your mind's receptivity to your positive suggestions. In the Aron's Depth Scale, Stage 3 is indicated by having temporary or selective amnesia, and the process of making the numbers disappear is a method of achieving this level of depth. This step is very important because successfully allowing the numbers to vanish indicates you just crossed the threshold of light hypnosis into deeper levels of hypnosis. In other words, when you are successful with this step, your brainwaves are now beginning to shift from alpha brainwaves into deeper states of mental relaxation and theta brainwaves begin to emerge. While in this state, your mind is highly receptive to new ideas and suggestions, and you are beginning to experience the brainwaves associated with the super learning states that children experience. Achieving this level of relaxation makes it easier to get maximum benefit from each suggestion for success, makes your visualization experiences more vivid and life-like, and accelerates your learning process in developing new skills.

The goal in providing this quick breakdown of what it taking place during this induction is to explain *why* you are doing these various steps and how they systematically work together to guide you into deep relaxation, both mentally and physically. Besides the systematic nature of the process, it also provides you ways to measure and determine the level of relaxation you are getting into when doing self-hypnosis. Everybody wants to know they are doing things right, especially when doing something new. This induction method provides that feedback to you and, with each successful step, it serves as a validation that you are using your mind in a different way than you normally do.

Step II: Hypnotic Deepener

There are two other important parts of a self-hypnosis session that need to be covered to complete this explanation of doing self-hypnosis. These two other phases, the deepener and the count out, are staples of a self-hypnosis session and should always be incorporated into each one of your sessions. First, let's go over the next step following the hypnotic induction, which is hypnotic deepener.

You may have noticed that I mentioned that the Aron's Depth Scale has 6 stages of depths in the hypnotic experience, and this induction method only went to Stage 3. While there are other depth levels and they can be beneficial for certain areas such as pain management hypnosis, when using self-hypnosis for golf improvement these other depths aren't necessary or required. The state achieved when the numbers disappear is a deep enough state to achieve a tremendous amount of success using self-hypnosis. You will naturally reach deeper states of relaxation simply by repeating the process as well as incorporating what is called a hypnotic deepener after the numbers vanished from your mind.

What is a hypnotic deepener? A deepener is exactly what the name implies, it is a way of deepening the level of relaxation after the induction process. While there are endless ways to deepen the state of relaxation, I will briefly discuss two of the most commonly used deepeners so that you can use them to enhance your experience and get into deeper states of mental relaxation.

The first and most common deepener is doing a countdown such as 10 to 1 or 5 to1 with suggestions for going deeper into hypnosis with each lower number. This may seem basic, yet it is very effective method of getting into deeper states of relaxation. Here is a simple example of how this works. After going through the induction, mentally say to yourself:

> *In a moment I will count from 5 down to 1. With each number I say, it causes me to let go more and more and relax completely. 5 – deeper and deeper relaxed; 4 – more and more relaxed; 3 – drifting deeper and deeper relaxed; 2 – really letting go now; 1 – more completely relaxed now.*

To make this countdown deepener even more effective, you can incorporate mental imagery into the process to stimulate your imagination and enhance the experience of going deeper. A common way to do this is imagining that each lower number is like walking down a staircase of relaxation with each step taking you down into deeper levels. Another example is imagining being at a beach and writing the numbers in the sand. With this imagery, imagine writing the number 5 in the sand then wiping it away, and relaxing deeper as it disappears. These are just two of the endless ways you can add mental imagery into the deepening process. Use your imagination to come up with something that resonates with you.

The second common way of deepening your state is giving yourself a few minutes after the induction to imagine a serene place. Everybody has a serene place, a place that makes them feel the most relaxed and at peace. This could be the golf course, the beach, a park, a garden, being on a boat, relaxing in a favorite chair, and so on. Your serene place can be a real place or an imagined one, it makes no difference. By giving yourself a few minutes to imagine being in this serene place of yours and experiencing the peace, it will naturally cause you to relax deeper due to the mental association of relaxation you have linked to this place as well as the stimulation of your imagination. When your imagination is stimulated it means that your subconscious mind is becoming more active and your left hemisphere activity has reduced. Getting lost in a serene place is a fun and effective way to deepen the state of hypnosis and make your mind even more receptive to suggestions.

When doing a serene place deepener, the goal is to be able to get into the experience of being there so deeply that it feels like it's real. It can take time to achieve this goal of making the experience vivid and life-like, however, you can accelerate this process by incorporating all of your senses into the experience. As you let your mind drift off into the serene place, imagine the sights, sounds, feelings, smells, and tastes of this place. For example, if your serene place is the beach then visualize the clear, blue water with the white foam of the crashing waves. Hear the sounds of the waves, the birds, and all other noises at the beach. Imagine feeling the heat of the sun, the sand contouring to your body, the feeling of the cool water, and the feelings of relaxation. Smell and taste the salt air of the beach. Incorporating all of your senses into the experience will greatly enhance your ability to connect with your creative mind.

A Quick Review of Hypnotic Deepener:

1. A deepener is designed to deepen the state of relaxation and this process is done after the induction of self-hypnosis. This is done to increase your receptivity to receiving suggestions.

2. An easy way to remember to do a deepener is to think of it as the final step to the induction after you let the numbers disappear out of your mind.

3. After doing the deepener, you will start giving yourself positive suggestions for improvements in your golf game. More on this in the chapters to come.

Step III: Hypnotic Count Out

The other important part of the self-hypnosis session is the count out. The count out is the process of emerging from this state of deep relaxation at the end of your self-hypnosis session. To do a count out is simple. What you will do at the end of the session is mentally count yourself up from 1 to 5 and open your eyes. To make this more effective, it is recommended that you add some success boosting suggestions when doing the count out from 1 to 5. Here is an example. When you are ready to emerge, mentally say to yourself:

In a moment I will count from 1 to 5. At the count of 5 my eyes will open and I will feel refreshed, revitalized, and full of energy.

- *1 – The next time I do self-hypnosis or get hypnotized, I get into deeper states of relaxation quicker and easier than the time before.*

- *2 – Coming up more and more now. I can feel the positive energy surging into my body.*

- **3** – *Feeling completely rejuvenated now as if I was waking up from a refreshing nap.*

- **4** – *All suggestions are accepted in my mind and I am ready to create more success. I am energized, excited, and feeling great.*

- **5** – *Eyes open, full of energy and motivated to succeed.*

Besides giving yourself suggestions for rejuvenation and increased energy, the most important suggestion to give yourself is what is called a post-hypnotic suggestion for getting into deeper states of hypnosis in the future. This suggestion will accelerate your learning process and make it easier each time you do self-hypnosis. We will discuss post-hypnotic suggestions in length in a future chapter, but for now, simply remember this suggestion during the count out so you can learn this new skill of doing self-hypnosis quickly and easily.

Quick Review of the Self-Hypnosis Process

Let's do one final quick review of the steps in the self-hypnosis process:

1. First, you are going to do a hypnotic induction which is the step-by-step process of relaxing the body and the mind to get into receptive states for learning.

2. After the induction, you will follow it up with a hypnotic deepener to enhance the relaxation and guide yourself into deeper levels of hypnosis.

3. Once you have deepened the state, this is the time you will be giving yourself positive suggestions or going through mental training exercises which we will cover shortly.

4. Finally, after the positive mental programming, you will do a count out to emerge from the relaxed state with suggestions for feeling great and energized as well as for getting back into self-hypnosis deeper and easier the next time.

Initial practice steps for learning self-hypnosis: As mentioned at the start of this chapter, the best way to learn self-hypnosis is to first get hypnotized by a professional so that you have a firsthand experience of being guided into this relaxed state of mind and body.

If you haven't done so already go to www.golfersguidetomentalfitness.com and download your free self-hypnosis starter audio that guides you through the process described in this chapter. You will want to start the process of learning by first using this audio so that little thought is required to do self-hypnosis. Simply follow the instructions on the audio and in just a few minutes you will be experiencing the euphoria of deep relaxation that self-hypnosis creates. This audio also incorporates all the different parts of the self-hypnosis process including the induction, deepener, and count out so you can learn through experience how these parts work together in a session.

After you have practiced with the audio several times, you should be very familiar with this process and it is a good time to begin practicing on your own. As you start practicing the process on your own, be aware of the familiar sensations you experienced when following along the audio recording as a way to indicate you are getting into a receptive state of mind. At first, just practice inducing a hypnotic state, deepening your relaxation, and then count yourself out to emerge from the relaxation.

As you become more proficient at getting into this relaxed state, the next step is to begin incorporating some positive mental programming into the session after the deepener. The easiest way to start is to pick an affirmation that you like or use the autosuggestion you were taught and repeat it to yourself 10-20 times. Simply allow this suggestion to roll around in your mind as if it was a mantra. To enhance the power of the suggestion as you mentally say it to yourself, allow your mind to get lost in the idea and begin to create experiences associated with it. For example, if you are using the affirmation, "I am confident on the tee" then imagine yourself executing on the tee box in a confident way. Allow your imagination to take this suggestion and bring it to life. So you aren't just saying the words, but creating an experience of the words as if acting it out in reality. If you are using a general autosuggestion like "Every day and in every way I am getting better and better", then allow your mind to think about all the different aspects you would like to improve and imagine these ideas coming to life in your mind. These examples are the simplest way to begin doing positive mental programming in your self-hypnosis sessions.

When beginning the process of learning self-hypnosis follow these simple steps and you will be on your way to becoming proficient at doing self-hypnosis in no time at all. Each time that you do self-hypnosis add in a little more and over time you will have a very evolved system of doing positive mental programming, a way to accelerate learning in your golf game, and a method of conditioning success in your mind so it becomes a habit.

As you continue on with this book you will discover many exciting and effective ways of enhancing the power of your mind and making maximum use of this new skill of doing self-hypnosis.

Necessary Precautions

I want to conclude this chapter by going over a few necessary precautions when doing self-hypnosis.

The first precaution is to never do self-hypnosis or listen to a hypnosis recording when driving a car, operating machinery, or doing anything that requires your full attention. Self-hypnosis brings about deep states of relaxation which makes it impossible to do things like driving your car safely. The author takes no responsibility for anybody neglecting this advice and doing so is strongly discouraged. Practice self-hypnosis at a time when you can relax and aren't doing anything that would require your attention.

The second precaution is to understand that hypnosis doesn't give a person abilities they do not have in a normal waking state. For example, if you can't normally lift 300 pounds, you can't do it in hypnosis either. Use your head and don't put yourself at risk. Hypnosis is very effective for goal achievement but it doesn't bestow superhuman qualities. In addition, self-hypnosis is not a magic wand that can turn an average golfer into the next PGA Tour superstar. However, it is a tool that can accelerate the process of making an ok golfer a good one, a good golfer a great one, and a great golfer an elite one in a much faster time than just doing physical practice.

The final precaution when doing self-hypnosis is to know that a common experience people have when getting into alpha and theta brainwaves is time distortion. What tends to occur is people *underestimate* the amount of time their self-hypnosis session lasts and it feels like just a few minutes passed, when in reality, an extended period has gone by. In my hypnosis office, when I ask my clients how much time they think has passed, they typically say 5-10 minutes, when in reality, the session lasted an hour. To overcome time distortion when doing self-hypnosis, simply tell yourself the amount of time you want to do self-hypnosis for before starting. By telling your mind the time frame prior to the session, you set your internal clock. When the time is up you will feel an internal signal go off letting you know it's time to wrap up the session. If time is of the essence or you have limited time to do self-hypnosis this is a necessary step to do. However, if you have flexibility with your time then this becomes less important. One thing to refrain from is setting an alarm unless it is a soothing sound. An alarm will abruptly take you out of the relaxed state with a shock and this can result in feelings of fatigue, headaches, or inhibit your ability of getting deeper into self-hypnosis in the future.

Common Sensations, Signs, and Indicators of Hypnosis

Every person will have a unique experience when doing self-hypnosis. Even though it is a subjective experience, there are sensations and signs that are commonly experienced when a person does self-hypnosis. You don't have to experience all of these in self-hypnosis and chances are you won't. What is important is to discover your familiar indicators of self-hypnosis so that you know how the process is going – how deep you are getting.

Experiencing any one of these common responses is your mind's indication of you letting go and your ability to enter into this state of deep relaxation and heightened suggestibility. This list comes from the National Guild of Hypnotists training manual from their hypnosis certification course.[4] Here are some of the most common responses:

➢ Time Distortion

➢ Tingling

➢ Numbness

➢ Dullness

➢ Heaviness

> ➤ Lightness

> ➤ Excessive Salivation

> ➤ Eyelid Fluttering

> ➤ Detached

> ➤ Imagery

> ➤ See a Place (feel, imagine)

> ➤ Color

> ➤ See Self Happy

> ➤ Feelings (happy, safe)

<u>Chapter Review:</u>

1. Download your free self-hypnosis starter audio that will guide you through the steps of the self-hypnosis method explained in this chapter and give you a firsthand experience of self-hypnosis.

2. The hypnotic induction is the process of mental and physical relaxation that guides you into alpha and theta brainwaves.

3. A hypnotic deepener is a technique for deepening the state of relaxation you are experiencing. This follows the induction and can be used throughout your session to keep deepening your relaxation.

   > ➤ Countdown from 10 to 1, with suggestions for going deeper relaxed.

   > ➤ Imagine a serene place to activate the imagination and enhance the relaxation.

4. Positive suggestions are used after the induction and deepener for positive mental programming, goal achievement, and to accelerate learning. More on this in later chapters.

5. The count out is the process of emerging from the relaxed state with energy and rejuvenation. To emerge from the relaxed state, count from 1to5 with

suggestions for increased energy, and a positive attitude, then open your eyes at the count of 5.

6. When initially learning self-hypnosis, it is best to start with the audio and then practice the induction, deepener, and count out without the audio to get used to getting into self-hypnosis.

7. Once familiar with the process, begin incorporating an affirmation or auto-suggestion into your session and repeat it 10-20 times in order to get used to directing your mind with suggestions. As you become more comfortable with this part of the session begin adding in other suggestions and techniques that will be described later in the book.

8. Practice, practice, practice. Self-hypnosis can't be learned by reading, only through experience. Commit to practicing self- hypnosis at least once a day for a few minutes. The results will get infinitely better and you will experience more positive benefits each time.

9. Refer to Appendix VII Hypnosis Induction Tips and Scripts for more helpful tips for self-hypnosis success, and scripts for inducing hypnosis, deepeners, and count outs.

10. Necessary precautions

   ➢ Don't do self-hypnosis or listen to a hypnosis recording while driving, operating. machinery, or doing anything that requires your full attention

   ➢ Hypnosis doesn't give you special abilities or superhuman qualities. You can't do things in a hypnotic state that you can't do normally. Use your head when doing self-hypnosis.

   ➢ Be aware of the time distortion element of doing self-hypnosis. Before doing self -hypnosis mentally set your internal clock by telling your mind how long you want to do your session for. When you feel the internal alarm go off it is time to end the session. Avoid using a real alarm clock when doing self-hypnosis because it can have negative effects.

11. List of common sensations, signs and indicators of hypnosis.

SEVEN

OTHER METHODS OF SELF-HYPNOSIS

"Golf is a game in which attitude of mind counts for incomparably more than mightiness of muscle."

--Arnold Haultain

Without knowing it, you have already learned a variety of ways of inducing self-hypnosis. The first method of self-hypnosis is doing positive mental programming through autosuggestion during the first 20 minutes upon waking up and the last 20 minutes before going to sleep. The induction with this process is a natural one that occurs as the brainwaves go through their natural cycles when waking up and resting at night. These are naturally occurring alpha and theta states each day and through the use of autosuggestion, the state of self-hypnosis is easily deepened and the mind conditioned with positive mental programming.

You also learned two self-hypnosis induction methods in the chapter on relaxation training. Both the tension-release technique and the passive progressive relaxation are commonly used induction methods for hypnosis. Both of these techniques are primarily focused on physical relaxation, but combine it with a deepener, and it's an effective way to slow down your brainwaves for positive mental programming to the subconscious mind.

Finally, you learned my recommended method of self-hypnosis which is using a version of the Elman induction to systematically guide yourself into self-hypnosis.

In this chapter you are going to learn a few other methods for doing self-hypnosis so you have a variety of tools to achieve alpha and theta brainwaves and a method that suits you the best.

Dr. Bakas's Forty Count Self-Hypnosis Method:

The first method I want to discuss was developed by Dr. Norbert Bakas, author of the *Self-Hypnosis: Your Golden Key to Self-Improvement and Self-Healing.* Dr. Bakas's method is called the Forty Count Method of Attaining Self-Hypnosis and it is based on the tension-release technique described previously in this book.

Let's go over the steps now.[1]

1.   Retire to a quiet, darkened room where you will not be disturbed.

2.   Loosen any tight or restrictive clothing and remove your shoes.

3.   Lie on a bed, sofa, or reclining chair.

4.   Tighten the muscles in your legs, apply as much tension as you can, hold the tension and count backwards from 10 to 2, take a deep breath, and at the count of 1, exhale slowly. Permit the muscles in your legs to slowly relax - relax completely. Feel and become aware of the last bit of residual tension fading away.

5.   Extend your arms upward, tighten the muscles of your forearms and upper arms, and clench your fists. Repeat the same counting procedure you did for your legs.

6.   Tighten the muscles within your abdomen and chest, bearing down as hard as you can. Repeat the same counting procedure as you did for your legs and arms.

7. Lastly, close your eyes tightly, tighten your jaw muscles, clench your teeth together, swallow, and then apply tension to your neck and throat muscles. Repeat the same counting procedure. At this point you should have accomplished complete physical relaxation; however, should you continue to still feel physical tension, repeat steps 4, 5, 6, & 7. With a little practice you will become very proficient in developing complete control over tensions and stress of your physical body.

8. After having mastered the state of complete physical relaxation, you are again ready to proceed to relaxing your mental self. Start counting, backwards, from 40. Many individuals prefer counting an inhale as 40, the exhale as 39, inhale 38, exhale 37, etc. You may even visualize erasing the numbers from a blackboard as you say them. With each count, permit yourself to mentally relax by imagining a perfect vacation, a golf game, or whatever imparts to you a satisfying and relaxed feeling. Continue this count down until you have reached the number 25. At 25 you pause on your magical plateau. Stop counting and implant into your mind the mental images, your unfulfilled goals, and that which you desire to accomplish. How long you remain at this plateau is optional. For some, perhaps as little time as five minutes will suffice, while others may remain and luxuriate for 20-30 minutes.

9. To exit this state of mind, you may prefer to doze off into a peaceful, restful, and rejuvenating sleep, awakening at a specified time feeling rested, invigorated, or revitalized. You will be ready to enjoy a more positive and self-directed life. However, if practicing this procedure at other than your regular sleeping time, you may easily bring yourself out of your self-imposed trance by continuing to reverse the count from 24 towards 1. As you count back, perceive the feeling of relaxation with a fresh alertness, revitalized body, and a great positive outlook. When you reach the number 5, breathe a little deeper while your body continues to absorb that fresh positive energy. Then feel more and more stimulated. At the count of 1, EYES WIDE OPEN - A WONDERFUL FEELING -ENJOY LIFE TO THE UTMOST.

10. **CAUTION** - Once you commence counting backwards from 40, avoid allowing anything or anyone to distract you. Do not open your eyes, not attempt to arise and move. Program your subconscious mind to accept the reality of turning over complete control to your inner self. You cannot react consciously to any given situation until you reach that 5-4-3-2- and - 1 - eyes open! Plan for the event of an interruption or an emergency situation. If someone should start knocking on your door, or the telephone should ring, you must terminate the session. Quickly but methodically resume the countdown back to 1. For example, if you were on the count 32 when the interruption occurred, mentally say "30-25-20-15-10" and then "5-4-3-2-1 - eyes open." To properly condition the subconscious mind, it is imperative that once you start the countdown from 40 you must always count back to the 5-4-3-2 and 1. The count back is not necessary when you are leaving the magical plateau at 25 to enter your evening's sleep. The countdown from 24-1 is an energizing experience and is designed to vitalize and energize. Use it for wakening up; do not count back when you are entering a state of slumber.

Silva Method Instructions

Another powerful method of training yourself to get into alpha and theta brainwaves to achieve a receptive state of mind is to follow the steps outlined by Jose Silva in his world renowned book *The Silva Mind Control Method.* I highly encourage you to pick up a copy of his book if you want to expand your knowledge on alpha and theta brainwaves and their benefits as well as to discover some additional ways to maximize your mind outside of golf.

For the purposes of this book, I will just cover some of the introductory steps Silva provides for achieving alpha brainwaves.[2] Let's go over the simple instructions now for training yourself to achieve alpha brainwaves so you can easily get into self-hypnosis and use it to transform your golf game.

> *"When you awaken in the morning, go to the bathroom if necessary, then return to bed. Set your alarm for fifteen minutes later in case you drift off to sleep during the exercise.* (Author's note: I am not a fan of using alarms

because they can jolt you out of the relaxed state abruptly however it is your preference when doing the exercise.) *Close your eyes and look upward, behind your eyelids, at a 20-degree angle. For reasons not fully understood, this position of the eyes alone will trigger the brain to produce Alpha.*

Now, slowly, at about two-second intervals, count backward from one hundred to one. As you do this, keep your mind on it, and you will be in Alpha the very first time.

In Mind Control classes, students show a variety of reactions to their first experience from "That was beautiful!" to "I didn't feel a thing." The difference is less in what happened to them than in how familiar they were with this level of mind in the first place. It will be more or less familiar to everyone. The reason for this is that when we awaken in the morning we are often in Alpha for a while. To go from Theta, the sleep level, to Beta, the awake level, we must pass: through Alpha, and often we linger there through our early-morning routine.

If you feel that nothing happened during this first exercise, it simply means you have been in Alpha many times before without being particularly aware of it. Simply relax, don't question it, and stay with the exercises.

Even though you will be in Alpha on the very first try if you concentrated, you still need seven weeks of practice to go to lower levels of Alpha, then to Theta. Use the hundred-to-one method for ten mornings. Then count only from fifty to one, twenty-five to one, then ten to one, and finally five to one, ten mornings each.

Beginning with the very first time you go to your Alpha level, use only one method to come out of it. This will give you a greater degree of control against coming out spontaneously.

The method we use in Mind Control is to say mentally. "I will slowly come out as I count from one to five, feeling wide awake and better than before. One-two- prepare to open your eyes - three - open eyes - four - five - eyes open, wide awake, feeling better than before."

The Silva Method is an easy way to train your mind to successfully achieve alpha brainwaves for positive mental programming. All you have to do is put in the time each morning for forty days and you will be one step closer to mental mastery and have the ability to get into receptive states at will. This is a great method for anybody to follow especially those who need a little more time to adequately train the mind to get into self-hypnosis.

On Course Self-Hypnosis Applications

After you have trained yourself to achieve a state of self-hypnosis through any of the methods described so far in this book and gained proficiency at relaxing the mind and body, you can use variations of these methods to put yourself into a state of relaxed awareness on the course, or waking self-hypnosis.

Below you will find two simple applications of these exercises so you can do self-hypnosis on the course to increase your focus, relaxation, confidence, and swing performance.

Both of these self-hypnosis course applications are highly effective but do require that you put in the time *off the course* doing self-hypnosis for the benefits to be fully realized *on the course*. Just like your swing needs to be practiced in order to swing your best, self-hypnosis also needs to be practiced to achieve the greatest success. Let's go over the on course self-hypnosis applications now.

The Elman Induction - On Course Version

After doing the Elman Induction, the recommended self-hypnosis induction method, and gaining proficiency using it, you can turn this into a powerful way to trigger alpha brainwaves, or the "zone", prior to every shot you take.

Here are the steps to using the Elman Induction On Course Version:

Step 1: When you are behind the ball preparing to take your shot, take a deep breath in, close your eyes for a moment, and relax your eyelids to the point they won't work and test them. Once you have achieved eye lock, you are now in self-hypnosis and your brainwaves instantly slow down into alpha, due to conditioning, and cause you to get into the zone state for your shot.

Step 2: Keeping your eyes closed, take another deep breath in and give yourself a positive suggestion about the shot you want to hit such as "I am striping this tee shot straight down the middle of the fairway," "I love holing out shots with my wedge," "I am making a confident swing on this shot," or "This shot is on the green." Any positive suggestion will work as long as it is focused on what you desire to achieve. Avoid using negative programming words and keep it focused on the positive.

Step 3: Open your eyes and stay in this state of relaxed awareness by suggesting to yourself, "When I open my eyes I stay deep in the zone and succeed" or some variation of this and continue the rest of routine in the zone state. Or, you can simply open your eyes, continue your pre-shot routine, step up to the ball, and execute in the zone.

This 3 step process is a powerful and simple way of deliberately putting yourself into a zone state before having to perform. It is effective because you have several elements at work when going through this process. First, the deep breathing will naturally calm and relax your mind and body which by itself will elevate performance. Second, most adults experience alpha waves when their eyes are closed. Closing your eyes for 1-3 seconds will slow down the brainwaves and elicit a state of relaxed awareness. Third, locking out your eyes like you did in the long Elman Induction will trigger the same relaxed state of mind due to mental association from your self-hypnosis practice. Finally, with consistent practice it is a way to trigger your mind into positive action because it turns into a mental cue for peak performance.

Each time you follow the same process, the subconscious mind will naturally begin to take over more and more because a habit is being established. This pre-shot routine starter is a covert and effective way to train yourself to perform without conscious effort on each shot. It is highly recommended to put this process into your game after you have gained proficiency with the long induction because it is a sure fire way to perform consistently in the flow state on the golf course.

The Silva Method – On Course Version

If you decided to use the Silva Method as your primary method of inducing self-hypnosis then you can use this variation to trigger yourself in the zone prior to performance. This method will follow the same basic steps as the Elman On Course Version, but with a slightly different starting step.

Let's go over the steps now for the Silva On Course Version:

Step 1: When you are behind the ball preparing for performance, start your routine by taking a deep breath in and close your eyes for a few seconds. With your eyes closed, mentally say to yourself "3,3,3...2,2,2...1,1,1" and visualize the numbers flashing in your mind as you say them. This will clear your mind, relax your body, and trigger the alpha state achieved through the Silva Method.

Step 2: Keep your eyes closed, and give yourself a positive affirmation about what you want to achieve on this shot. Be sure to keep it in a positive direction and focused on what you desire to do so your mind can direct the body to produce a successful result.

Step 3: Open your eyes and stay in this state of relaxed awareness by suggesting to yourself, "When I open my eyes I stay deep in the zone and succeed" or some variation of this and continue the rest of your routine in this flow state. Or, you can simply open your eyes, continue your pre-shot routine, step up to the ball, and execute in the zone.

There are countless methods of inducing self-hypnosis that you can learn to do besides the ones revealed in this book. The ones presented here are only a tiny sample of what's available today. However, these methods were chosen due to their strong track record of success, how easy they are for anybody to do, and the applications that they can provide golfers on the course to increase performance once they become proficient with the mental skill.

Bottom line, these methods were selected because they work. Commit yourself to using one of these methods, or all of them, and develop the ability to do self-hypnosis. Will it take some work and practice? Yes, but learning self-hypnosis is one skill that is definitely worth the effort because it will put you on the path to mental mastery on and off the golf course.

Chapter Review:

Without knowing it you already learned several ways of inducing self-hypnosis throughout this book. Let's review the various ways you can physically and mentally relax and slow the mind down into alpha brainwaves.

1. **AM/PM Autosuggestion:** The first 20 minutes when you wake up and the last 20 minutes before bed, your brainwaves are in alpha due to the natural cycles of the brainwaves. In Chapter 4, you learned a routine that you can do in the mornings and evenings using autosuggestion and self-talk to program your mind for success.

2. **The Tension-Release Technique:** Doing the long version of this technique will guide you into a relaxed state where you are receptive to positive mental programming. See Chapter 5.

3. **The Passive Progressive Relaxation:** This is a commonly used technique by professional hypnotists as a way to guide a person into a relaxed, receptive state, as discussed in Chapter 5. After you finish the passive progressive relaxation, it's a perfect time to do positive suggestions.

4. **The Elman Self-Hypnosis Induction:** This is the recommended method of self-hypnosis described in depth in Chapter 6.

5. **Dr. Bakas's Forty Count Method** as discussed in this chapter

6. **The Silva Method** as discussed in this chapter.

You also learned several ways to do self-hypnosis on the course once you have practiced the induction methods. Let's do a quick review:

1. **The Tension-Release Technique Short Version:** You can turn the tension-release technique into a rapid way to relax on the course in 15 seconds. Close your eyes, take a deep breath in and squeeze the muscles of your legs, hold your breath while continuing to squeeze the muscles tight for 5 seconds, exhale slowly through your mouth and release all the tension instantly letting the muscles relax. Repeat this for the mid-region of the body, and finally the neck and shoulders. This is the 15 second tension cure as discussed in Chapter 5.

2. **The Elman Induction On Course Version** as discussed in this chapter.

3. **The Silva Method On Course Version** as discussed in this chapter.

EIGHT

HYPNOTIC SUGGESTIONS AND POSITIVE MENTAL PROGRAMMING

*"Your ego is everything. And if you don't get that
pumped up regularly you can't last."*

-- Dave Marr

Now that you know a variety of ways to do self-hypnosis and relax your mind into alpha and theta brainwaves, it is time to learn how to communicate to your mind for success on the golf course through hypnotic suggestions. Dr. Norbert Bakas, author of *Self-Hypnosis Your Golden Key to Self-Improvement and Self-Healing,* said[1],

> **"The success or failure of self-hypnosis is manifested by the types of suggestions that are programmed into the subconscious mind."**

In this chapter, you will learn the proper way to structure and use hypnotic suggestions so that you can make maximum improvements in your golf game and experience the positive benefits from your self-hypnosis sessions.

What is a hypnotic suggestion? A hypnotic suggestion is a positive suggestion that is given while a person is hypnotized. Hypnotic suggestions are similar to affirmations but with a few distinct differences.

> ➤ The primary difference between an affirmation and a hypnotic suggestion is the state of mind that they are given and received in. An affirmation is a positive suggestion delivered to the mind, while in beta brainwaves, or when fully alert. A hypnotic suggestion is a positive suggestion delivered to the mind in hypnosis or a state of alpha and theta brainwaves.

> ➤ The second difference between an affirmation and a hypnotic suggestion is since an affirmation is dealing with the conscious mind and its analytical filters, will power is needed to get the message into the subconscious mind whereas hypnotic suggestions require no force or will power in order to be effective. When doing affirmations it is almost like selling your mind on an idea where a more active and aggressive approach is needed, but hypnotic suggestions are more powerful when you are receptive, open, and passive.

> ➤ Lastly and most importantly, affirmations and hypnotic suggestions deal with different parts of the mind. The conscious mind is more an adult mind that analyzes, judges, and critiques information and needs convincing whereas the subconscious mind is more child-like in nature and takes information literally and simply acts upon it. The subconscious mind doesn't discern connotations in language and responds to the literal nature of the suggestion.

Tebbetts' Rules for Hypnotic Suggestions

Before getting into the different types of hypnotic suggestions, it is important to understand the proper structure and rules for creating positive suggestions that effectively impact the subconscious mind. Legendary hypnotist, Charles Tebbetts, in his book titled *Self-Hypnosis and Other Mind Expanding Techniques* provides 9 key principles to follow when creating your hypnotic suggestions. Let's go over these 9 rules now and expand on the important points.

Tebbetts' rules are:[2]

#1. *The motivating desire must be strong.* Before you start to write your suggestions, choose a reason or a number of reasons why you want your suggestion carried out. This must be a counter-emotional motivator to replace the behavior pattern you are intending to eliminate. If you are overeating, your present emotional motivator may be the enjoyment you derive from tasting certain foods. The emotions that might be chosen to replace this habit could be a desire for better health, a pretty figure, looking better in clothes, or becoming more attractive to a person you care for.

#2. *Be positive.* If you say "I will stop eating too much" you are REMINDING the subconscious mind that you eat too much, thereby suggesting the very idea you want to eliminate. If you say "My headache will be gone when I come out of hypnosis" you are suggesting a headache. To frame these thoughts positively, you should say, "I am always well satisfied with a small meal, I enjoy eating only at meal times, and after I have eaten food amounting to approximately four hundred calories, I push my plate away and say that's enough. I get up from the table feeling entirely satisfied and enjoy the resulting loss of weight." If you wish to suggest that your headache will go away you should say "My head feels better and better. It is clear and relaxed. My head feels good. It will continue to feel good after I come out of hypnosis, because all of the nerves and muscles are rested, relaxed, and normal. **Never mention the negative idea you intend to eliminate**. Repeat and emphasize the positive idea you are replacing it with.

#3. *Always use the present tense.* Never say "Tomorrow I will feel good" but rather "Tomorrow I feel good."

#4. *Set a time limit.* Remember, your subconscious mind is a goal striving mechanism, and once programmed toward a goal it never stops until it achieves it. Set a realistic time limit, and you will find that the goal is usually reached well before the time you set!

#5. *Suggest action, not ability to act.* Don't say, "I have the ability to dance well" but rather "I dance well, with ease and grace."

#6. *Be specific.* Choose a self-improvement suggestion you are anxious to carry out, and work with that one suggestion until it is accepted. While learning, it is best to start with suggestions that are easier to carry out so that you can see more immediate results.

#7. *Keep your language simple.* Speak as though your subconscious were a bright ten-year-old. Use words the average ten-year-old would understand.

#8. *Exaggerate and emotionalize.* Remember, your subconscious mind is the seat of the emotions, and exciting, powerful words will influence it. Use descriptive words such as wonderful, beautiful, exciting, great, thrilling, joyous, gorgeous, and tremendous! Say or think these words with feeling.

#9. *Use repetition.* When writing your suggestion, repeat it, enlarge upon it, and repeat it again in different words. Embellish it with convincing adjectives - the more often you are exposed to an idea, the more it influences you. - THE BRAIN WILL ALWAYS SEND OUT A MESSAGE TO ACT UPON ANY SUGGESTION, UNLESS CONFLICTING SUGGESTIONS INHIBIT IT. That all forces act along the line of least resistance is a fundamental law of matter. This is also a law of mind, since mind is merely the activity of matter - the result of stimulating nerve cells. The more often a card is creased, the more likely it is to bend in the same place again. And the more often a suggestion is acted upon by the UNCRITICAL MIND, the more certain the suggested response is to repeat itself.

How to Structure Hypnotic Suggestions for Golf

I want to elaborate now on some of these points to show how they relate to your golf game and suggestions for golf improvement.

Tebbetts' first rule states that the motivating desire must be strong. This is an important rule to follow because it sets the tone for creating improvements in your golf game. It is of great significance that you are very clear on your motivations and the reasons "why" you desire to achieve the goal. The "why" behind the goal is 90% of goal achievement because it is the force that keeps you moving forward on an unstoppable path. Truth be told, you will encounter roadblocks, some big, while others small, on your pursuit to your goals in golf. It is unavoidable. Without a strong motivator driving you to success, these roadblocks can inhibit your progress or even stop it all together. It is the motivators and reasons "why it is important to achieve this" that will give you the power to plow through all obstacles that appear on your path to greatness. When you have a strong motivation behind your goals you become like a powerful river that has the ability to flow through, around, over, and under anything that gets in the path.

Use Emotional Motivators for Your Golf Game

There are two types of motivators people come up with, practical ones and emotional ones. Practical motivators are doomed for failure because there isn't a compelling force behind them, whereas emotional based motivators have the power to move a person past even insurmountable obstacles on the way to the goal. Let's go over a simple example to explain the difference between practical and emotional based motivators. A simple example is to imagine a person who wants to quit smoking. The reason why they are still smoking isn't because there is a lack of desire to stop smoking, the problem lies in the motivation behind the goal. Most people have practical motivators when it comes to quitting and when asked why they want to achieve this they say things like "It's too much money" or "I want to be healthier." As you can tell these practical motivators have very little power and lack the ability to move a person into action.

The people who are successful at becoming a non-smoker have completely different motivators. Their motivators are emotionally driven, and invoke a sense of power and drive to achieve the goal. These people when asked why they want to be a non-smoker say things like: "I want to be around to see my children graduate high school"; "I am sick of being out of control to this behavior, I am ready to be the boss of my life"; "I am pregnant and my baby deserves to be healthy"; "I want to be a role-model for my kids"; "I want to prove to everyone at work that I can do it." This list can obviously go on forever, but I am sure that you are getting the idea. These motivators go beyond the practical and inspire action.

Let's assume now that Person A has a practical goal of stopping because smoking is too expensive and Person B has an emotional driven goal to succeed because they want to have a healthy baby and pregnancy. When faced with a craving or difficult situation who do you think will make it through and be successful at overcoming it? In difficult situations, practical motivators never even show up on a person's mental radar and doesn't get them taking action. Whereas the emotional driven motivators come up in the mind almost instantly and remind the person on why it is important to succeed.

All of this holds true in golf as well. Many golfers when asked about making improvements in their golf game come up with practical motivators and as a result end up making very little progress on their goals. They say things like "I just want to play better" "I just want to figure this game out" "I just want to lower my score by a stroke or two." These motivators lack power and won't get a golfer off the couch to go practice or take action.

The most successful golfers I work with when asked what their motivation is to get better, give responses like: "I want to be the best golfer in the world"; "I am working on turning pro and I am determined to make it"; "I want to prove to everybody in my hometown that I can do this"; "I am tired of getting beat by my playing partners and I want to beat them by lots of strokes"; "I want to win and make my name known to the world." These are obviously much more compelling motivators that inspire action and build intrinsic motivation to achieve the goals.

How do you determine good motivators to use in your self-hypnosis sessions? The best way to determine motivators is to ask yourself a series of questions. These questions will help you pin point your true motivators and help you enhance your practical motivations into emotional driven ones. Sometimes all that is required is to go from general to specific in your thinking and asking quality questions will help you to do this. Let's assume you have a general and practical motivator "I want to play better." To enhance this into a real motivating factor that inspires you to take action in your golf game, ask yourself the following questions and write out your answers. Be sure to be specific in your answers.

- Why is it important to me to play better?

- What excites me about playing better?

- How will playing better enhance my experience on the golf course?

- What are the rewards for playing better?

- How will I be empowered by playing better?

Answering questions like these will help you discover your real motivation behind your goals. Later on in this chapter you will learn how to incorporate these motivators into your suggestions to supercharge their effectiveness and accelerate the achievement process.

Use Positive Suggestions for Your Golf Game

The next point that I want to expand on and reinforce is the importance of your suggestions being positive in nature to create peak performance on the golf course. This is such a crucial thing for golfers to internalize because golfers think in pictures and these pictures direct our body's in how it is to perform the task at hand. Many golfers inadvertently direct their minds in a negative way and as a result end up hitting poor shots by thinking or suggesting to themselves things like, "I got to hit a shot a 170 yards to clear the water hazard." What does this type of suggestion imply and what type of picture does it create in the mind? Obviously, the dominant thought that enters into mind is the water hazard. Another example is a golfer who wants to use self-hypnosis to eliminate a slice. A negative suggestion that could hurt their game and actually increase the likelihood of more slices is to suggest something like "I no longer slice the ball." This example is an obvious one, the thought of the slice is the dominant focus of mind and what the mind focuses on expands.

Believe it or not, most people are so focused on the negative aspects their game that they want to improve and as a result that they are actually creating mental momentum in a negative direction. When I ask my clients what they want to improve upon, they typically respond with all the things they "don't want" such as "I don't want to be stressed on the course," "I don't want to slice the ball," or "I don't want to feel uncomfortable on the greens" to name a few.

My job as a performance coach and hypnotist is to help golfers identify the positive side of things to do effective mental programming. The way I get my clients to identify the positive direction of what they want to achieve is I say to them, "Great, you just told me what you don't want. Can you please tell me what you *do want*?" This may seem basic but it is very important for successful programming because you don't want to get better at the problem or make it more powerful which is what most golfers do. So if you are a person who knows what you don't want to do, simply flip it into a positive direction and in a way that will produce positive pictures in the mind of what you want to accomplish. Here are some simple examples:

Negative	**Positive**
I don't want to slice the ball.	I hit shots straight to my target.
I don't want to feel stressed on the greens	I feel relaxed on the greens.
I don't want to be embarrassed.	I am confident in my golf game.
I need to stay away from all hazards.	I play golf from the fairway and hit all the greens.
I keep missing putts to the left.	I roll putts into the center of the cup.

When you determine the positive aspects of the areas you want to improve, now you are one step closer to formulating effective suggestions for your self-hypnosis sessions.

Use Specific and Focused Suggestions for Your Golf Game

The next principle of proper suggestion structure I want to expand on is the aspect of being specific with your suggestions. In my experience working with clients for more than a decade, I have learned it is important to have a specific focus for each hypnosis and self-hypnosis session. While it is possible to cover and address a lot of different elements of your golf game in a self-hypnosis session, it is less effective if you take a shotgun approach whereas it is much more effective if you take a laser-like focus for the direction of your session and suggestions. It is important that you narrow your focus and work on enhancing a few specific aspects of your game before moving onto other areas.

Here is a simple way to narrow the focus of your sessions so you are addressing the most important aspects of your golf game.

The first step you want to take is to identify the 3 areas of your golf game where improvement would provide the greatest strides forward in your performance on the golf course and consequently will lower your score. These areas of improvement can include things that are related to behaviors on the course, mental attitudes, controlling emotions, or any other area that you feel needs improved. Take a moment to review your present golf game and write out all the areas of improvement that you would like to achieve. Next, review this list and circle the top 3 areas that would create the most significant improvements. Once you have done this, you now have identified the focus and direction of your sessions. Less is more in hypnosis and by having a clear, specific focus, it gives you the ability to keep your suggestions directed towards the greatest success boosters and makes it easier to formulate effective suggestions.

The second step in honing the focus of your session and making it more specific is to identify the 3 top motivators for improving these 3 areas of your game you just identified. I ask my golfers, "What are the top 3 reasons why you are ready to make these improvements starting right now, not tomorrow or next week? Why is it important to you to start improving now?" This question will help you to determine your motivators in regards to these areas of focus. Remember to make them emotionally charged motivators as discussed previously. After you write out your answers you will have your top 3 performance areas for the session and the 3 top motivators on why it is important.

The third and final step in narrowing the focus of your session is to determine 3 success symbols. Success symbols are indicators of your improvement and the signs that will let you know that you are on track. These success symbols are not your long term goals, such as becoming a scratch golfer, they are simple success markers that let you know you are making progress. An example outside of golf that makes this easy to understand is to imagine a person wanting to become a non-smoker. Obviously the main goal is to quit smoking. However, when asking my clients about their success symbols, I am looking for are the signs that let them know the suggestions are working in their life. For example, a smoking client might say, "I will know the session is working for me if I can get in my car and drive home without a craving or stopping to get cigarettes."; or "Tonight as I go out with friends, I remain calm and comfortable as a non-smoker, and when I wake up tomorrow I just get started doing my daily activities without desiring to smoke." These success symbols are important to identify because it gives you the ability use post-hypnotic suggestions to ensure that these symbols are achieved on your way to your long term goal.

Here is an example of what these steps look like when completed:

- ➢ **3 Performance Areas of Focus:**

  - Confidence on the tee box.

  - Consistent pre-shot routine on each shot.

  - Steady head while putting.

- ➢ **3 Top Motivators:**

  - To beat my playing partners.

  - I deserve to play golf well because of all the hard work and practice I put into my game.

  - To show everyone my true talents and prove it to myself.

- ➢ **3 Success Symbols:**

  - Making confident, relaxed swings on the tee box.

  - Going through my full pre-shot routine on each shot regardless of the difficulty the shot.

  - Rolling in more putts because my head is steady and calm.

A list like this provides you with a plan of action for your self-hypnosis session. Use your answers to create powerful suggestions for enhancing your golf game that are specific to your goals and will motivate you to greatness on the course. This laser-like focus will keep your suggestions on target and address the most important aspects for you and your success.

Use the Law of Compounding for Your Golf Game

The final principle I would like to expand on is the aspect of repetition of suggestions. In today's world, we are bombarded with advertisements that try to get us to take action on buying a product. Marketers know that the key to getting a person to take action is repetition of their message. In fact, there is a rule in marketing advocated by experts which states a person needs to be exposed to a product or company 7-10 times before a person will feel comfortable with it and act on what they are offering. Marketers and advertisers know that repetition sells and the more they can expose a person to what they are offering the more likely there are to follow through.

This same principle is at work with hypnotic suggestions and hypnotists call this the law of compounding suggestions. The law of compounding states that each time the subconscious mind is exposed to a suggestion it strengthens the power of the suggestion through reinforcement.[3]

There is a common technique, called the direct drive technique, used by hypnotists that applies this law of compounding to embed a suggestion deep into the subconscious mind through reinforcement and repetition. The direct drive technique is repeating the same suggestion 10-15 times in a row.[4] This is an effective technique for delivering suggestions because, just like in marketing, the more you are exposed to an idea the more likely you are to act on it.

During a hypnosis training to medical professionals, Dave Elman explains to the doctors how the law of compounding works.

> "Why was I able to get deeper anesthesia every time I gave a suggestion? Because suggestions can be compounded. The first one you give may be relatively weak. It becomes stronger, however, when you follow it with a second suggestion, even though the second one may be entirely different. You give suggestion one and that's weak. Then you give suggestion two and number one gets stronger. Then you give suggestion three and numbers one and two get stronger. Give suggestion four and one, two, and three all get stronger. Give suggestion five, and one, two, three, and four get stronger. Always, the first suggestion gets stronger. The progression extends back to the beginning."[5]

This direct drive technique is one of the easiest and most effective ways to turn a simple suggestion into a power-packed suggestion that makes a big impression on the subconscious mind to influence your behavior in a positive way. Repetition sells in marketing and in hypnosis so, repeat, repeat, repeat. Think of the law of compounding as the mind's version of compounding interest in the financial world

Direct Hypnotic and Post-Hypnotic Suggestions

Now that we covered the proper structuring of hypnotic suggestions, let's go over some of the different suggestion types for your self-hypnosis sessions. For the purposes of this book we are going to cover two different types of hypnotic suggestions: direct suggestions and post-hypnotic suggestions.

Direct Suggestions: Direct suggestions are suggestions that are delivered while in a hypnotic state that are to the point, direct, and have no ambiguity. Here are a few examples of direct suggestions: "I am confident on the golf course,"; "I make rhythmic swings and strike the ball on the sweet spot each and every time I am on the tee box,"; "I make the right read on every green and roll it straight into the center of the cup."

Besides the variety of ways to formulate direct suggestions which you will learn shortly, there are two main types of delivering direct suggestions that have different tones: Authoritative and Permissive. Authoritative suggestions are a direct command while permissive suggestions are more of a request. For example, "do it" versus "let's do it." Both are effective and it is your personal preference which style you want to use.

Post-Hypnotic Suggestions: Post-hypnotic suggestions are suggestions that are delivered during the hypnosis session, but the effects of the suggestion are to be carried out after the session is done. The best example of post-hypnotic suggestions comes from the entertainment side of hypnosis, the hypnosis stage show. For example, a stage hypnotist might give their hypnotized volunteers a suggestion like "In a moment I will count from 1to 3 and at the count of 3, you will open your eyes and emerge from hypnosis. When you do, any time you hear the word microphone, you will stand up and sing "The Star Spangled Banner" as if you were a famous singer. The hypnotist will repeat this suggestion a few times and then count from 1to 3. All the volunteers open their eyes and when the hypnotist says the keyword microphone, everyone stands up and starts singing. This is an example of a post-hypnotic suggestion. The suggestion is given while in hypnosis, but the effect is carried out when the person(s) emerge from the relaxed state.

Another example of a post-hypnotic suggestion is the one mentioned earlier in regards to Louie Oosthuizen and the red dot on his golf glove. In his sessions working with a hypnotist or a psychologist, a post-hypnotic suggestion was conditioned into his mind so each time on the course he stared at the red dot for 5 seconds, it triggered a state of calmness, focus, and grounded him in the present moment. To effectively use post-hypnotic suggestions, you will need to determine the way you want to feel, perform, or think, and then have a specific trigger that will set it into motion such as the word microphone and the red dot, as in the examples.

There are two primary types of post-hypnotic suggestions; A Carry-Over Effect and a Triggered Effect. A carry-over post-hypnotic suggestion is one that causes the feelings experienced in your session to continue after the session is over. For example: *"After I emerge from hypnosis, these confident thoughts and feelings will stay with me long after the session has completed. As I go about my round and take it shot by shot, these same confident feelings and thoughts will grow and grow and grow."* The triggered effect post hypnotic suggestion is like the examples above and use a trigger or a cue to elicit the effects of the suggestion. For example: *"When I grip my club, it triggers my perfect swing,"; "Anytime I say the words "confidence now"; confident thoughts and feelings instantly come over me."*

Using Hypnotic Suggestions: Examples of Positive Mental Programming for Your Golf Game

Now that you are familiar with the two primary types of suggestions you will use in your self-hypnosis sessions, let's review examples of different ways to use these suggestions for positive mental programming.

Swing Performance Direct Suggestion Examples:

➢ I make confident, full swings on every shot that I take.

➢ I love striping tee shots straight down the middle of the fairway.

➢ On every shot, I know what to do, how to do it, and I do it to perfection.

➢ I am confident with any club in my hand.

➢ I execute my swing with effortless power and precision.

➢ I love sticking approach shots tight to the hole.

➢ I consistently play from the fairways.

➢ I am so accurate that I hit every fairway and green in regulation.

➢ From tee to green I am unstoppable, confident, and determined to succeed.

➢ My swing is smooth, effortless, and consistently great.

➢ I connect with each shot and release my best swing.

➢ I visualize the perfect shot clearly and vividly, and produce what I picture.

➢ My swing always stays on perfect plane.

➢ I trust my swing and make confident swings on each shot.

➢ My best swing is released into every shot and I produce outstanding results.

➢ When I am positive I swing and play my best.

Putting Performance Direct Suggestion Examples:

➢ I am a fearless putter and know I can make putts from anywhere on the green.

➢ It's easy for me to get the perfect read and roll it in.

➢ I am calm, relaxed, and confident on every green and every putt.

➢ I love rolling in birdies.

➢ I am a birdie-making machine.

➢ My head stays steady and still on each putt.

➢ Every putt I take I roll it pure and perfect.

➢ I always have the right read, the right line, and the right speed on each putt.

➢ I visualize the entire putt and then roll it in.

➢ I consistently make one putt after one putt.

➢ I can make any putt so I step up and sink it.

➢ I am the best putter in the world.

➢ I believe in my skills, I focus my mind, and I make putts.

➢ I know putting is all mental and my mind serves me on each putt I take.

➢ I am consistently great on the greens.

➢ I clearly see the line and roll my ball into the hole.

➢ I love hearing the ball drop into the cup.

➢ I trust my putter.

➢ When I am on the green the hole seems to be twice the size and my ball easily finds the bottom of the cup.

➢ I always perceive the hole to be bigger than it is.

Pre-Shot Routine Direct Suggestion Examples:

➢ I do a pre-shot routine on every shot and make confident swings.

➢ I program my mind for success before every shot I take and my body follows the pictures in my mind.

➢ Before every shot, I tell myself what I want to do, I visualize it, and I execute the shot.

➢ I always remember to do a pre-shot routine before every shot.

➢ My pre-shot routine focuses my mind, relaxes my body, and I enter the zone.

➢ I have an unbreakable habit of doing a pre-shot routine.

➢ I visualize my success before each shot, step up, and perform perfectly.

➢ Each time I do my pre-shot routine I enter the zone and succeed.

➢ Every shot is important to me and I give it my full focus by doing a consistent pre-shot routine.

➢ My routine gives me confidence, determination, and the best opportunity to succeed.

➢ Before each shot I see the perfect ball flight, I get the perfect feel, and I execute the perfect swing.

➢ My pre-shot routine is automatic and my habit of success on the course.

➢ Each time I do my pre-shot routine I get deeper and deeper into the zone.

➢ I commit to doing my full pre-shot routine on every shot I take.

Short Game Direct Suggestion Examples:

➢ My short game is solid, consistent, and accurate.

➢ I love holing my chips and pitches.

➢ My short game always gives me great opportunities.

➢ I am calm and comfortable with my wedges in my hand.

➢ I visualize the ball landing and releasing into the hole and my short game produces success.

➢ I have amazing control of the ball around the greens.

➢ I have incredible touch and feel.

➢ I can get up and down from anywhere around the green.

➢ I love making sand saves.

➢ I love showing off my short game skills.

➢ My wedges are always on fire.

➢ I can always trust my short game.

➢ I am so confident with my wedges.

➢ I visualize it and I execute around the greens.

➢ I have perfect feel around the greens.

➢ I have great touch.

Course Confidence Direct Suggestion Examples:

➢ I have unlimited confidence in all aspects of my game and every day my confidence gets stronger and stronger.

➢ When I have a golf club in my hands confidence flows throughout my body and mind.

➢ I believe in my game, in my talents, in myself. From tee to green I am confident, calm, and consistent.

➢ Each time on the course I tap into more and more of my unlimited confidence.

➢ My confidence on the course produces lower and lower scores.

➢ My body language reflects my high level of confidence.

➢ I move on the course as if I was the most confident golfer in the world.

Emotional Control Direct Suggestion Examples:

➢ I am in complete control of my emotions on the course at all times.

➢ I am calm, confident, and in control on the course.

➢ I handle adversity in a positive, confident way and keep myself in the zone.

➢ I release negative shots through acceptance and keep myself moving in a positive direction.

➢ I am in complete control on the course and I choose to be positive at all times.

➢ My golf game doesn't determine my attitude, my attitude determines my game and the way I play.

➤ I commit to being the most positive golfer on the course.

➤ My calm, cool, confident approach to my game produces better and better results each time on the course.

➤ I handle every situation on the course with confidence, optimism, and determination.

Present Moment Golf Direct Suggestion Examples:

➤ I stay in the present moment on the course and take it one shot at a time.

➤ Every shot is important to me and I give each shot my full 100% focus and concentration.

➤ The only shot that matters to me is the one that I am taking.

➤ I stay in the moment, execute one shot at a time, and I produce the best results.

➤ The more present I am on the course the lower the score I produce.

➤ I succeed on the course one shot at a time.

➤ I love executing shots so much that I devote my full focus to each shot.

➤ Each shot is important and I release my best into every shot I take.

➤ Staying in the present keeps me focused, relaxed, and full of confidence.

➤ My pre-shot routine keeps me in the present moment and lets my best swing be released.

On Course Visualization Direct Suggestion Examples:

➤ I visualize clear, vivid pictures before every shot.

➤ I see the shot in my mind and I execute.

➤ I visualize the perfect ball flight and the ball landing precisely on my target.

➤ I always get clear visual images of the shot before executing.

➢ On the greens, I visualize the perfect putt and roll it home.

➢ Each day on the course my ability to visualize gets better and better.

➢ I always visualize my success and then do it.

➢ Each time I do self-hypnosis it gets easier and easier to visualize before every shot.

➢ What I visualize on the course I produce perfectly.

Self-Image Enhancer Direct Suggestion Examples:

➢ I am a champion, a winner, and victorious in all ways on the course.

➢ I can achieve anything that I put my mind and energy to.

➢ I am on the path of fulfilling my greatness.

➢ I am a success on and off the course in all that I do.

➢ Every day my inner confidence grows to new heights.

➢ I can do anything and now actively achieving all my goals.

➢ I believe in myself, in my talents, and my personal power.

➢ I am an empowered golfer who plays like a champion.

Direct Suggestion Examples Using Repetition:

➢ Every time on the course my confidence grows, and grows, and grows.

➢ My score is consistently getting lower and lower and lower.

➢ On the greens I make putt after putt after putt.

➢ I am constantly getting better and better and better, every time on the course.

➢ Going low on the course is easy, easy, easy.

➢ I love making birdie after birdie after birdie.

➢ I consistently hit fairway after fairway after fairway.

➢ My inner confidence is building and building and building.

➢ I am so focused on every shot that I produce success, success, success.

Direct Suggestion Examples Using "Because":

➢ I make confident swings on every shot BECAUSE I always do a pre-shot routine.

➢ I produce accurate and precise results BECAUSE I visualize my success and do it.

➢ I roll in putt after putt BECAUSE that is what confident putters do.

➢ I execute at a high level on each shot BECAUSE I am confident in my game.

➢ I succeed on the course BECAUSE my game is solid tee to green and my mind is positive and confident.

➢ I always do a pre-shot routine BECAUSE it releases my best into the shot.

➢ I always stay in the present moment BECAUSE the shot I am taking is the most important shot of the round.

➢ I am confident on the course BECAUSE I am in control of my mind and my game.

➢ I handle adversity in a positive way BECAUSE that's what the champions do.

➢ I go low on the course BECAUSE I know what to do, how to do it, and I do it perfectly.

➢ I maintain confident, positive body language on the course BECAUSE it keeps me in the zone.

➢ I am motivated to practice BECAUSE each day I get better and better.

➢ I play my best golf each and every time out BECAUSE (insert one of your motivators).

Embedded Command Direct Suggestion Examples:

- ➢ I NOW play golf with confidence.
- ➢ I NOW release my best into every swing.
- ➢ I NOW sink more and more putts.
- ➢ I NOW relax and focus on every shot.
- ➢ I am NOW making great improvements in my game.
- ➢ I NOW do a pre-shot routine on each shot.
- ➢ I NOW commit to staying present on the course.
- ➢ I am NOW in control of my thoughts and emotions while playing golf.
- ➢ I NOW play golf in the zone consistently.
- ➢ I NOW make confident swings on each shot.
- ➢ I NOW believe fully in myself.
- ➢ I NOW go low on the course.
- ➢ I NOW tap into my greatness.
- ➢ I NOW visualize success and then do it.
- ➢ I NOW feel confident from tee to green.

Examples of Carry-Over Post-Hypnotic Suggestions: (The effects of the positive suggestions continue on after the session)

- ➢ After I emerge from self-hypnosis these confident feelings will stay with me and get stronger as I step on the course.
- ➢ When I emerge from self-hypnosis I continue to feel calm, confident, and unstoppable long after this session.
- ➢ These confident, strong feelings of being a champion stay with me after the session and out on the course.

➢ When my eyes open I continue to feel my level of confidence growing and growing, and growing.

➢ This deep inner zone state continues to get deeper the moment I open my eyes.

➢ After I open my eyes I remain positive, optimistic, and motivated to achieve my goals.

➢ As I return to the here and now, I will remember all the positive suggestions and they make a deeper impact in my mind.

➢ Once I emerge from my session my subconscious mind continues to think about and reinforce all suggestions and makes me feel more and more confident in my golf game.

Examples of Triggered Response Post-Hypnotic Suggestions: (The effects of the positive suggestions are activated with a specific trigger)

➢ Whenever I say to myself RELAX NOW, I instantly feel a wave of relaxation wash through my mind and body.

➢ Each time I grip my club, I immediately feel confident and positive.

➢ The moment I step foot on the tee box, I immediately begin visualizing my shot.

➢ The moment I step foot on the greens I instantly and automatically feel confident, fearless, and determined to sink the putt.

➢ Every time I grip my club, my subconscious triggers my perfect swing into action.

➢ Each and every time I take a deep breath, I automatically feel in control, calm, and confident.

➢ Each and every time I say the words CONFIDENCE NOW, I instantly and automatically shift into a confident state and execute like a champion.

➢ From this moment on anytime I say FOCUS NOW, my mind instantly focuses on the shot at hand.

➢ The moment I grip my club, my mind and body relaxes and I execute my best swing.

➢ Every time I address the ball my mind instantly becomes quiet and still allowing my body to perform my best swing.

➢ The moment I grip my club I immediately enter the zone and perform without conscious effort.

➢ When I address the ball, my perfect swing just happens.

➢ Every swing I take produces greater and greater confidence.

➢ Every time I do self-hypnosis I go deeper and deeper into this state of relaxation.

➢ Every time I do self-hypnosis it gets easier and easier to succeed in all I do.

➢ Every time I do self-hypnosis, the suggestions make a deeper and more lasting impression in my subconscious mind.

The above are all examples of different ways to use direct suggestions and post-hypnotic suggestions in your self-hypnosis sessions. This is just the tip of the iceberg in regards to hypnotic suggestions and there are lots of books written on hypnotic suggestions and language patterns for those who want to dive deeper into the subject.

However, these two main suggestion types form the foundation of hypnotic suggestions and you have more than enough to get started using powerful suggestions that make an impact in your self-hypnosis sessions.

Now that you know how to do self-hypnosis and create positive suggestions for yourself, an important topic to discuss at this point in time is the correct mental attitude to maintain as you deliver suggestions to yourself.

Renowned hypnotist, Gerald Kein, said "When an individual is in hypnosis and hears a suggestion she/he must take one of four mental attitudes about that suggestion. Which mental attitude the person takes will determine whether the suggestion is accepted or rejected."

Kein describes the 4 mental attitudes as follows:

> ➢ Mental Attitude #1 - "I like that suggestion. I know it's going to work for me!"

> ➢ Mental Attitude #2 - "I don't know; it sounds a little uncomfortable to me. It just doesn't fit me."

> ➢ Mental Attitude #3 - "I'm neutral about it. I don't care if I get it or don't get it."

> ➢ Mental Attitude #4 - "I like that suggestion. I hope it works!"

He continues, "The only mental attitude that will cause the suggestion to be accepted is #1. Any other will cause the suggestion to be rejected and there will be no change."[6]

Chapter Review

At this point in time, it is recommended that you begin writing suggestions that resonate with your golf game and areas of your game you would like to improve. Use the examples from the above lists or follow the rules to proper suggestion structure to formulate your own personal suggestions. The possibilities are endless in creating suggestions, so let your creativity take over to create your ideal script.

1. According to Dr. Bakas, "The success or failure of self-hypnosis is manifested by the types of suggestions that are programmed into the subconscious mind."

2. A hypnotic suggestion is a positive suggestion that is delivered to the subconscious mind while in self-hypnosis.

3. When creating hypnotic suggestions, keep Charles Tebbetts' 9 principles in mind to create effective suggestions:

   > ➢ The motivating desire must be strong.

   > ➢ Be positive.

   > ➢ Always use present tense.

   > ➢ Set a time limit.

➢ Suggest action, not ability to act.

➢ Be specific.

➢ Keep your language simple.

➢ Exaggerate and emotionalize.

➢ Use repetition.

4. The "why" behind any goal or suggestion is 90% of its achievement. The best motivators are ones that are driven by emotion instead of being practical. Your motivators must be compelling enough to plow through obstacles on your path and to get you excited to take action.

5. Be sure to always keep your hypnotic suggestions focused on what you do want to create and not on the problem. For example, suggesting to yourself, "I don't slice the ball anymore", will create pictures of the problem and more of it. Instead, keep your suggestion focused on what you want such as "I stripe tee shots straight to my target."

6. Be specific and narrow the focus of your self-hypnosis sessions. Less is more in self-hypnosis and it is better to focus on 1-3 key performance areas, instead of all aspects of your game. Follow the steps listed in the chapter to determine your focus areas, motivators, and success symbols and use this information to create a successful self-hypnosis session.

7. Repetition of suggestions is an easy and powerful way to program the subconscious mind. Each time the same suggestion is given it gets strengthened and reinforced through the law of compounding.

8. Direct Drive Technique: Repeating the same suggestion to yourself 10-15 times in a row. This is a simple and yet highly effective technique for delivering suggestions in self-hypnosis that is based on the law of compounding. Include the direct drive technique in each one of your self-hypnosis sessions so you can embed the most important suggestion of your session into your subconscious to ensure it will be acted upon.

9. Two primary types of hypnotic suggestions are Direct Suggestions and Post-Hypnotic Suggestions.

➤ Direct Suggestions are suggestions that are delivered while in the hypnotic state that are to the point, clear, and direct. For example, "I am a confident golfer on the course."

➤ Post-Hypnotic Suggestions are suggestions that are delivered during the hypnosis session, but the effects are to be carried out after the session is finished.

10. Two types of post-hypnotic suggestions

➤ Carry-Over Effect: Post-hypnotic suggestions that cause the feelings experienced during the session to continue after the session is finished. For example, "After the session is over, these wonderful feelings will stay with me throughout the day."

➤ Triggered Effect: Suggestions that fire off a post-hypnotic effect when a cue triggers the suggestion. For example, "When I step up on the first tee, I instantly feel calm and relaxed." Or, "Anytime I say the words 'Confidence Now', instantly and automatically I feel surges of confidence flow through me."

➤ Write up a self-hypnosis script using the examples provided in the chapter or with your own unique suggestions that follow the principles for proper suggestion structure. Once you wrote your script, you can record it and play it during your self-hypnosis time, memorize the key ideas so it is easier to deliver suggestions in the sessions, or use it as a reference before starting your session.

11. Examples of Positive Mental Programming for Your Golf Game: This section provides 16 exercises and examples of Direct Hypnotic Suggestions, Post-Hypnotic Suggestions, and emotion-driven motivators for a range of performance issues from the pre-shot routine, to swing performance to the short game to putting.

NINE

CONDITIONING AND ANCHORING

*"The mind is your greatest weapon. It's the greatest club in your bag.
It's also your Achilles' heel."*

--Steve Elkington

In the early 1900's, an incredible discovery was made by a Russian scientist that when applied to your golf game can make your best swing more repeatable, and create powerful mental programs. Ironically, this discovery in human behavior occurred not by working with athletes or even studying people, it came by researching dogs. This scientist stumbled across what is called classical conditioning and this breakthrough in understanding human nature is a powerful tool that you can use to enhance your game. In this chapter, you will learn the basics in classical conditioning, how to condition your best swing, and ways to trigger it into action consistently on the course. In addition, you will learn how to create anchors, or mental triggers to instantly create focus, relaxation, or any other emotion or mental state of your choice.

Classical Conditioning

What is classical conditioning? Classical conditioning was discovered by Ivan Pavlov who was originally studying the digestive system in dogs, but stumbled across something much more interesting. Pavlov noticed that when he brought food out to his dogs they would naturally begin to drool at the sight and smell of the food. After sometime, he became curious to see if he could trigger this same response from an unrelated stimuli, in this case a ringing bell. So here is what he did. Each time he brought food out to his dogs, he would ring a bell before giving them the food. Pavlov did this every day for a period of several weeks. Then one day, he just rang the bell and the dogs began to drool without the presence of food. Here is a link to a short YouTube video clip on Pavlov if you are interested in learning more about classical conditioning and the original experiment: http://www.youtube.com/watch?v=hhqumfpxuzI[1]

This process of conditioning behaviors doesn't just apply to animals, it also applies to human behavior as well. An easy everyday example of classical conditioning outside of golf is again looking at the behavior of a smoker. The exact same process is at work, as in Pavlov's experiment, that creates a powerful and, often times, unbreakable habit. For example, a smoker gets in a car and lights up a cigarette. The next time they get in the car, they light up another smoke. They do this again and again, each time they get into their car. It doesn't take long for the mind to create a link between getting in a car and smoking, even though they are completely unrelated things. This just doesn't happen with smoking, this process of classical conditioning is underlying just about all of your habits.

Without even knowing it, you have already conditioned yourself to think, feel, and behave in certain ways while playing golf. These conditioned responses are either positive or negative, and are unconsciously at work influencing you while you are performing on the course.

Have you ever wondered why there are some tee boxes that regardless of how well you are playing golf, you step up and hit a poor shot? And then why is it that on other tee boxes, even if you are not playing golf well that day, you stripe it every time?. This occurs because of the pictures you are holding in your mind, but where do they come from? They are generated from the subconscious mind due to the past conditioning and reinforcement from previous results from the past. The subconscious mind is quick to create mental connections and associations to things. Performance on the tee box is a common example of this. The moment you step foot on tee box, you respond to the conditioned response, just like a smoker who gets in their car and it triggers them to light up.

Another example of this type of conditioning can be found in golfers who are struggling with their putter. When a person is in a slump on the greens, unless it's a tap in, more often than not have a lack of confidence over the ball and have a hard time seeing the ball going in. Here is what happens. They get their ball on the green and when they reach for their putter, they immediately begin having doubts about their ability to make the putt. By the time they get on the green, these negative thoughts have expanded, and they have already convinced themselves they aren't going to make the putt. They attempt to make themselves feel better by thinking, "I should just try to get it close to avoid a 3 putt." They make a read, but second guess it and doubt the line. Then they stand over the ball, hope for the best, and proceed to hit a bad putt. When this happens, they criticize themselves and reaffirm their inability to make a putt. Without clearing away all this negative energy and doubt, they step up hit another bad putt and repeat the cycle of negativity all over again. They finally tap in their 3 putt and walk off cursing the green and their putting ability, which only adds more fuel to fire. This pattern of behavior gets repeated again and again until it becomes second nature and the slump settles in, due to the subconscious mind linking up the feelings of negativity to the action of putting. It can even get to the point that even though the golfer is striking the ball awesome and feeling confident on the course, that just the act of taking their putter out of their bag can begin to change their state in a negative direction. The end result is a negative conditioned response that unconsciously triggers feelings of doubt and insecurity when the putter is in their hands and while on the green.

Now that you are aware of conditioned behaviors and their potential negative programmed effect, you can change them by breaking the old patterns and regaining control. In a later chapter, you will learn a process called pattern interrupts and this technique is one of the most effective ways to break these old negative patterns of behavior. However, this chapter is going to teach you how to do positive conditioning in self-hypnosis as well as on the range, so that you can create mental triggers of success and patterns of positive behaviors to increase your level of performance.

Self-Hypnosis Can Accelerate the Conditioning Process

Self-hypnosis can be used to accelerate the conditioning process since you have more direct access to the subconscious mind while in the learning states. In addition, the subconscious mind doesn't know the difference between real events or vividly imagined ones. For example, visualizing your ideal swing develops the mind in the same way as actual performance and, oftentimes better, since you can make the experiences perfect in your mind every time. Through the use of self-hypnosis and providing perfect feedback to the mind, you can condition patterns of success in less time than through normal means of conditioning.

Let's go over ways to do accelerated conditioning now so you can apply this power in your golf game.

Conditioning Mental Movies of Success

I first discovered this method of conditioning early on during my initial work with golfers. This process proved to be highly effective at speeding up the learning curve and one that proved successful over the course of time. It is a simple method to take experiences of your past successes or even imagined visualizations of success in a particular aspect of your game and make it a mental program for your subconscious mind to act upon.

Let's go over the steps now to this two phase process.

Phase 1: Establishing a Mental Movie of Success and Increasing the Playback Speed:

Step 1: While in self-hypnosis, let your mind think back to a time of success on the golf course or at the range when you executed a perfect swing. If you can't remember a time when this occurred then you can imagine an experience and the same purpose will be served. Once you have identified an experience, make a mental movie of it in your mind with a beginning and end point.

Step 2: Now that you have a mental movie of this successful moment, start at the beginning of the movie, and watch this movie as vividly as possible from start to finish in 10 seconds.

Step 3: Next, rewind the mental movie back to the beginning of the experience and increase the speed of the playback. Imagine that the mental movie is playing on fast forward and this time watch the mental movie from start to finish 2 times in 10 seconds.

Step 4: Rewind the movie back to the beginning and continue to speed up the playback of this mental movie of success. This time watch the mental movie 4 times in 10 seconds.

Step 5: Go back to the beginning of the movie and continue increasing the speed of the movie. This time watch the mental movie 10 times in 10 seconds as vividly as possible.

Step 6: Rewind the movie back to the beginning and this time put the mental movie on super-fast forward and watch the mental movie of success 30 times in 10 seconds.

Phase 2 Decreasing the Mental Movie Playback Speed:

Step 7: Repeat step 6 and one more time, watch the mental movie 30 times in 10 seconds.

Step 8: Slow down the playback speed of the movie and watch the movie more vividly 10 times in 10 seconds.

Step 9: Continue to slow down the playback of your mental movie and watch it 4 times in 10 seconds. As you slow down the movie, imagine it more vividly and with more and more detail.

Step 10: Slow down the mental movie even more and watch the entire movie 2 times in 10 seconds in richer detail and more vividly.

Step 11: Continue this slowing down of the playback and watch the mental movie of success in its entirety 1 time in 10 seconds. This time be sure to make it as real as possible as you watch this perfect swing and experience take place from start to finish.

Step 12: Finally, imagine floating into the movie and go through an experience of the success through your own eyes to get you fully associated and connected with the experience. This is done to give you a firsthand experience of the success and embed these patterns and images into your subconscious mind from a performance perspective.

Step 13: Establish an anchor, i.e., pressing your thumb and index finger together, to trigger these thoughts, feelings, behaviors, and all other mental associations connected to this success whenever you need it or want it. More on creating anchors later in this chapter.

Important Notes on this Mental Conditioning Process:

> ➤ Your subconscious mind has an internal clock built-in and requires no conscious thought to keep track of time. When the 10 seconds are up, your subconscious mind will indicate this to you on its own. All you have you do is use your intention to set the clock in your head.

> ➤ It is important to understand there is no right or wrong way to do this and to simply do each series of playback as best as you can. When it gets to 30 times in 10 seconds, it is almost impossible to imagine the entire experience because it's going too fast. However, the subconscious mind will identify the most important aspect of the experience and will repeat it over and over in a lightning like fashion. This process is ingraining these successful images deep into the subconscious mind and accelerates the conditioning process by continuously presenting the images to the subconscious. This will naturally begin to create mental links of these positive images of success to the action of swinging your club. When it's time to perform because of this conditioning, your subconscious will immediately conjure up these successful pictures whether you are consciously aware of it or not.

> ➤ This process accelerates conditioning because it exposes your subconscious mind to mental movies/images of success 94 times in less than 2 minutes. The more you do this process in self-hypnosis the greater the impact it will have. Once you do this a few times, you will easily memorize the process and as a result this memorization will increase your ability to get into the experience more deeply. With practice, you will know how to use this technique of accelerated conditioning to program your mind with mental movies of success for any aspect of your game or in life.

Anchoring and Post-Hypnotic Triggers

Anchoring is another conditioning process that operates on the law of association which occurs whenever a person experiences one stimulus in the presence of another one, and the mind creates a connection between the two. After the anchor or this connection has been established, whenever you do one behavior it triggers the other one into action.

The Global NLP Training Institute says that:

> *"Anchoring is a process where a specific stimulus (cue, trigger) is connected to a memory recall, state or state change, or another response."* They go on to say that *"Anchoring occurs naturally all the time. You likely have several powerful anchors in place; a certain smell may remind you of a specific person (moth balls, perfume, etc.) Each time you see something, it brings you back to the state or a past memory (a photograph, a living room, etc). The same occurs when you hear a certain sound or piece of music."*[2]

How are anchors created? Anchors are created one of two ways. Either naturally or deliberately.

Anchors are naturally created when we have a peak experience on the golf course or in any other area of life. The more intense the peak experience the quicker and stronger the mind creates links to it. Let me give you a personal example. Ever since I was a kid, I have been an athlete and just loved playing all sports. My favorite sport growing up was basketball. When I was in eighth grade, I had a peak experience that was so awesome it has stayed with me to this day. It was the school assembly game and we were playing our rival school in front of all my classmates. With just seconds left on the clock and down by three points, I grabbed the rebound and took off down the court to try and get a shot off. As I neared the center of the court, I looked up at the clock, and realized I had to put up a shot. I saw the hoop and launched up a shot from half court. As the ball was flying through the air, I knew right away that it had a chance. Everything feel silent in my mind, time seemed to slow down, and all I was focused on was watching that ball going right towards the hoop. Then the ball swished through the hoop and, in an instant, everything erupted. The silence stopped and the cheers roared through the building. As I was running over to my teammates to celebrate, I can remember pumping my fist and yelling "YES, YES, YES!" The experience was so awesome, that without any conscious effort on my part, my mind immediately linked up my fist pumping and saying "yes, yes, yes" to the intense feelings of success, and triumph in moment.

From then on I noticed that whenever something great happened in any sport I was playing, I always did the same fist pump and said "yes, yes, yes!" This gesture got so conditioned from these peak experiences that to this day, anytime I do the same thing, regardless of where I am or what I am doing, the fist pump and "yes, yes, yes" triggers a surge of adrenaline through my body, my mind gets flooded with confident thoughts, and my state instantly changes in a positive direction. That one peak experience got anchored into that gesture and from then on, I used that powerful anchor to feel good anytime I needed to or wanted to.

You probably have similar experiences in your past and have already created positive anchors without even knowing it. Go back into your memory and re-call some of your peak experiences and notice what type of gestures you did or things that you said to yourself during these awesome times on the course. When you identify a moment like this in your life, close your eyes and mentally go back into that peak experience. Then fire off the anchor by doing what you did or said at the height of the peak experience and feel yourself instantly get into that same positive state.

The other way anchors are established are deliberately, and can be used to anchor and condition in a specific state that you would need or want to have at your beck- and- call on the course.

For example, you can anchor a feeling of calm confidence. Imagine that you are in a pressure situation and need to make a big putt. And, as you approach the putt your nerves start getting out of control rather than feeling the calm confidence you want to experience. In this situation, you can "fire off" the anchor you created and trigger a state of calm confidence within yourself, so you have the best opportunity to sink the putt. Any time a specific state needs to be accessed for whatever reason on the course, anchoring is a useful and effective tool.

You can elicit a specific mental or emotional state as well as specific behaviors that you want to anchor by:

> ➢ Going back in your memory to a time that you felt a particular way – in the zone, confident, focused, relaxed, determined, or any feeling/state of your choice.

> ➤ Talking about peak experiences out loud to somebody and allowing yourself to really get into the experience, so you generate lots of positive thoughts and emotions.

> ➤ Display a certain behavior to put yourself into the state such as moving around excitedly, laughing and joking, or perhaps completely relaxing.

> ➤ Look at pictures of past successes and relive the experience all over again

These are all examples of ways to get yourself into re-experiencing a peak moment in your life when you felt a certain way. It is important that you not just think about it, but really feel the excitement, or the confidence, or the success, etc. The better you are at eliciting the state that you want, the more powerful the anchor will be and the easier it is to set. *You have to make it a peak experience to set a successful anchor.*

The Steps to Setting and "Firing Off" an Anchor

There are 4 simple steps to "firing off" an anchor:

1. A specific state of peak experience that is either naturally occurring or deliberately elicited by you.

2. When you feel the state rising in its intensity, it's time to set the anchor. An anchor can be a visual cue (like Louie Oosthuizen and the red dot), an auditory cue (a keyword), a kinesthetic cue (like a gesture or behavior similar to Brandt Snedecker's shoulder and hip waggle), or a combination of the three, such as pumping your fist, saying yes, yes, yes.

3. Right at the peak of intensity, before it goes down, it's time to remove the anchor, so you are only anchoring the highest peak of the experience.

4. Then, while in a neutral state, fire off the anchor again and you will re-access and re-experience the state.

Let's go over a quick example to demonstrate this process of setting and firing off anchors. For this example, the anchor that will be established is the action of pressing the thumb and index finger together and saying a keyword, in this case "Power." Imagine that you are playing in a "big money" game against some competitive friends. It's coming down to the end and you need to smash a drive down the middle of the fairway to put the pressure on the other golfers. You step on the tee, go through your routine, and smash one of your longest drives perfectly down the middle of the fairway. As you feel the tremendous waves of positive emotions and thoughts coming over you, and feel the experience rising to the peak, press your thumb and index finger together and say "Power" in a strong tone to yourself. Continue to press the fingers together and keep saying "Power" until the feelings begin to subside, then release the anchor. You have now successfully installed an anchor. As you get ready to take your second shot, you can then re-access those same feelings from your drive by pressing your thumb and index finger together and saying "Power". Then after you stick your approach shot tight to the pin and you feel the peak experience coming over you again, reinforce your anchor by pressing your thumb and index finger together saying "Power" and do this until the feelings are ready to fade and release the anchor.

The Global NLP Training Institute says that effective and successful anchors have the following characteristics:[3]

> ➤ Purity of state (not diluted with other states).

> ➤ Intensity of the state.

> ➤ Uniqueness of the anchor (unique for that particular state only). So an anchor for confidence is different than an anchor for relaxation.

> ➤ The accuracy of replication, firing the anchor in the exact same way.

> ➤ Timing of the anchor.

Before you get started creating anchors through the self-hypnosis exercises in this chapter, here are some additional notes on anchoring.

1. Anchors can be used to condition and trigger positive mental and emotional states as well as behaviors to a unique action. Prior to starting the exercise, it is recommended to determine the anchor that you will be using. Remember each mental or emotional state you anchor needs to have a

unique trigger. Here are a few common examples of anchors that you can use or to help you figure out what will work for you.

➤ Pressing your thumb and index finger together, and saying a keyword.

➤ Rubbing one of your knuckles and saying a keyword.

➤ Squeezing your fist and saying a keyword.

➤ Doing a fist pump with a keyword.

➤ Squeezing the brim of your hat with a keyword.

➤ Snapping your fingers twice with a keyword.

➤ Gripping your club with a keyword.

➤ Tucking your sleeves in under your arms with a keyword.

➤ Any other unique behavior you come up with.

2. You probably noticed that all of these examples include a keyword. This is recommended because it makes the behavior more unique, which will make it a more effective anchor. In addition, it incorporates more than one cue, which is important because the more senses you can get involved, the more powerful the anchor becomes. When you combine an action (kinesthetic cue) with a keyword (auditory cue), it increases the effectiveness of the anchor. If possible, also add in a visual cue, like a positive outcome picture then it will become even more powerful in eliciting the state you desire.

3. The more intense the experience, the quicker and more powerful the anchor will be set. Be sure that if you are eliciting the state deliberately on your own that you really make the experience intense and take it to a peak experience before setting the anchor.

4. The more you use your anchor and reinforce it the stronger it gets.. Think of it like a muscle. The more you work the muscle the stronger and more powerful it becomes. However, if you don't use the anchor or reinforce it, then it can be extinguished. Once you set an anchor, you must either use it

or lose it. If you lose it, simply follow the same steps as before to reinstall the mental program in your subconscious mind.

5. It doesn't matter when you experienced the desired state or pattern of behavior. For example, if your desired state is confidence, but you never experienced a high level of confidence on the golf course, then you can use other areas of your life where you felt confident to establish the anchor. If you are very confident when you are at work, then you can use anchoring to trigger that same confident state from work while performing on the golf course. Anchoring works on the law of association which means the mind can create connections between unrelated events.

    Confidence is confidence and success is success regardless of where and when it's experienced. Through a little bit of training, your subconscious mind is able to link up things that are unrelated, and has the ability to bring that same confidence you experience in your work and transfer it into your golf game through anchoring.

6. When eliciting states to anchor in self-hypnosis, be sure to incorporate as many senses as you can into the experience to relive it as real as possible. A good way to do this is to suggest to yourself, *"Feel what I would feel, see what I would see, hear what I would hear."*

7. When setting anchors in self-hypnosis, repeat the process and suggestions at least 3 times in your session. Each time you repeat the experience, make each experience more intense and more exciting to install a good anchor and triggered response. While in self-hypnosis, let your imagination add more and more elements into the experience that would make it even better. There are no rules and you don't have to stay limited to what actually happened. Do what you need to do and add whatever is needed to make it a peak experience.

Anchoring Your Perfect Swing

One of the key's to successful swing execution is to think as little as possible while addressing the ball and let the subconscious perform the swing it was trained to do. It is important to know that every golfer has hit a perfect golf ball before either on the course, at the range, or even in the backyard and the subconscious mind remembers these experiences. Your subconscious mind records and stores every experience that you have in your life. Since every golfer has hit perfect shots before that means this pattern of success is stored in the mind and just needs to be recalled to release it more consistently on the golf course.

With this is in mind, a powerful way of increasing swing execution and the ability to perform without conscious effort is through anchoring your perfect swing pattern into an action like gripping your club, with a keyword, so that when addressing the ball you don't have to think, you just execute this ideal pattern of success. With a little conditioning, this simple action of gripping your club can be used to activate the subconscious pattern of success that will enable you to execute a smoother swing, better shots, more confidence, lower scores, and more.

In this section, you will learn how to create anchors and trigger these patterns of success in action through post-hypnotic suggestions. For this exercise, have one of your clubs handy so that you can anchor your ideal swing pattern into the action of gripping your club.

The Anchoring Process:

Step 1: After you get into self-hypnosis and a receptive state of mind for training, begin to think back to times of your perfect swings. An easy way to identify these experiences is to think about how great it feels to stripe a perfect shot. As you feel those feelings, focus on them and imagine following those feelings back to times you experienced them while playing golf.

Step 2: Once you have identified a memory of a perfect swing and shot, begin to re-experience the successful shot in very rich detail and make it as real as possible in your mind. Incorporate all of your senses into the experience and become aware of the day, what you were seeing, what you heard, and what you felt during this moment. The more real you make the experience the more you will benefit.

Step 3: After you re-experienced the successful shot the way it was, use your imagination and repeat the experience again, this time intensifying it and making it even better in every way. Make the scene brighter, bolder, more colorful, and more magical in your mind. Intensify all the sounds of the experience and make them louder, more harmonious, add in your favorite music, more compliments, and cheers. Increase all the positive feelings of the experience by adding in more positive emotions, maximize the excitement, boost all the happiness, and pride of hitting the perfect shot.

Step 4: Once you have intensified and maxed out the experience, and everything is even better than it was originally, anchor this state into a unique action, such as gripping your club. While staying in self-hypnosis, grip your club and say to yourself a keyword like "Power", "Confidence", "Success" or any keyword of your choosing. (What you have done here is created a peak experience *and* created a link to the action of gripping your club. This is the first step of setting the anchor.)

Step 5: Clear your mind, relax your grip on the club, and repeat the same process, but making it more of an intense, peak experience. Recall another successful swing, or continue using the same experience, and as you re-experience the success make it better and better in all ways. Max out the experience and once you feel yourself at a peak state, grip your club, say your keyword again, and set the anchor into the gripping of your club.

Step 6: Once more, clear your mind, relax the grip on your club, and repeat the same process. This time use your imagination and make it the most powerful and greatest peak experience you can make it. Really get into the experience and add in any element that would make the experience even greater. There is no limit to your imagination, so do whatever is needed to maximize everything, make it more exciting, more awesome, and more successful. Again, once you have taken the experience to another level of excitement and performance, anchor the state by gripping your club and saying your keyword.

Step 7: Relax your mind and grip on the club, and then use post-hypnotic suggestions to drive in the anchor and solidify it. Here are examples of post-hypnotic suggestions for this exercise:

- *From this moment on and for the rest of my life whenever I grip my club and say the word, INSERT KEYWORD, instantly, automatically, and without thinking, my perfect swing pattern is released in my mind and in my performance.*

- *The moment I grip my club and say, KEYWORD, I instantly feel confident, relaxed, focused, and my subconscious mind produces my best swing.*

- *From this moment on and for the rest of my life, anytime I grip my club and say the word, INSERT KEYWORD, instantly, automatically, and without thinking my perfect swing pattern is released and I execute my best swing and the highest level of performance.*

- *The moment I grip my club and say, KEYWORD, I instantly feel confident, relaxed, focused, and my subconscious mind produces my best swing easily and effortlessly.*

- *From this moment on and for the rest of my life, the moment I grip my club and say the word INSERT KEYWORD, instantly, automatically, and without thinking my perfect swing pattern is triggered into action and I execute my best swing and the highest level of performance.*

- *The moment I grip my club and say KEYWORD, I instantly feel confident, relaxed, focused, and my subconscious mind produces my best swing and it continuously gets better and better and better.*

- *My mind is now programmed to trigger my best swing into action the moment I grip my club and say, KEYWORD. Whenever I do this, my subconscious mind instantly and automatically thinks about my perfect swing, puts it into action, and I execute it at the highest level.*

- *Just like a muscle that gets stronger with use, every time I grip my club this KEYWORD gets more powerful and instantly, automatically, and without thinking, triggers my perfect swing into action. This always occurs because my mind is now programmed to do this and my mind works in my favor and for my advantage.*

Step 8: Emerge from self-hypnosis and test your results. If you have successfully installed the anchor then when you grip your club and say your keyword, you should experience a state of confidence and notice the images of that perfect swing coming into your mind.

If you aren't noticing changes then that means one of two things. First that you simply need to do more conditioning in self-hypnosis to reinforce the anchor and the new triggered response. Second, it could mean that you need to intensify the experience. Remember, the more intense the experience and the more exciting and successful you can make it the faster the conditioning takes place. In either event, continue to use self-hypnosis and repeat the experience until a powerful anchor gets established.

Trust me, this is one exercise that is worth putting time and effort in because when you create a successful anchor like this, it will give you the ability to consistently release your best swing simply by gripping your club and saying a keyword. In my first season of using this technique in my own game, I successfully took 7 strokes off my scoring average and to this day when I address the ball, I make confident swings and produce consistent results. Do you remember researcher John Pates and the Senior European Tour player referenced in Chapter Three? This process is a similar technique to the one used in their hypnosis sessions to lower the golfer's scoring average and achieve their first professional victory on tour.

This technique is an example of deliberately eliciting the state of peak performance and anchoring the state so that you can consistently repeat this high level of performance on the course.

Remember there are two ways to create an anchor, deliberately which we just covered, and when the states occur naturally. Let's go over a way to anchor your perfect swing when the state of peak performance naturally happens. When you are on the course, at the range, or even blasting shots in your backyard and you execute a perfect shot, the moment you begin to experience the positive emotions and thoughts, is a perfect time to anchor this state that is naturally occurring. To do so, simply follow the same process as described earlier. As you feel the rush coming over you, squeeze the grip of your club and say your keyword, and continue to do this until you feel the intensity of the emotions ready to subside and then release the anchor. Keep repeating this process after every peak experience on the course or shot at the range to successfully set and create an anchor of that high level of performance. Once you have done this several times, the subconscious mind will naturally begin linking up the two experiences, and the anchor will be established.

After you do this, you now have a powerful tool that you can use to trigger your best performance whenever it is needed. Now when you are in a situation when you are experiencing doubts about the shot or lacking confidence in your swing, you can grip your club say your keyword, and instantly trigger into action your best swing full of confidence and positive energy. However, you don't have to wait until you are feeling insecure to fire off your anchor. It is recommended that once your anchor has been set that you fire it off before every shot so that you put forth your best ability and effort into every swing.

Use both the natural states of peak performance and the deliberately elicited states to create effective anchors for your game. By using both methods, it is the fastest and easiest way to reinforce the anchor, make it more powerful, and trigger your best consistently on the course.

Anchoring Mental and Emotional States

Besides anchoring your perfect swing patterns, there are other useful states to anchor to help you stay at your best on the course. Anchoring states like relaxation and focus can be very beneficial to create since these are two key aspects of success in golf. Self-hypnosis is an easy way to create these types of anchors because while in a relaxed state of mind you have access to your permanent memory bank and can recall experiences that you can use to set anchors. Remember that you can use unrelated events outside of golf when you experienced certain states, perhaps relaxing at the beach, and use these states to create anchors for your golf game. Below you will find examples of suggestions to use to create and set anchors during self-hypnosis.

Anchoring States Using Post-Hypnotic Suggestions:

Here are two examples using post-hypnotic suggestions to set and create anchors for relaxation and focus. Once you internalize this basic process you can use it to create anchors for any other state of you're choosing such as confidence, empowerment, and so on. Both of these examples will be using the same anchor for explanation purposes. Be sure to change the anchor if you desire to set one for each of these states so that each state has a unique trigger. Use the examples previously mentioned in the chapter, or simply use a slight variation of the anchor for eliciting different states such as pressing the thumb and index finger together for one state and pressing the thumb and ring finger to anchor another state.

Example #1: Relaxation Anchoring Process and Suggestions:

Once you have relaxed your mind and body and are in a state of self-hypnosis, give yourself suggestions like this:

> *I am directing my mind to drift back to a time in my life when I felt the most relaxed, comfortable, and tranquil. This could be a time relaxing on the beach, a time on the golf course, a time on vacation, relaxing in my favorite chair, or any other time when I felt completely peaceful, relaxed, and comfortable. As my mind drifts back to a relaxed time of its choosing, I experience the peace of the moment all over again completely and totally.*
>
> *Now that I am beginning to think of this experience I will count from 1 to 3 and at the count of 3, I will be there as real, as real can be, all over again.*
>
> *1...I am now drifting back...2...I am touching down into the experience now...3 I am back in a time when I was completely and totally relaxed, comfortable, and tranquil. I give myself full permission to get completely into this moment and I am now seeing what I was seeing, feeling what I was feeling, and hearing what I was hearing.*
>
> *Now that I am experiencing this all over again, everything gets more comfortable, more tranquil, and more relaxed RIGHT NOW.* **(As you are feeling the relaxation at its peak, breathe in deeply, press your thumb and index finger together and as you exhale say to yourself, RELAX NOW, and let the feelings become even more peaceful and tranquil.)**
>
> *Now that I am experiencing deeper feelings of peace, comfort, and relaxation these feelings get even more powerful, RIGHT NOW.* **(As you feel the feelings of relaxation reaching a higher peak, breathe in deeply, press your thumb and index finger together, and as you exhale say to yourself, RELAX NOW, and let the feelings become more peaceful and tranquil.)**

Now I am experiencing deeper feelings of peace, comfort, and relaxation these feelings get even more powerful, RIGHT NOW. **(As you feel the feelings of relaxation reaching a higher peak, breathe in deeply, press your thumb and index finger together, and as you exhale say to yourself RELAX NOW and let the feelings become more peaceful and tranquil. Now relax your fingers and let go even deeper.)**

From this moment on, any time that I breathe in deeply, press my thumb and index finger together, and say the words, RELAX NOW, instantly, automatically, and without thinking waves of relaxation will wash through my mind and body, and I relax completely and totally.

From this moment on any time that I breathe in deeply, press my thumb and index fingers together and say the words, RELAX NOW, instantly, automatically, and without thinking waves of relaxation wash through my mind and body making me instantly feel calm, comfortable, and completely and totally relaxed.

From this moment on and for the rest of my life, any time that I breathe in deeply, press my thumb and index finger together and say the words, RELAX NOW, instantly, automatically, and without thinking waves of relaxation wash through my mind and body making me instantly feel calm, peace, and completely and totally relaxed.

My subconscious mind is now programmed to bring forth complete relaxation, peace, and tranquility the moment I press my thumb and index fingers together and say, RELAX NOW.

This is acted upon anytime I need to relax or want to relax on the golf course. I now have the power to instantly and completely relax mentally and physically anytime I use this anchor. My mind is now programmed with this mental trigger and it is available anytime I need it or want it when I fire off my anchor for relaxation.

Example #2: Anchoring Process and Suggestions for Intense Focus:

Once you have relaxed your mind and body and are in a state of self-hypnosis, give yourself suggestions like this:

I am directing my mind to drift back to a time in my life when I had the most intense level of focus and concentration I have ever felt. This could be a time when I was working on a specific project, completely engrossed in a hobby, reading my favorite book, a time on the golf course, or any other time when I was completely focused and in a state of supreme concentration. As my mind selects this time of perfect, intense and unbreakable focus, I will experience the same level of focus of that moment all over again completely and totally.

Now that I am beginning to think of this experience I will count from 1 to 3 and at the count of 3, I will be there as real as real can be all over again. 1...I am drifting back now...2...I am touching down into the experience now...3...I am now back in a time when I was completely and totally focused, concentrated, and engrossed in the moment. I give myself full permission to get completely into this moment and I am now seeing what I was seeing, feeling what I was feeling, and hearing what I was hearing.

Now that I am experiencing this all over again, my mind becomes even more focused and concentrated, RIGHT NOW. **(As you are experience the level of focus at its peak, breathe in deeply, press your thumb and index finger together and as you exhale say to yourself, FOCUS NOW, and let the feelings become even more powerful and concentrated.)**

Now that I am experiencing more intense and powerful levels of focus and concentration, this level of focus gets even more powerful, RIGHT NOW. **(As you experience the level of focus and concentration reaching a higher peak, breathe in deeply, press your thumb and index finger together, and as you exhale say to yourself, FOCUS NOW, and let the feelings become more powerful and concentrated.)**

Now I am experiencing even greater levels of focus and concentration this level of focus gets even more powerful RIGHT NOW. **(As you experience greater levels of focus and it reaching a higher peak, breathe in deeply, press your thumb and index finger together, and as you exhale say to yourself, FOCUS NOW and let focus and concentration become more powerful, intense and laser like. Now relax your fingers and let go even deeper.)**

From this moment on any time that I breathe in deeply, press my thumb and index finger together, and say the words, FOCUS NOW, instantly, automatically, and without thinking my mind focuses, concentrates fully, and I enter the zone of unbreakable focus completely and totally.

From this moment on, any time that I breathe in deeply, press my thumb and index finger together, and say the words, FOCUS NOW, instantly, automatically, and without thinking my mind focuses, concentrates fully, and I enter the zone of unbreakable focus completely and totally.

From this moment on and for the rest of my life any time that I breathe in deeply, press my thumb and index finger together and say the words, FOCUS NOW, instantly, automatically, and without thinking I enter the zone of perfect focus, intense concentration, and all that matters is the shot at hand.

My subconscious mind is now programmed to bring forth complete and total focus and concentration the moment I press my thumb and index fingers together and say, FOCUS NOW.

This is acted upon anytime I need to focus or want to focus more completely on the golf course. I now have the power to instantly and completely focus my mind and enter the zone of unbreakable concentration anytime I use this anchor. My mind is now programmed with this mental trigger and it is available anytime I need it or want it when I fire off my anchor for perfect focus and concentration."

Chapter Review

Who would have thought that a discovery made while studying dogs would give us such a great insight into the nature of human behavior? Conditioning and anchoring are things that are naturally occurring all the time and you now know how to harness these processes to deliberately condition your mind for success.

In addition, you learned how to create anchors to trigger positive thoughts, feelings, and behaviors as well as how to use post-hypnotic suggestions to embed keyword triggers into your mind to produce desired results in an instant.

1. Classical conditioning discovered by Ivan Pavlov is a form of learning in which a conditioned stimulus triggers off an unrelated stimulus. For example, the ringing bell triggering the dogs to drool in Pavlov's study, sitting in the car triggering a smoker to light up a cigarette, or stepping on a specific tee box and executing poorly.

2. Self-hypnosis is a way to dramatically accelerate the conditioning process to increase your performance on the course and condition patterns of success in the subconscious mind.

3. Conditioning Mental Movies of Success:

   ➢ While in self-hypnosis, recall a successful memory of a perfect shot you executed.

   ➢ Make this memory into a 10 second mental movie.

   ➢ Condition this mental movie into your mind by accelerating and slowing down the playback as described in the exercise steps.

   ➢ Establish an anchor to trigger this conditioned mental movie into action on the course.

4. Anchoring is another conditioning process that operates on the law of association. Whenever a person experiences one stimulus in the presence of another one, the mind creates a connection between the two. It is a process where a specific stimulus, cue, or trigger is connected to a memory recall, a specific state, or another response.

5. Anchors are created in one of two ways: naturally when a peak state occurs; or deliberately when you choose the state you want to condition and anchor.

6. Steps to Setting and Firing an Anchor:

   ➢ A specific state of peak experience needs to occur either naturally, like in the basketball example in the chapter, or deliberately elicited.

   ➢ When you feel the state rising in its intensity, it's time to set the anchor. An anchor can be a visual cue (like Louie Oosthuizen and the red dot), an auditory cue (a keyword), a kinesthetic cue (like a gesture or behavior like Bryant Snedecker's shoulder and hip waggle), or a combination of the three, such as pumping your fist saying yes, yes, yes.

➤ Right at the peak of intensity, before it is going down, it's time to remove the anchor, so you are only anchoring the highest peak of the experience.

➤ Then while in a neutral state, fire off the anchor again and you will re-access and re-experience the state.

7. Effective and successful anchors have the following characteristics:

➤ Purity of state, not diluted with other states.

➤ Intensity of the state.

➤ Uniqueness of the anchor (unique for that particular state only.) So an anchor for confidence is different than an anchor for relaxation.

➤ The accuracy of replication, firing the anchor in the exact same way.

➤ Timing of the anchor.

8. Use anchoring in self-hypnosis to:

➤ Anchor your perfect swing.

➤ Anchor mental and emotional states for peak performance.

9. Use post-hypnotic suggestions to anchor keywords to trigger focus, confidence, relaxation, etc.

TEN

THE POWER OF VISUALIZATION: EXERCISES AND APPLICATIONS

"Visualization is the most powerful thing we have."

--Sir Nick Faldo

This chapter is all about developing one of the most important mental skills for peak performance on the golf course; the power of visualization. Visualization is a tremendous tool on the course to increase accuracy and swing execution as well as off the course in your self-hypnosis sessions to program your mind for success and develop areas of your golf game.

In this chapter, you are going to learn more than just basic visualization scenarios. *You are about to discover how your mind codes and stores information, and how you can use this information to enhance your success, get rid of negative pictures and feelings, and identify your mental swing signature.*

In addition, you will learn ways to incorporate visualization into your pre-shot routine, fun ways to use visualization at the range to increase the quality of your practice as well as various exercises to practice visualization.

The Typical Questions About Visualization

When discussing visualization with golfers, there are three common questions that typically surface in golfers who aren't using visualization in their golf game. Before diving into this topic and going through exercises for development, I feel it is important to quickly address these common questions.

The first question is "Why is visualization so important for my game?" By now, you should have a very good idea on the importance of your thoughts while performing from the research in Chapter One and all the supporting evidence throughout the book. Remember that golfers think in pictures and these pictures are literally programming your mind and body how to perform. The problem is most golfers are not actively creating visualizations of the type of shot they want to hit in their mind's eye and, as a result, their subconscious mind runs off of old patterns of behavior or negative pictures. For example, imagine a golfer teeing off on a par 3 with a water hazard in front of the green. The golfer with an untrained mind in this situation typically has pictures flashing in their minds of their ball going into the water and unconsciously reach into their bag to get out a "water ball" to hit. Unaware of what they are visualizing, they step up take their shot, and put it in the water because the subconscious was programmed with the thoughts and images of the negative shot. Your subconscious doesn't know the difference between good and bad and simply follows through in producing the most powerful and compelling thought. This is why developing the skill of visualization is vitally important – so you are using this power of your imagination to direct the body on how to perform the way you want.

The second question that usually comes up is "I can't visualize...will this still help my game?" Everyone has the ability to visualize whether they are aware of it or not. Some people are just more naturally gifted at visualizing while others need more time to develop the skill just like learning anything new. However, everyone does in fact visualize things in their mind. For example, have you ever got lost in a great book? When you read a story, your mind naturally begins to create visual images in your mind of the characters, the events, and the setting. Oftentimes the books you read are turned into movies; however, when you go to see the movie, the characters and scenes are different than what you visualized while reading the book. Reading is an excellent example of demonstrating that everybody does in fact visualize.

Let's do a quick exercise now that will also demonstrate this point. This exercise requires that you close your eyes, so read over the steps first.

➢ Step 1: Close your eyes and take a deep breath to clear your thoughts.

➢ Step 2: Begin to think about your golf bag and imagine how it looks.

➢ Step 3: As you think about your golf bag, answer the following questions:

• What color is your golf bag?

• Do any of your clubs have head protectors on them? If so what do they look like?

• Is your bag a full sized bag, a cart bag, or a walking bag?

• Is there anything unique about the way your bag looks?

• What do you keep in the front pocket?

Answering these questions proves that you have the ability to visualize because in order to answer them, you have to visualize and mentally picture your bag to retrieve the information. It is important to note that some people have the ability to close their eyes and vividly picture elaborate and detailed scenes in their mind's eye. While others close their eyes and see only black behind their eyelids. If this is the case with you, understand that you are still visualizing and the clarity of the mental imagery will increase with practice. However, as long as you just *think* about the exercises and mentally go through them, it will produce the same results. You will discover later that visualization goes beyond just having mental imagery and actually incorporates all your senses. So no matter how skilled you are at visualization, you will benefit from these techniques and constantly improve the more you practice.

The last question that is commonly brought up is "I tried visualization before but didn't notice much improvement. Was I doing something wrong?" It is important to understand that visualizing success is not a one-time thing. Visualization is a tool that needs to be done consistently before every shot and in daily self-hypnosis using the mental training exercises. I know this sounds like a big commitment, and it is at first, until visualization becomes a habit. However, understand that whether you are directing your mind or not, it will do it anyways.

Golfers who fail to see improvement from visualization do so because of inconsistency and, as a result, the mind stays on auto-pilot and runs off old mental programs, which for the untrained mind, is typically in a negative direction. Besides consistency, sometimes it is the type of visualization that needs to be changed. There are a variety of different ways to visualize and by changing the type it can change the result.

The effectiveness of visualization has been proven in research studies in virtually all sports. So it isn't a question of "if" visualization is effective or produces better results. It is a question of finding out what type of visualization is best suited for you and taking the time to develop the skill.

The Most Common Ways Golfers Visualize

Now that these frequently asked questions have been answered and clarified, let's go over the most common ways golfers visualize.

A Basic Visualization Exercise:

Let's start with a basic visualization exercise. Follow these simple steps.

1. Find a comfortable place to relax and close your eyes for a few minutes. Start by doing one of the methods for self-hypnosis or do a few minutes of deep diaphragmatic breathing before starting the exercise.

2. Once you are in a relaxed state, imagine looking through your forehead, and imagine a movie screen 6 to 8 feet in front of you.

3. Next, think of someone that you know very well and imagine their face on the screen in front of you. Visualize their face as clearly as possible. If you are having a hard time visualizing and imagining their face, begin to ask yourself questions about the appearance of the person you are thinking about. Ask yourself things like: "What color are their eyes?"; "What does their hair look like?"; "What is their smile like?" As you think about the answers, imagine the way they look and begin getting a visual image on the screen. Another thing that you can do is imagine them in a context, by recalling a memory of them on the screen.

4.   After you have clear visual image of their face, begin to imagine the whole person and visualize their entire body on the screen. Imagine it as vividly as possible and hold that image on the screen. If you are having any trouble doing this, again ask yourself questions or recall a memory of them to get the visual image of them.

You can also use this basic movie screen visualization exercise to hold other images in mind. Practice visualizing objects in great detail, such as a golf ball and visualize all the dimples, the type of ball, the number, etc. Work on both creating clear mental images as well as holding these images in mind.

Once you are able to get a clear mental picture of a golf ball, see how long you can maintain this visual image in perfect detail on the screen. Can you maintain full focus on that image without the mind wandering for 10 seconds? 30 seconds? A minute? *The goal is to be able to maintain the image as long as possible. Why is this beneficial? Because it will train your mind to be able to hold clear, and vivid outcome images all the way through your pre-shot routine and during your shot which will increase focus as well as execution.*

This is a skill that all the great golfers have developed. By practicing this simple technique and challenging yourself to make clear images and hold them for longer periods, you will train yourself to do the same thing in your golf game. Spend 5 minutes a day doing this exercise and you will notice great improvements in your ability to visualize and focus more powerfully.

A Variety of Types of Visualization

Visualization is not limited to imagining things on a screen. For example, visualization experiences can often be life-like and appear in your mind as if you are in the situation. There are many different ways that people visualize. Let's discuss these various types of visualization you can use to enhance your golf game on and off the course.

Visualization with Associated View: This is visualizing the experience through your own eyes as if you were actually executing your swing. When doing this type of visualization, everything appears as it would in reality. You would see your hands gripping the club, the ball positioned between your feet, the way it looks as you make impact, and watching the flight of the ball as you normally do on the course. This type of visualization is a firsthand experience of taking the shot. Sports psychologists call this Internal Perspective.

Visualization with a Dissociated View: This is visualizing yourself taking your shot as if you were watching yourself on a movie screen or television. In this type of visualization, you are witnessing the shot and the experience, instead of being in it. Sports psychologists call this External Perspective.

Standard Trajectory Visualization: This type of visualization is when you imagine watching the ball flight as it travels towards the target. During golf tournaments on television, they have technology called "Shot Tracker" which traces the flight of the ball. This is a perfect example of a Standard Trajectory Visualization.

Reverse Trajectory Visualization: This type of visualization starts with the ball already resting on the target and you visualize the ball traveling backwards from the target back to where you are. For this type, you start with the end in mind and let your mind retrace the flight on how it got there. This is an excellent type of visualization to use when you are putting. Visualize the ball sitting in the bottom of the cup and coming out of the hole, rolling back along the perfect line to your putter. This is effective because the mind has to visualize the ball in the cup, which will naturally increase accuracy, and it shows the mind the exact way to make it a reality as it retraces the line.

Becoming the Ball: This type of visualization is when you visualize yourself as the ball and traveling the ball flight to the desired target, as if doing a fly-over of the shot. It is similar to playing a video game that follows the ball and its flight after you take the shot. This type of visualization can help you imagine more of the course and creatively determine the best shots, strategies, and targets.

Outcome Visualization: This type of visualization occurs when you address the ball and you lock the image of your outcome in your mind. As you address the ball, visualize your outcome while over the ball and let your swing rip. The basic visualization exercise described earlier will help you develop this skill.

Mental Imagery Visualization: This type of visualization occurs when you use mental imagery on the course to help you execute. Here are a few examples: When lag putting, golfers will sometimes imagine a hula hoop around the hole, or a 50 gallon drum over the hole they want to bump. Some golfers imagine red and white targets to hit to out on the course, or imagine sweeping out a dollar bill behind the ball when they have a sand shot out of a bunker. This type of visualization is a great way to activate your subconscious mind on the course and use your imagination to increase performance, accuracy, and creative shot making.

These are some of the most common ways to visualize on and off the golf course. However, there are endless ways to visualize. This is just a sample of how your creative mind can utilize the power of visualization to increase your results on the course. I want to encourage you to always allow your creative mind to have fun visualizing successful shots and outcomes, and give it the freedom to do it in a way that best serves you.

Identifying Your Ideal Visualization Perspective

Now that we have covered the different types of visualization, the most natural question that emerges is what is the best way to do it?

Visualization is a subjective and personal experience, and the right way to visualize is different for everybody. Your subconscious mind is the world's most powerful bio-computer on the planet. However, nobody has given us a user manual on the best ways to use this incredible machine between your ears. Neuro-Linguistic Programming, or NLP, is literally the "first edition" user manual for your brain and you are about to learn some powerful NLP techniques that you can use in your self-hypnosis to take control of your mind and direct it towards greatness.

Experts in NLP have identified that your subconscious mind stores information in strings of coding, the same way a computer does. So this means your subconscious mind has a very specific way that it mentally codes success and a specific way it codes failure, and all other experiences.[1]

Throughout this chapter we will be progressively building on this concept of mental coding. You will be given exercises on how you can identify your ideal visualization style, how to enhance the power of your visualization experiences, as well as how to change and eliminate negative images that have made imprints in your mind.

Visualization Perspective Determiner Exercise

Let's start with an exercise that will identify the best perspective to use during your visualization experiences: associated (internal) or dissociated (external).

Step 1: Find a quiet place to relax and do self-hypnosis for a few minutes.

Step 2: After you begin to relax, let your mind wander back to some of your best memories and experiences on the golf course.

Step 3: Let yourself re-experience those incredible moments on the course all over again.

Step 4: After you have gone through a couple memories of success, notice whether you are visualizing and remembering the events through your own eyes like you are re-living them or whether you see yourself on a screen, like watching a movie or TV. Make a mental note of any other similarities you notice about these successful moments.

Step 5: Now let your mind think about some of the bad, embarrassing, or disappointing shots you have made. If you can't remember a time like this, just imagine a situation that is similar to something you have experienced, and it will serve the same purpose.

Step 6: As the images of the disappointing moments and poor performance flow through your mind, notice if experiencing them through your own eyes or if you are watching yourself on a screen. Also, take notice of the other ways they are different from the successful memories.

Step 7: Once you notice the differences and determine which perspective you were visualizing both experiences, open your eyes, and write down your findings.

The goal of the above exercise is to begin to identify some of the differences in the way your mind visualizes patterns of success versus patterns of poor performance. The most common difference that people experience is which perspective, associated or disassociated, they use to visualize success versus failure. For example, you might have been associated in your successful memories, but when you recalled negative events, it was like watching yourself on a screen, or vice versa.

When you become aware of this difference, you have just discovered a piece of mental coding that can make you instantly feel more confident and experience more success.

I will explain why. First, by identifying how your mind visualizes success, you know the right perspective to use when visualizing in self-hypnosis, during your pre-shot routine, and during mental exercises to elicit more success, since it's aligned with the preexisting mental coding. Second, it will give you the ability to shift from negative mental states to a state of confidence simply by changing the way you are visualizing the shot or experience. For example, let's say you determined that when you visualize success, it is through an associated perspective or through your own eyes, and the negative situations were visualized in a dissociated perspective, like watching yourself on a screen. When you are in a situation where you are having doubts or insecurities, you can change the perspective of the thoughts and visualizations occurring in your mind from dissociated to associated, and by doing so you will change the way think, feel, and perform. So for this example, if you notice that you're imagining yourself on a screen, then you are visualizing in the coding of a negative state. Take a deep breath, clear your mind, and shift the perspective so you are visualizing the experience through your own eyes, or the way your mind codes success and confidence. Again, as you do this it will immediately change the way you think, feel, and consequently the way you will perform on the shot.

How the Mind Codes in Size and Location of Mental Images

In the mind's eye, size matters and bigger is always better and more compelling to the subconscious mind. When you feel good about something, get excited about an idea, or driven to take action, your subconscious mind produces images that are right up in the forefront of the mind, huge in the mind's eye, and very appealing. On the contrary, things that you really don't care about or have much interest in, or unmotivated to take action are typically way in the back part of the mind, smaller in size, difficult to see or imagine, and not very appealing in the mind's eye and, as a result, they don't compel us to into action.

An exercise to demonstrate how the mind codes in size and location:

Step 1: Take a moment to close your eyes and vividly think about one of the following:

- A person you love.

- A dream or goal of yours.

- Something you are very motivated to do and do consistently.

Step 2: As you think about and visualize this person or thing you absolutely love, become aware of the size of the mental image or thought. Because it is something appealing to you, it is probably big, vivid, and right up in the front of your mind. Like when a person says "I have a BIG idea!" Notice what you notice about the size and location of this positive mental image.

Step 3: Clear your mind and this time when you close your eyes think about one of the following:

- A garden hose.

- A lawn chair.

- A tire.

- A fire hydrant.

- Something you are unmotivated to do but want to do.

Step 4: As you think about one of these things, notice the difference in size, location, and clarity. Because this is something that you are indifferent about, or unmotivated to act on, the mental image is probably much smaller, way in the back of your mind, and difficult to visualize clearly. ***Take notice of the differences.***

This simple exercise demonstrates a few of the differences in the way your subconscious mind codes things that you find inspiring, appealing, and compelled to act upon versus things you are indifferent about, and unmotivated to do. There is a clear difference in the size and location of these different mental images. Compelling images are BIG and in the forefront of your mind. Images that don't motivate you are small and way in the back of your mind.

An important rule to follow while doing your visualization exercises during your self-hypnosis sessions, your pre-shot routine, and mental rehearsal exercises is to make the positive mental images BIG and right in the forefront of your mind.

This will make the thought more compelling, and cause your subconscious mind to more readily act upon them.

It is important to always remember that the subconscious mind doesn't discern good or bad, right or wrong, it just acts upon the most compelling and powerful images held in the mind. *Therefore, it is important to understand that negative images oftentimes are BIG and in the forefront of the mind, if it is a recurring problem. In order to eliminate the compulsion to act on these negative images, you must change the picture and way it is coded in the subconscious in order to create new responses and behaviors.*

The Switch Technique: Rewiring Your Brain

Let's take this information to the next level with another exercise that you can do right now that can eliminate unwanted behaviors and responses on the course by changing the coding in your subconscious mind.

Step 1: Identify an unwanted behavior or response that you want to change in your golf game.

Step 2: Identify a **trigger image**, this is image #1. Your trigger image needs to be:

- A visual image that occurs right before you experience the unwanted behavior or response that you have on the course. To determine your trigger image, ask yourself these two questions: "How do I know that I need to start doing (insert unwanted behavior or response)? What do I see right before this occurs?

- An associated view, which means what you see through your own eyes right before the behavior or response takes place.

Step 3: Identify the **ideal image** of the way you would like to be. This is image #2. To identify your ideal image:

- Make an image of the "new you", who no longer has this problem and has not only overcome this challenge but has evolved way beyond it. Create an image of you the way you really want to be and make it so attractive and appealing that you have to have it now, not tomorrow or next week, but you want to be that now! Make that image of the most successful, resourceful, and powerful you.

- Be sure that this image is in a dissociated perspective meaning you are seeing yourself like on a screen. Make it realistic. A person who has many choices.

- Have no background, and preferably neutral of any location.

- Finally check to see if this is what you truly want by asking yourself, "Do I have any objections about becoming this person?

Step 4: Mental Setup of the Technique: In your mind, create a bright, and colorful image of the trigger image that you identified in Step 2 and put it in the front of your mind. Now, next to it, in the distance of your mind, put the ideal image of the "you" that you would like to be, in black-and-white. This will be called the "original setting."

Step 5: Making The Switch: Now you are about to begin the process of rewiring your brain and creating a new behavior or response. Here is how it is done:

- Start with the original setting, meaning the trigger image, Image #1, which is close, colorful, and in the forefront. The ideal image, Image #2, is small, in the distance and in black-and-white.

- Next, you are going to rapidly switch the images by doing the following. The trigger image moves into the distance and becomes black-and-white. The trigger image will lose all color as it shrinks and moves extremely fast far away into the distance. Simultaneously, the ideal image moves to the forefront of the mind, getting bigger and closer, and gains full color. So once the switch is made, the new setting will be the ideal image is bright, colorful, big, and in the forefront of your mind, and the trigger image is way in the distance, small, and black-and-white, or even gone altogether. Note: It is important that when you do the switch that you do it in a split second and super-fast.

- Finally, let's go over how to do the switch. Start with everything in the original setting. Count from 1 to 3, then mentally say "switch," and instantly make the images switch perspectives extremely fast, in a split second, as described above. Then make your mental screen go blank, reset everything back to the original setting, and repeat this process 5-10 times. Note: Be sure to remember to blank out the screen in between switches before repeating to ensure success.

Step 6: Test Results: To test the results, clear out your mind and think about the trigger image. What happens now? When done successfully, you will experience one of two things. Either you will not be able to re-access the trigger image in any way, or it will instantly and automatically switch into the ideal image, or Image #2. What has just occurred is the subconscious mind has created a new association to the trigger image and a new response has been established. Now that you have made this shift in mental coding, the subconscious mind has a new mental program to operate with and move towards that is in alignment with what you actually desire. Basically, this technique updates the bio-computer with the new and right information to act upon instead of the old conditioned patterns of behavior and responses.

To drive this technique home, let me provide an example of this process in action when I was working with one of my golfers. The first thing we did was identify the unwanted behavior and response that he wanted to eliminate. In this situation, when the golfer would see a white out of bounds stake while waiting to tee off, it would immediately trigger a state of anxiety and mental images of the ball either going out of bounds or going dramatically the other way, which in either case are both negative performance pictures. Normally in this situation on the course, the anxiety created tension in his body, the negative pictures directed his mind in a negative direction, and inevitably he would step up and hit a bad shot.

Obviously, he wanted to change this unwanted pattern of behavior and we achieved Step 1 by clearly identifying the negative behavior. Next, I asked him to recall a time on the course when this situation occurred and asked him, "How do you know you need to start experiencing the anxiety and negative pictures?" He responded, "When I see the out of bounds stake." I followed up by asking him, "What is the last mental image you have before you start experiencing the unwanted behavior?" Again, he said, "The white out of bounds marker." Now we achieved Step 2 which is to identify the trigger image. So I had him create an image of seeing the out of bounds marker in an associated view or through his own eyes, just like on the course. Next, I instructed him to create an ideal image of himself on a screen that has evolved way beyond the problem and is responding in the perfect and most desired way. Once he created this image, I instructed him to make the image even more appealing in every way so that he really wanted that right now. After he did this, he described his ideal image as seeing himself holding the strong, confident finish that he has when he stripes the ball to the middle of the fairway. Now we just achieved Step 3 and created an attractive, appealing, and compelling ideal image.

Then I instructed him on how to create the original setting for the exercise. I had him visualize the trigger image of the out of bounds stake big, and colorful in the front of his mind, while off in the distance I had him make the ideal image small and in in black-and-white. Next, I told him at the count of 3 and when I say "switch", he is to make the trigger image lose all its color and move way back into the distance, while simultaneously adding color to the ideal image, making it huge, and moving it to the forefront of the mind, and do this in a split second. Once he understood the directions, we began the process. I counted 1, 2, 3, **"Switch"** and he mentally swapped the pictures.

Then I had him clear his mind, reset it to the original setting, and we repeated this about 10 times for approximately 3-5 minutes. Finally, I had him take a deep breath in, clear his mind, and then I told him to think about a white stake and tell me what happens. He immediately responded by saying all he could see or think about was the ideal image and he wasn't able to even see the old image at all. The next day, I asked him to think about a white stake and he said he immediately thinks about his ideal image and sees himself striping it down the fairway. This simple technique completely changed his behaviors and responses to that old trigger, and now it has become a positive trigger that produces pictures of success instead of stress.

Enhancing and Desensitizing Mental Images

You are now becoming aware that changing the mental pictures changes the entire experience. So far, you have learned that your mind codes positive and negative experiences differently such as the perspective (associated or dissociated) as well as the size and location of the image. Let's continue building on this information and discuss some other ways that you can enhance positive pictures of what you desire so that the subconscious mind acts upon them, and desensitize the effects of negative pictures that hurt performance and hold you back on your journey to your goals.

The first element that can enhance or desensitize mental images is color. When things are highly appealing to you, your subconscious mind naturally creates bright, clear, and colorful mental images of these things you are drawn to. Things that you aren't drawn to or compelled to act on naturally show up in the mind as black-and-white images, or in shades of grey as well as typically appear fuzzy, dim, and difficult to see clearly. The same way changing the size and location of the mental image can change your experience, when you add or remove color from mental images and visualizations it also changes the experience and the way you perceive it.

Let's do a quick mental exercise to enhance positive images and remove any emotional charges to the negative ones.

Desensitizing Negative Mental Images:

Step 1: Visualize a situation that has been troubling you on the golf course and create a mental image of it. Chances are if this is something that has been consistently bothering you on the course, then it's probably a bright and colorful mental image of the experience.

Step 2: With your eyes closed and while holding that mental image in mind, begin to imagine the picture losing all its color and becoming black-and-white, or turning shades of gray. After you remove the color from the negative situation, notice how it immediately makes you feel differently about the situation.

Step 3: You can desensitize any negative effects from this mental image even more by altering the picture in other ways. For example, you can make it dimmer, darker, and put it in very low light. You can add static to the image like you would see on a TV with no reception. Or, even changing the color to something like solid pink or blue. These are just a couple examples of the countless ways that you can change the appearance of an image. Anytime you remove color from an image, make it harder and more difficult to see, and blur out the image, the more it will desensitize any negative emotions associated with that mental image.

Step 4: Mentally lock in the changes to keep this image in this perspective so that you are no longer affected by it in the same way again. An easy and fun way to do this is to imagine putting an old frame around the picture and store it away in your mental archives or museum of past thoughts that is way in the back of your mind.

Notes: General Points to Desensitize Mental Images:

- Remove color and make it black-and-white.

- Dim and darken the image to make it harder to see.

- Add in static.

- Make it small and way in the back of the mind.

Enhancing Positive Mental Images:

Step 1: Visualize a situation that is positive but you don't consistently do enough on the course. Or visualize a behavior that you would like to do more of, but you aren't very motivated to take action on, perhaps exercising or practicing more hours. Chances are that even though these are positive things you want to do, since you haven't been acting on them, it is very likely that these images are harder to see, less colorful, or even black-and-white.

Step 2: Now let's enhance this image to make it more appealing in your subconscious mind and make it more compelling to act upon. To do this start by making the image bigger and adding bright color to the image. After you made it bigger, brighter, and in full color, become aware of the difference in your level of excitement about the image. Is it more compelling, exciting, and motivating now that it is full of color and bigger?

Step 3: You can enhance this image even more by allowing your imagination to add in more elements that make it more exciting, appealing, and something that you really want right now. Increase this image in any way that is right for you to enhance the positive feelings that are now being associated with it.

Step 4: Once you have maxed out this mental image and it is highly compelling and exciting to you, lock and store this image in your mind. Make it huge, with no borders, move it to the forefront of your mind, and imagine locking it in this position. This will keep this mental image in the right frame of reference to keep you excited about acting on this.

Notes: General Points to Enhancing Mental Images:

- Make it colorful.

- Make it bright and bold.

- Make it high definition and ultra-clear.

- Make it huge, borderless, and in the front of your mind.

Additional Ways to Enhance Your Visualization Experiences and Mental Images

A great way to enhance the overall effectiveness of visualization is to think of it as an experience that you want to make as real as possible that goes beyond just visualizing but incorporates all of your senses. Your experiences in life and out on the golf course are not experienced only through sight, but also through all of your 5 senses; sight, sound, touch, taste, and smell. In Neuro-Linguistic Programming (NLP) we call the senses "modalities" and have slightly different names for the senses which are visual, auditory, kinesthetic, gustatory, and olfactory.

How does this apply to your golf game? The answer is simple. By incorporating all of your senses, or modalities, into the experience, the greater the impression it makes in your subconscious mind.

This is important because your subconscious doesn't know the difference between fact and fiction, and by creating visualization experiences that are life-like and use all the senses, the subconscious can be trained in a similar fashion as if you were actually performing.

The goal is to always make your visualization experiences as real as you can and to achieve this goal be sure to:

- ➢ Incorporate the Visuals: Visualize in as much detail as you can all the sights, images, colors, and objects on the golf course.

- ➢ Incorporate Feelings: Feel the movements of your swing, the grip of the club, the heat of the sun, the success of hitting a great shot, the pride of draining a putt, the joy of a low round, and so on.

> ➢ Incorporate Sounds: Hear the sounds of the experience such as the sound of your swing, the contact with the ball, sounds of the birds, compliments from playing partners, and the noises out on the course.

Make the experience even more appealing, exciting, and compelling by enhancing all these different elements:

> ➢ Make the visual images brighter, more colorful, bolder, bigger, more detailed, clearer, etc.

> ➢ Intensify the feelings by imagining more power being added to all the positive feeling making them stronger. The more emotional power you can put into your visualizations the greater the impact it will have on your subconscious mind since your subconscious is fueled by emotions.

> ➢ Amplify the sounds by imagining turning up the volume to all the positive sounds of the experience. Make the sound of perfect contact, the cheers from your friends, your positive self-talk, and all other sounds louder and more harmonious.

The last thing that I want to mention as a way to enhance the effectiveness of your visualization is self-hypnosis. Visualization exercises off the course are always most effective in a state of self-hypnosis or while in alpha and theta brainwaves. Self-hypnosis activates the creative functions of your subconscious mind which enhances the visualization experience, makes it more life-like, and develops neural pathways in your brain similar to actual performance due to the formation of perfect mental images and experiences.

Journey of Success Exercise

It's time for another self-hypnosis mental exercise. This exercise is a powerful way to enhance your level of success and desensitize negative experiences that could be potentially holding you back from greater success.

Before getting into the exercise, I want to share with you a belief system of the most successful golfers and individuals from around the world. **The belief is there is only one form of failure – which is inaction – otherwise failure doesn't exist.**

I will assume that you are an action-taker since you are reading this book which means failure doesn't exist in your life or in your golf game.

"How can this be?" you might ask. Because you either succeed in your endeavors or you have a learning experience that will get you one step closer to your goals. With this type of belief system you are always succeeding or learning which will keep you motivated to achieve your goals and positive as you pursue your dreams. It is one thing to know this is true and it's another thing to feel *and* know it's true.

The Journey of Success Exercise Steps:

The Journey of Success exercise is designed to enhance all the positive moments of success in your golf game, or in life in general, as well as to remove all negative emotions connected to the difficult moments and transform them into learning experiences so you can find the positive lessons that you gained from each experience.

Step 1: Find a quiet place where you can relax, focus your attention, and won't be disturbed. After doing some deep breathing to begin the relaxation process, do your favorite method of self-hypnosis to get yourself into a receptive and creative state of mind.

Step 2: Once you successfully induced self-hypnosis and now, with your eyes closed, begin to imagine in vivid detail the room that you are sitting in. Next, imagine and pretend floating out of your body, and up to the ceiling. Imagine looking down at yourself from this perspective and visualize yourself relaxed and peaceful in the chair you are sitting in.

Step 3: As you float above the present moment, imagine that you are now connected to the timeline of your life and you can move freely to any experience in your life. You are now ready to take a journey into your past to re-experience some of the greatest moments of your golf career. To drift back in time to positive memories and experiences, give your subconscious mind suggestions like this:

> *In a moment, I will count from 1 to 3 and at the count of 3, I will instantly and automatically travel back into my past and float above a positive*

experience on the golf course just as I am floating above this moment right now. At the count of 3, I will travel back to a time when everything was going right on the golf course and I was performing my best. I give my mind permission to travel back to a great memory and float above it so I can recall a time of great success on the golf course. This occurs instantly and automatically at the count of 3. 1...I am drifting back now. 2...I am just about there. 3...I am there and now floating above a positive experience of the past.

Step 4: Now that you are floating above this past experience of success, imagine floating back down into your body so that you can re-experience the success and greatness of this time in your life. As you touch down into the experience, make it as real and as vivid as possible and give yourself permission to really get back into this moment in your life.

Step 5: Now that you are experiencing the moment all over again, begin to enhance the experience to make it even more amazing and exciting. To do this, begin to enhance all the modalities especially the visual, auditory, and kinesthetic aspects. Make all the colors brighter, bolder, and more colorful. Increase all the positive feelings of this moment and make everything feel even better, more successful, and more positive. A great way to do this is imagine plugging these feelings into a power outlet and turning up the voltage so that these positive feelings are flowing more powerfully through all parts of you. Increase all the positive sounds in the experience by increasing the volume, intensify the volume of your positive self-talk and the compliments, and add in your favorite upbeat and inspiring music to the experience. Do whatever you need to do or want to do to make this experience 10 times better than it was. Finally, once you have maxed out the experience and it is even more powerful, successful, and positive, float back up and out of the experience, but leave everything enhanced and highlighted on the timeline of your life.

Step 6: Now you should be floating above the positive experience you just went through and it is all lit up and highlighted on your timeline. Drift back to another memory now by suggesting to yourself:

In a moment, I will count from 1 to 3 and at the count of 3, I will instantly and automatically travel back into my past and float above a positive *experience on the golf course just as I am floating above this moment right now. At the count of 3, I will travel back to a time when everything was going right on the course and I was performing my best. I give my mind permission to travel back to a great memory and float above it so I can recall a time of great success on the golf course. This occurs instantly and automatically at the count of 3. **1**...I am drifting back now. **2**...I am just about there. **3**...I am there and now floating above a positive experience of the past.*

Once you identified and are floating above the next successful memory, follow the same steps as previously mentioned. Drift and touch down into the moment, re-experience the success again, and enhance all the modalities making the experience 10 times better than what it was. After it is maxed out, lock in the enhancements, float up, and see this experience highlighted and illuminated on your timeline just like the first experience. Repeat this 1-3 more times so that you have a total of 3-5 positive experiences enhanced, highlighted, and illuminated on your timeline.

Step 7: As you float above the timeline of your life now, you should see the 3-5 successful moments bright, big, colorful, and highlighted on your timeline. Now, you are going to follow the same process of traveling on your timeline, but this time you are going to float above those times in the past that you perceived to be negative events. You can't change the past, but you can change the perception of it. All experiences serve you because learning experiences are necessary in your development and journey as a golfer. To identify these negative experiences so you can transform them into positives, mentally suggest to yourself:

In a moment, I will count from 1 to 3 and at the count of 3, I will instantly and automatically travel back into my past and float above a negative experience on the golf course just as I am floating above this moment right now. At the count of 3, I will travel back to a time that I thought was negative but was in fact a learning experience in my journey. I give my mind permission to travel back to a memory of a negative experience and float above it so I can take in the positive lessons I learned on the golf course during that experience. This occurs instantly and automatically at the count of 3.

1...I am drifting back now. 2...I am just about there. 3...I am there and now floating above a learning experience of the past.

Step 8: As you float above a negative experience, stay floating high above the moment and observe it from this bird's eye perspective instead of touching down into the moment. Remain floating above the experience, and become aware how at first glance this experience may appear to be negative. However, as you observe the experience from this detached perspective above the situation, it is easy to realize the positive lessons that was acquired from having gone through this.

Step 9: Remain floating above the negative experience and it is now time to begin eliminating the negative effects of this experience so that more lessons can be gained from it. To do this, begin removing all the color from the experience. Let all the color fade away, becoming shades of grey, and eventually black-and-white. Disconnect all the negative feelings from the event by imaging pulling out the power cord that is feeding this experience energy, and remove the energy source. Silence and mute out all the sounds of the experience. Make the experience neutral by making the color, the feelings, and sounds fade away completely.

While this is occurring, imagine that rising out of the fading memory are big, bright, and colorful bubbles of knowledge and positive lessons rising up like bubbles of a soda floating above the experience. As all the negatives are fading away to nothing, more and more big, bright, colorful bubbles of learning are rising up to you and blocking out all other perspectives. All you can see now are these big bubbles filled with positive lessons and knowledge gained from the experience, nothing else remains. After you have done this, you will have one of two experiences. The memory will be neutral or transformed into a positive and perceived as a needed experience on your journey to becoming the best golfer you can be.

Step 10: Now as you observe your timeline, you have 3-5 big, bright, highlighted experiences of success, and now a big cluster of bubbles containing the positive lessons from the learning experience. Repeat this step with 2 more learning experiences so that you desensitize any negative experiences and put things in the right perspective by bringing forth the positive lessons.

Step 11: After you have done this for 3 negative events turning them into learning experiences on the course, float back to the present moment and back to the room in which you are sitting in. Now as you look back on your timeline, all you can see are the big, bright, colorful highlighted experiences of success and all the colorful bubbles of the positive lessons that rose to the top and you gained from the learning experiences.

Step 12: Take a deep breath in and as you exhale, imagine that all the positive energy from the past successes and the successful learning experiences are accelerating and pushing you into the future. Imagine all this positive energy is skyrocketing you to all your goals and dreams on the golf course and let it take you to a moment in the future where you can experience the success, perhaps an upcoming round of golf or a tournament.

Step 13: Now touch down in this future moment and experience what it is like performing on the golf course as your ideal self of the future, the one who achieves all their goals and experiences tremendous success on the course. Experience life as your ideal self as vividly and as real as possible. Really get into the experience of achieving this level of success and what it's like. Make it compelling, attractive, and so appealing that you have to experience this. Notice the way the ideal self moves, acts, walks, and talks. Become aware of the things you do to create such high levels of success. Experience how positive, confident, and powerful you are in this future moment. Make all aspects of this future success even better by enhancing the colors, the feelings, and the sounds, and make a mental memory of this incredible experience to bring back with you to the present moment.

Step 14: Float out of the future experience, locking in all the enhancements and storing it in your memory. Drift back to the present moment and back down into your body feeling more confident, positive, and certain of your success. Take a few deep breaths and store this experience into your mind. Emerge yourself from self-hypnosis by doing a count out and return the world energized and fueled by your past and future success.

This exercise is a longer one and may seem like a lot of steps. However, it is simple and easy to do once you have internalized the process. Before doing the exercise, it is recommended that you read through the steps several times to become familiar with them and then proceed to doing the exercise in self-hypnosis.

This exercise is an example of how to enhance positive aspects of experiences and make them more compelling as well as how to desensitize the effects of negative images and experiences. You can use these steps by themselves at any time to change the mental coding in your subconscious mind by altering the modalities so that you can make successful experiences better and eliminate any negative effects from experiences you have on the course. This exercise also boosts success simply by recalling your successes of the past and putting your mental spotlight on these experiences. What you focus on expands and by recalling, enhancing, and focusing on your success, your subconscious mind will be directed to produce more of it in your golf game.

In-Depth Approach to Determining Your Mental Coding

The **Mental Swing Signature Exercise** is a more in-depth look at the way your mind codes success, so that you can identify your unique mental swing signature, or the specific coding of success, that is congruent with achievement in your mind's eye. This exercise is best done with a partner who can guide you through the questions and write down your answers. If you don't have a person to assist you, it is still possible to do the exercise successfully. However, it is recommended that you record the steps and listen to it as you do self-hypnosis so you can be guided through the steps without having to think about them.

In this chapter, we have been discussing how the subconscious mind creates strings of codes to mentally represent the experience. There is another sub-set of coding below each of the modalities (visual, auditory, kinesthetic, gustatory, and olfactory) which are called sub-modalities. Sub-modalities are what make up the various strings of mental coding in the subconscious mind and by identifying the coding of positive and negative states you can make rapid shifts in behaviors and feelings simply by altering these sub-modalities.[2] This exercise will help you identify, in a very specific way, the coding of success and failure and how you can enhance success in all aspects of your golf game with this information. Since this chapter is devoted to visualization development, this exercise will focus only on the visual aspects of your performance. If you want to get into this exercise even deeper to determine additional strings of internal coding, I suggest contacting my office or another performance coach trained in NLP.

Because this exercise is intended to be done with a partner, you will notice that the steps are written in third person and not first person, so the partner is not confused when going through the steps with you. Let's go over the steps now so you can determine your mental swing signature.

Your Mental Swing Signature Exercise Steps:

Step 1: Identify the negative state that is hindering performance on the course. For the purpose of this example, we will use self-doubt.

Step 2: Identify the positive state that would boost performance on the course. For this example, we will use confidence.

Step 3: Do self-hypnosis to relax the mind and body.

Step 4: Bring up the negative state: The assistant is to instruct the golfer to think about a negative situation on the course that caused them to feel self-doubt (or another negative state) and to visualize the situation occurring.

Step 5: Identify the Visual Coding of the Negative State: To do this, the assistant will direct the golfer to focus fully on the negative event and go through the series of questions below to determine how the mind coded the experience visually. The assistant also needs to write down the answers from the golfer. As the golfer focuses on the experience, ask these questions:

- As you visualize the experience, is it in color or black in white?

- Is the image moving or still?

- Is the experience bright or dim?

- Is it focused or unfocused?

- Are you associated in the experience (seeing it through your own eyes) or is it dissociated (watching yourself on a screen)?

- Is it 3D or flat?

- Is it close or distant in the mind?

- Where is the image located in the mind (Front, back, left, or right)?

- What is the size of the image?

- Is it framed in or panoramic extending beyond borders?

Note: There are no wrong answers. Simply write down the answers that come up without analysis.

Step 6: Clear the Mind. To do this, simply ask the golfer a random question to change the mental focus and clear the mind. For example, ask the golfer "What would you do if you woke up and the sky was a different color than blue?" Any random question will clear the mind and thoughts of the negative experience so that the mind can accurately think about the next step. If you are doing this exercise without an assistant then simply open your eyes, think of something random like your favorite color, and close your eyes and proceed to the next step.

Step 7: Bring up the Positive State: Once the mind of the golfer is cleared, instruct the golfer to focus on a positive situation when they felt confident. Tell them to think about one of their best experiences on the course and to focus their full attention on it.

Step 8: Identify the Visual Coding of the Positive State or Your Mental Swing Signature: To identify the visual coding, have the golfer focus on the positive event that created the confidence and ask them the following series of questions and write down the answers.

- As you visualize the experience, is it in color or black in white?

- Is the image moving or still?

- Is the experience bright or dim?

- Is it focused or unfocused?

- Are you associated in the experience (seeing it through your own eyes) or is it dissociated (watching yourself on a screen)?

- Is it 3D or flat?

- Is it close or distant in the mind?

- Where is the image located in the mind (Front, back, left, or right)?

- What is the size of the image?

- Is it framed in or panoramic extending beyond borders?

At this point in time, you should have two lists of answers; a list of the visual sub-modalities related to the negative state and the positive state. These two lists reveal the exact way your mind visually codes these different states. *What you will notice is that some of the elements are the same and others are different. These subtle differences are what create success verses failure. This information is extremely valuable to know because it identifies the exact way you visualize success in your mind's eye.* With this information you can immediately shift mental states by making your visualization experience match your success coding in your mind. Let's go over how you do this now so you know exactly how to apply this information.

Step 9: Bring up the negative state again: Instruct the golfer to think about the experience of self-doubt again. To help them re-access this state fully, go down the list of their answers to provide the framework of the experience you identified in the exercise.

Step 10: Alter the Experience: Once the golfer is visualizing the negative experience as they normally do, begin to change the visual codes to match the ones of the positive experience. For example, if the negative experience was in black and white, but the confident experience was in color, then instruct the golfer to use their imagination and add color to the experience. Do this for all the mismatches until the golfer is thinking about the negative experience with the same coding as the successful experience. These simple adjustments will change the coding of the experience and transform it instantly from a negative one to a positive, confident experience.

Step 11: Test the Results. Have the golfer think about the old negative experience in this new framework of the golfer's mental swing signature, and ask what differences they notice in the way they think and feel about the situation. Another way to test the results is to go out to the range or the course. While practicing or playing, deliberately visualize your shots in the framework of your mental swing signature and notice the differences you experience in your performance as well as in your state of confidence.

This is powerful information to know about your mind and will produce tremendous improvements in your game as long as you take the time to identify your coding of success and then practice it, practice it, practice it! This is also the way you want to do visualizations during your self-hypnosis sessions so that you are conditioning you mind for success based on the specific coding of your mind.

Visualization Exercise for Focus and Execution Enhancement

Focus is vitally important for success in golf and visualization can be used to enhance your level of concentration on the course. A round of golf takes 4 hours to play but your scorecard is determined by just a few minutes of performance. Every golfer knows that it is next to impossible to maintain intense focus throughout a 4 hour round of golf. However, it is possible to train your mind to have unbreakable, laser-like focus for 60 second intervals. Being able to create one minute of intense focus is more than enough to boost your performance because most pre-shot routines take 40 seconds or less, and it takes only 1-1.5 seconds to execute your actual golf swing.

It is possible to train your mind to have an intense level of focus on each shot. This next visualization exercise can help you achieve just that. It is called the 5 Minute Performance Enhancer. This powerful mental drill takes only 5 minutes to do and, with daily practice, can benefit your game in a significant way. Some of the benefits of this technique include:

> ➤ An increase in your ability to focus your mind fully on every shot as well as block out distractions.

> ➤ It increases the execution of your swing due to the benefits of mental rehearsal in the subconscious mind. Mental rehearsal of the golf swing is proven to increase motor skills, coordination, ball striking, and execution.

> ➤ It increases your ability to relax your body and release stress.

> ➤ It increases your ability to visualize shots on the course so that you can have clearer and more vivid visualizations in your pre-shot routine.

5 Minute Performance Enhancer Exercise Steps:

Step 1: Find a quiet place where you can sit back and relax for 5 minutes. This technique can be done with or without self-hypnosis since the technique itself will also guide you into alpha and theta waves. If you choose not to do self-hypnosis prior to this exercise be sure to do some deep diaphragmatic breathing to relax the mind and body, and begin the process of getting into a receptive state of mind.

Step 2: Close your eyes to block out distractions and let yourself relax more. With your eyes closed, begin to imagine as vividly as possible being all alone on your favorite golf course. Give your imagination the freedom to be child-like again and do your best to make it as real as possible by incorporating as many senses as you can. Take a few minutes to create an experience of being on the course. Visualize what you would be seeing, feel the sun on your skin, hear the sounds of the golf course, and really imagine what it would be like to be out there. Doing this stimulates your imagination, activates the creative subconscious mind, and slows down your brainwaves so you are more receptive.

Step 3: Imagine that you are standing on the tee box and there is a bucket of brand new golf balls with numbers 25-1 on them. As vividly as you can, imagine picking up the golf ball numbered 25 and tee it up. Next, visualize yourself executing your perfect swing and striking the ball right on the sweet spot. As you complete your swing and watch the ball get striped down the fairway, simply allow your mental and physical relaxation to increase. Once the ball hits your target, powerfully declare in your mind a keyword, such as power or confidence. By declaring a keyword, you are beginning the conditioning process to turn this keyword into a mental trigger for success.

Step 4: When you are ready, imagine picking up the ball numbered 24 and repeat the same process. Experience, as real as you can, swinging your club perfectly and hitting another beautiful golf shot directly to your target. Again, double your mental and physical relaxation as the ball travels down the fairway on the perfect path. Once it hits the target declare your keyword.

Step 5: Continue this process of visualizing yourself executing your perfect golf swing, doubling your mental relaxation during the ball flight, and declaring your keyword after your shot landed perfectly on your target. Do this until you have successfully hit all 25 golf balls perfectly in your mind.

Step 6: After mentally hitting all 25 golf balls, you will be in a receptive state of mind regardless if you started with self-hypnosis or not. This is the perfect time to repeat a positive suggestion to yourself a minimum of 10 times to do mental programming for success in your game.

Step 7: Take a few deep breaths to re-energize your body and mind. Then do a count out from 1 to 5 and open your eyes.

This exercise should take around 5 minutes to complete. However, it may take a little longer the first few times until you get proficient with the exercise.

Important Notes on the 5 Minute Performance Enhancer: The ultimate goal is to complete this exercise without distractions or deviating from the task in any way. If you find your mind wandering during this exercise, as soon as you realize that your mind has wandered from the task, immediately go back to where you left off and continue the exercise until completion. This exercise is an excellent way to train your mind to increase your level of focus and keep your mind from drifting to different thoughts. On the course, this skill will help you stay focused on the shot at hand as well as maintain positive thoughts about the shot, without your mind slipping back into old mental programming.

As you begin to gain proficiency with this exercise, put yourself in more challenging situations and work on blocking out distractions. For example, find a bench on a busy street corner to practice the exercise or play loud music in the background. This will increase your ability to focus in any situation and handle anything you could possibly encounter on the golf course.

Have fun with this exercise! After learning the basic exercise, as described above, let your creative mind take over and imagine hitting other types of shots. If you are learning how to shape your shots, then visualize yourself fading and drawing the ball perfectly. You might imagine holing 25 shots from the sand or hitting 25 perfect approach shots from various distances. Perhaps you imagine hitting 25 precise shots in a competition setting or draining 25 winning putts in front of huge galleries and TV cameras. The possibilities are unlimited so let your imagination run wild. Just make sure that every shot you hit mentally is perfect in every way. It is important to understand that every shot you hit vividly in your mind is building neural pathways in your brain similar to what occurs during actual performance.

The great thing about visualization and mental rehearsal is you can hit every shot perfectly which gives your subconscious mind the correct reinforcement of what you want to create on the course.

When you are on the course, declare the keyword you used in the exercise before taking your shot to trigger the confidence, focus, and relaxation that you have conditioned into yourself through practicing this exercise.

To develop unbreakable focus and vivid visualizations, you must work on developing it just like you work on your golf swing. The top pros do mental fitness exercises every day to improve their focus and performance. *Since you are looking for major breakthroughs in your game, begin incorporating this exercise into your daily practice routine. The more you do it, the more you will improve.*

The Sunday Afternoon Success Generator Exercise:

Another great way to improve your golf game and condition your subconscious mind for success from the comfort of your favorite chair is a technique I call the Sunday Afternoon Success Generator. The technique is based on a NLP technique for creating new behaviors. I thought if this could help my clients learn new behaviors and eliminate negative ones, why couldn't it help my golf game? When I put it to the test, it worked better than expected and literally transformed my swing performance in a short period of time and it will do the same for you.

You might be wondering why I used the words 'Sunday Afternoon' in the title of this technique. I did that because it was on Sunday afternoons that I got some of my best practice. My best practice sessions didn't come from going to the range on Sunday afternoons, it came from watching the professionals on TV, closing my eyes, and applying the technique I am going to share now. I found this to be a great time to do mental drills because after witnessing great shots on TV it was easy to close my eyes, get into self-hypnosis, visualize the same success in my mind, and do this technique to enhance my game. This technique can be applied to any area of your game and once you do it a few times it will be easy to do anytime you wish.

Sunday Afternoon Success Generator Exercise Steps:

Step 1: Identify an area of your game that you want to work on and improve such as better performance and accuracy with your driver.

Step 2: Do self-hypnosis and get into a relaxed state of mind and body.

Step 3: Once in a relaxed state, begin to imagine the area of your game that you want to improve, but in the way you are currently experiencing it on the course. (Let's use a simple example to make things very clear.) Let's pretend a golfer is hitting worm-burner tee shots and they want to strike the ball better of the tee. In this step, the golfer would imagine an experience of hitting the worm-burner since it is their current state of performance.

Step 4: After visualizing the negative performance, clear your mind, and begin to think about one of your hero's in golf in the same situation. Now begin to imagine how the pro does things in in this situation. Notice the way they move, what they do before the shot, witness the beautiful execution of their swing, and the ball going directly to the target.

Step 5: Now imagine rewinding the experience and go back to the beginning of the professional's shot. This time as you visualize the experience, imagine that a hologram of yourself is lightly over top of the professional and you are able to experience going through the movements and swing execution in the same way they perform. Now imagine the golf shot, with the hologram of yourself over the pro, and the perfect results of the swing.

Step 6: Go back to the beginning again and this time imagine that the hologram is a becoming more solid and you can begin to see more of yourself in the scene. Now imagine the same golf shot, this time seeing more of yourself executing the swing of the pro, and the ball going directly to the target.

Step 7: Rewind the experience once again and this time the hologram is so solid that you can barely see any of your hero underneath the hologram of yourself. Imagine the same beautiful golf shot, seeing the perfect execution, and the desired result.

Step 8: Again, go back to the beginning of the experience, but this time all you can see is yourself doing things now exactly like the pro. Visualize yourself approaching the ball with confidence just like the pro, executing that perfect swing, and producing the desired outcome of the swing.

Step 9: One last time, go back to the beginning, and imagine floating down into your body so that you can experience through your own eyes the movements, the experience, and the execution of this shot. Imagine everything as real and as vividly as you can entering into the person you were watching and go through the successful experience in an associated view.

Step 10: Finish this mental training exercise with positive suggestions that affirm that this is your new reality. Give yourself 5 minutes or so of positive suggestions and then emerge from self-hypnosis.

At first, this technique may appear to be a number of complicated steps. In reality, it is very simple once you go through the process a couple of times. The Sunday Afternoon Success Generator is a powerful way to condition your mind for better performance in any situation in your game. Use this technique on Sunday afternoons relaxing on the couch, and watching your heroes conquer the course. When you see results that you want to replicate, close your eyes, get into a relaxed mental state, and go through this exercise. It will make it much easier after seeing it on TV because the images will be fresh in your mind which will make it easier to visualize and go through the process. Of course, this exercise isn't limited to Sunday afternoons and can be done at any time to accelerate the learning process of your physical skills. This exercise can help you make improvements in any aspect of your game that is important to peak performance on the course, such as your swing, the pre-shot routine, handling pressure, and performing in the clutch.

Incorporating Visualization into Your Pre-Shot Routine

In this section, I want to go over some basic steps to incorporate visualization in the *programming zone* of the pre-shot routine so that your routine can be more effective and you can direct your subconscious mind to high level performance on each shot.

Recall that in Chapter Three, we discussed the three phases of the pre-shot routine: *the thinking zone, the programming zone, and the performance zone.* The thinking zone is where you use your conscious mind to analyze the situation and determine the distance, the best club to use, select the type of shot you want to hit, etc. The next phase is the programming zone and this is the time you want to start to actively programming your subconscious mind on the way you want to perform the shot in the performance zone.

The Performance Bubble

The first concept to enhance the *programming zone* is visualizing or imaging a performance bubble around your ball. The performance bubble is an imaginary bubble that extends 10 feet in diameter around your ball. A bubble is visualized instead of a circle because a bubble surrounds you in all directions and through hypnotic suggestions delivered while in self-hypnosis, this bubble can be transformed into an imaginary force field that blocks out all outside stimuli and distractions. You want to train yourself that when you step foot inside the performance bubble, it's time to enter the zone fully, and program your mind to execute your ideal swing for the situation. Also, when you leave the performance bubble, it signals to your mind to turn off the intense concentration until the next shot.

Before going over suggestions to program and anchor this concept into the subconscious mind, let's go over some of the characteristics of the performance bubble so you can create powerful suggestions to drive this into your mind.

➢ The performance bubble extends 10 feet in all directions around the ball.

➢ Entering the performance bubble activates intense focus and triggers you to program your mind for success.

➢ Everything inside the bubble is consistent and the same; it triggers your pre-shot routine into action.

➢ Performance without conscious effort occurs inside the performance bubble.

➢ When you leave the performance bubble, your focus turns off until the next shot.

➢ When you leave the performance bubble, it disappears, all energy from the shot leaves with it, and it signals that the shot is over and finished.

Sample Hypnotic Suggestions for Performance Bubble: After the induction and deepener, suggest to yourself the following:

> *As I continue to relax deeper and feel more comfortable...I now accept all of these positive suggestions...because...I want to play better golf...and...lower my score. From this moment on when I am playing golf, I allow myself to think about, imagine, and pretend that surrounding my golf ball is a huge bubble 10 feet in diameter in all directions. As I imagine this bubble now...I understand that this is my performance bubble. From this moment on anytime I step in my performance bubble, my mind immediately focuses on the shot at hand. I notice that all distractions, outside noises, and all other things focus my mind even more on the shot or get completely blocked out by the bubble. When I am in the performance bubble all that matters...all my mind focuses on is the shot at hand. Inside the bubble, everything is calm and peaceful. This energy flows through my body and I relax into my game. I do the same thing every time I enter into the performance bubble. I do the same routine every time and this routine enables my subconscious mind to be fully present on the shot at hand. I trust my smart decisions, I visualize my perfect shot, and address the ball fully focused and fully relaxed. Inside the bubble my mind is completely focused and all outside distractions get blocked by the bubble. All that matters is the shot. After I hit a beautiful golf shot and I exit the bubble, my mind relaxes, I release the shot, and remain calm until I enter the next performance bubble on the shot ahead. With each and every shot this gets better and better, and my performance continues to improve.*

This is just a short script of suggestions to use to create a powerful performance bubble for peak performance and to trigger a consistent pre-shot routine. Use your creativity and come up with you own unique way of using this concept. After a little bit of conditioning, this easy to remember concept becomes a very effective way to increase your focus, consistency of your routine, and higher execution of your shot.

<u>The Double Snap Pre-Shot Routine Starter</u>

Another great pre-shot routine starter is to create a mental trigger to turn on and off focus with a double snap. Each time you enter into the performance bubble, do a double snap and mentally say to yourself something like, "Focus Now," "Time to Focus," or "Turn It On." After the shot and when you leave the performance bubble, bring closure to the shot by doing another double snap and mentally say to yourself something like, "Focus Off," "Time to Relax," "Turn It Off Now," or "Shot's Done, Move Forward."

There are many benefits to using a double snap to start and end your performance routine. First, the double snap acts as a mental trigger to turn on and off focus. After a little bit of conditioning, this double snap becomes a powerful anchor and gives you the ability to instantly get into a focused state of mind and then calm down just as quickly by snapping your fingers. The double snap also becomes a powerful anchor because it has auditory triggers, the suggestion and sound of the snap, as well as a kinesthetic trigger, the feeling of the finger snap together. Next, it acts as a reminder to stay in the present moment and to execute your pre-shot routine. Finally, it is a way to bring closure to the shot and shift your focus to the next shot. Many golfers would benefit from doing this to put the shot behind them, mentally. Too many golfers drag the past shots with them to the next shot which hurts their performance and results in lack of focus and wasted strokes on the scorecard.

Use post-hypnotic suggestions during your self-hypnosis time to enhance the power and effectiveness of this mental trigger. Here is a sample suggestion script for you to use:

> *From this moment on I have the power to turn on and off intense levels of focus anytime I snap my fingers twice. Anytime I snap my fingers twice and say "Focus Now" instantly, automatically, and without thinking my mind focuses, zeroes in, and I enter the zone. The moment I snap my fingers twice and say "Focus Now" I instantly, automatically, and without thinking enter the zone, my mind focuses fully, and I concentrate on the shot at hand. The moment I snap my fingers twice and say "Focus Now" instantly, automatically, and without thinking my mind focuses, I enter the zone, and start my pre-shot routine completed focused on the shot at hand. As I breathe in deeply now, this information is accepted into my subconscious mind and acted upon the moment I snap my fingers twice and say "Focus Now."*

> *The same way I have the power to instantly turn on my focus I also have the power to turn off my focus too. After each shot and when I leave the performance*

bubble, the moment I snap my fingers twice and say "Focus Off" my mind instantly relaxes and I end the shot. The moment I snap my fingers twice and say "Focus Off" my mind instantly and automatically relaxes, I end the shot, and move on to the next one. Each time I snap my fingers twice and say "Focus Off" my mind instantly and automatically relaxes, I end the shot, and move on to the next one. As I breathe in deeply now, this information makes a powerful impression in my mind to be instantly acted upon when I step foot on the course and at all times from tee to green.

<u>Keys to the Pre-Shot Routine:</u>
<u>AFFIRM IT, VISUALIZE IT, FEEL IT, AND COMMIT TO IT</u>

When you are in the *programming zone* during your pre-shot routine, it isn't time to think about club selection or make decisions. This is the time in the routine to program your subconscious mind on how to perform the shot at hand. In order to best program the subconscious mind during this period of time, I believe there are 4 key points to focus on to prepare your mind and body for success.

➢ **The First Key: AFFIRM IT:** The first key to success is mentally affirming what you want to accomplish in a positive way to instruct the subconscious mind on the direction to move in and to begin creating successful pictures in your mind. Remember to refrain from using negative words like, "don't" and state what you want in a clear, concise, and direct way. For example, "I am ripping this drive straight down the middle of the fairway." or "This approach shot is going right to the hole." Step one of the *programming zone* is to affirm in a positive way exactly what you desire the outcome to be.

➢ **The Second Key: VISUALIZE IT:** The second step is to visualize the perfect shot in rich detail in your mind's eye. The easiest way to ensure that you visualize your shot prior to performance is to identify two targets. The first target to identify is your ending target. Then identify a starting target, the spot to start your shot over to successfully hit your ending target. When you identify these two targets, your mind naturally begins to visualize the ball flight and path of the ball. The subconscious naturally wants to connect the dots, and as it does, it is being programmed to execute what it is creating and visualizing in your mind's eye.

➢ **The Third Key: FEEL IT:** Once you have affirmed what you desire, picked your two targets, and visualized the perfect shot, now it is time to program the body on how it's to perform by getting a good feel for the shot. Keep visualizing the perfect shot, seeing that ball tracing right over the starting target and flying pure to your end target, while you groove in your perfect swing to physically connect to shot that you are holding in your mind. Take a few practice swings while visualizing, and connect with the right feel to produce that perfect shot.

➢ **The Fourth Key: COMMIT TO IT:** After you have gone through the first 3 steps in the *programming zone*, your mind and body are now programmed to execute the shot at hand. At this point no more thought is required about the shot, it is now time to step up and make it reality by committing fully to the shot. Imagine crossing over an imaginary commitment line as you address your ball, commit to the shot, and hold in your mind the perfect shot/outcome you have been visualizing. Step up over the ball, fire off your anchor for your perfect swing pattern, visualize the shot one more time, and let your swing rip with confidence. Remember the goal is to execute your swing and perform without conscious effort. Trust in the mental programming you did in steps 1-3 and know that your subconscious mind will cause your body to respond in the perfect way to produce the desired result. All you have to do is commit to the shot, hold the mental images in your mind, and your subconscious will do the rest of the work in the performance zone.

<u>Incorporate Visualization into Your Putting Routine</u>

Research has proven that visualizing successful putts prior to putting the ball increases accuracy and the percentage of made putts. Tiger Woods said, "A pre-putt routine helps you stay nice and relaxed so you can make the best stroke possible." Let's go over a simple, and proven successful putting routine that incorporates visualization into the routine and produces results.

Step 1: Get a Good Read. To determine the best line to hole a putt, it is advantageous for you to read the putt from 3 locations each time in this order:

- Read #1: Behind the hole to determine the break and slope of the green

- Read #2: From the side of the hole on the low side to determine your distance and speed.

- Read #3: Behind the ball to determine the line.

Step 2: Visualize the Entire Putt: After the line is determined and you are standing behind or beside the ball, visualize the entire putting sequence to completion while you are finding the right putting stroke. It is important to visualize all aspects of the entire putt from start to finish. Visualize the entire stroke, the ball rolling pure and dropping into the center of the cup at the perfect speed. Research shows this increases accuracy and success.

Step 3: Visualize the Ball Coming Out of the Hole: Once you visualized a successful putting sequence, address the ball and while gazing at the target visualize the ball *coming back out of the hole* and rolling back along the perfect line to the face of your putter.

Step 4: Hold the Outcome Image and Putt: Now your mind is programmed to perform. Mentally hold the outcome image in your mind of the ball dropping in the hole perfectly and then putt. By holding onto the outcome image, it will temporarily still the conscious mind, activates the subconscious, and gives you the ability to perform without conscious effort on the greens. Or, once your eyes trace the line from the hole back to your putter, simply take your stroke and send the ball back down that same line you just visualized.

Brad Faxon once said, "Believe or not, I'm not really thinking about anything when I putt. I let my instincts take over. When I'm putting well, I feel like I can make everything." This putting routine will help you achieve the same type of results in your game. It keeps you focused on the target, activates your creative mind, and gives your subconscious a clear goal to achieve. Most importantly, this routine keeps your conscious mind out of the way. Masters champion Jack Burke Jr. said it best, "Bad putting stems from thinking "how" instead of "where." If you are thinking about "how" then you are using your conscious mind, or the thinking part, which is what most amateurs do. However, by incorporating this routine into your game you will naturally use more of your subconscious mind and your imagination which will increase your ability to execute on the greens without conscious effort.

Research shows that having a pre-shot routine that incorporates both *cognitive and behavioral* aspects, like the ones outlined here for swing and putting performance, are shown to significantly increase focus in the sport of golf.[3] In addition, it has been shown that pre-shot routines will increase focused attention, reduce anxiety, eliminate distractions, enhance confidence, and help mental preparation for future performance situations. [4]

How to Determine Targets for Shots and Putts

When selecting targets on the course there are two things you want to do. First, you want to determine your general ending target, i.e., the fairway, the green, or the hole. Second, you want to narrow your focus and select the smallest possible target inside this general area and make it your main target for the shot. For example, when you are getting ready to take a putt, instead of making the hole your main target, select a speck inside the hole to zero in on and make that your dominate target to focus on.

Why is it important to narrow your focus like this? Ben Hogan said it best, "This is a game of misses. The one who misses the best wins." *When you narrow your focus and select a very small target to focus on, it decreases your margin of error and increases the likelihood of success.* For example, when you are putting and you are aiming for a small speck inside of the cup, if you miss that mark your ball still finds the hole and drops in the cup. Whereas if you made the hole your main target and you miss your mark, you miss the hole all together and miss the putt.

This narrowing of focus doesn't just apply to putting, it applies to all shots you take on the course. Why do you think the average golfer is more likely to hit a fairway that is tree lined versus a fairway that is wide open with lots of room? The answer is simple, the tree lined fairway forces the golfer to narrow their focus and be more precise in determining their target. As a result, this smaller, more precise target decreases their margin of error and if they miss their line slightly then their ball only misses their target by a few yards which will still results in hitting the fairway and a good shot.

However, when the average golfer is looking at a wide open fairway on the tee box, they typically have some of their worst misses that end up going way off track and deep into the rough. Why does this occur? It happens because on wide open shots, most average golfers get lazy with selecting their target. They think that they can just step up and hit it because there isn't much trouble to get into and lots of fairway to hit to. As a result, their target is the big fairway which now increased their margin of error tremendously. Since they have such a big, general target, if they miss hit the ball they end up going way right or left, and completely miss the fairway all together.

The same thing happens with approach shots to the green. Most average golfers just want to hit the green and the green as a primary target is way too big to be accurate. With targets of this size, more often than not, the green is missed and instead of having a birdie opportunity somewhere on the green, the golfer is trying to get up and down to save par. By narrowing your focus and selecting a precise target on the green, your success will increase tremendously because the margin of error has just been dramatically reduced. So even if you miss your mark, you will have an accurate miss, and be left with a putt on the green versus having to chip or pitch on.

In his book, *Golf Is Not a Game of Perfect*, Dr. Bob Rotella shares this advice in regards to targeting on the course.

> *"Locking your mind onto a small target will help you deal with looming hazards. The brain tries to be an accommodating mechanism. It will try to send the ball in the direction of the last thing you look at or think about. If that happens to be a pond, you can find yourself in severe trouble. So if you're preparing to hit an approach shot over water, or a pitch over a bunker to a pin, it's important that you have an established habit of focusing your mind firmly on your target."*[5]

Besides focusing on a hazard instead of the target, many amateur golfers will spend a great deal of time focusing their attention on the ball prior to taking their swing which also can be detrimental to performance. However, the elite ball strikers and putters do the complete opposite. They direct the majority of their mental energy to focusing on their target, they fixate on it for longer periods, and have more consistent viewing sequences.[6] A simple way to increase your accuracy on the course and do the same thing is to follow the 80/20 rule in the *performance zone*. This rule means when you are addressing the ball during a performance round of golf that you use 80% of your energy and time focusing on your target and 20% of your mental energy on the ball for proper setup.

Here is an example of a targeting sequence to use in the *performance zone:*

1. Approach the ball focusing on your target.

2. Focus down on the ball and do your proper setup and alignment. (Ball Focus - 20 %.)

3. Visualize your line and the ball flight then fixate your gaze on your target in a relaxed yet focused way. Take your time and really get a clear picture of your target in your mind's eye while imagining the perfect shot. (Target Focus - 80 %.)

4. With your eyes slowly trace the line back to your ball, settle in, and release your most natural swing.

This type of targeting sequence in the *performance zone* will definitely boost your accuracy and results. One of the many reasons this type of process works is because it keeps your mind focused on the target and what you want to accomplish instead of getting distracted or conjuring up negative pictures because you are staring at the ball. Apply this 80/20 rule next time you are on the course and start hitting more fairways and greens right away.

Reverse Visualization Strategy For Lower Scores

The last few sections have mentioned visualizing your shots and putts backwards while addressing the ball. Reverse visualization is such an effective way to increase performance because the human mind tends to work backwards. Your mind always starts with the end in mind, or the ultimate goal, and works back through the steps to turn it into reality. For example, when you plan a vacation, you don't start the process by packing your bags first. That would be impossible since you would have no idea if you should pack clothes for skiing or the beach. When planning a trip, the first thing you do is determine your destination and then work backwards to figure out the means to getting there. Another example of the mind working backwards is when you set out to go see a friend at their house. You wouldn't focus on how to get out of your driveway or think much about what turns to make. Instead, you get a mental image of your friend's house in your mind, and the rest naturally seems to take care of itself. This same mental principle holds true on the golf course too.

Let's go over another way of using reverse visualization on the golf course to formulate a strategy on each hole and make more birdies.

When you are on the tee box, take a deep cleansing breath, and let your mind relax. With your eyes either open or closed, visualize yourself standing on the green and tapping in a putt for birdie. Then visualize backwards from the green by mentally tracing the line of the shot back to the ideal spot on the fairway you took the shot from. Next, imagine the approach shot you hit to stick it close to the pin and have that tap in. Finally, visualize backwards from this spot in the fairway by mentally tracing the shot back to the tee box. Again, imagine your swing, the ball flight, and the club used on the tee to execute this tee shot. Do this process of reverse visualization on every hole to prepare your mind to perform. Then do your normal pre-shot routine when it is your turn to tee off.

Some of the many benefits of this reverse visualization strategy include:

- It creates a birdie minded focus on the course and embeds your end goal into your mind prior to starting each hole.

- It forms positive mental images in your mind of your ball on your desired targets and positive swing performance. (Remember all golfers think in pictures. These pictures must be positive for peak performance.)

- It provides a game plan for you to follow on each hole. Having a strategy is an easy way to elevate confidence and keep you playing golf instead of worrying about results.

- It activates your imagination prior to performance which makes it easier to visualize more vividly on the upcoming shots.

- Finally, it serves as a reminder of the most important goal while on the golf course; get the ball in the hole. When you stay focused on this goal it is much easier to play golf in the present moment, maintain a positive mental attitude, and execute better on the course.

Next time you tee it up, apply this reverse visualization strategy, and enjoy greater success in your round.

Visualization Exercises to Increase Your Quality of Practice at the Range

Visualization and mental training exercises are not limited to your self-hypnosis time or the pre-shot routine. In fact it is important to incorporate visualization exercises into your practice time so it becomes more of a natural thing to do while performing on the course. In this section, we will go over some fun ways to use visualization to improve the quality of your practice.

An important mental paradigm to adopt in your game is "mindless practice doesn't improve skills, quality practice does." One of the most common mistakes amateur golfers make is going to the range and just whacking one ball after another. They don't practice their pre-shot routine, take the time to evaluate their shot, or even take a moment to step back to take a breath in between shots. Most amateur's simply rake and hit, rake and hit, rake and hit, and as they do this they condition poor habits, both physically and mentally, into their game.

A truth that you need to understand if you want to make serious improvements in your game is *what you do at the range, you will do on the course.* Let's go over a few simple examples to demonstrate this key point.

First, if you are the type of golfer who after hitting a poor shot at the range quickly tees up another ball without thinking and simply whacks away, then you will have the tendency to speed up and eliminate part or all of your pre-shot routine when faced with adversity or a poor shot on the course. When this happens on the course, the typical result is more bad shots, just like at the range, because of the tendency to speed up and take shots with a lack of focus.

Another example is when you let yourself get frustrated at the range and let your emotions and thoughts get the best of you. This creates a carry-over effect in your performance on the course. When something doesn't go your way on the course then the tendency is to get overwhelmed with negative thoughts and emotions because of the conditioning that occurred on the range.

What you do at the range you will do on the course, and since this is a truth, it is essential that you practice the way you want to perform. If you want to have a solid pre-shot routine like the pros then you must practice it every time at the range. *If you want to master visualization and do things like 'will' the ball to your target then you must practice and apply it at the range first before you will see it emerge in your course performance.*

Remember the earlier quote from Jack Nicklaus that provides insights into his practice philosophy. Nicklaus said,

> *"I never hit a shot, not even in practice, without having a very sharp, in-focus picture of it in my head. First, I see the ball where I want it to finish nice and white and sitting up high on the bright green grass. Then the scene quickly changes, and I see the ball going there: its path, trajectory, and shape, even its behavior on landing. Then there is a sort of fade-out, and the next scene shows me making the kind of swing that will turn the previous images into reality."*[7]

This high level of quality practice is one of the reasons why Nicklaus currently holds the record for the most major victories. Every golfer can benefit from taking his philosophy with them to the range, however until the mind has become trained it will take discipline to achieve this state of quality practice.

To elevate the quality of your practice time incorporate these visualization exercises the next time at the range. These exercises are an excellent way to increase the effectiveness of your practice sessions and boost your level of enjoyment at the practice range. Let's go over them now.

Practice Exercise #1: Visualize a Virtual Caddie

Step 1: When you get to the range, imagine that you have a virtual caddie with you for your practice time. Make a mental commitment before hitting any balls that you are going to consult with your virtual caddie before every shot, just like the pros do with their coaches during practice and with their caddies during competitive rounds of golf.

Step 2: Before every shot, have a conversation in your mind with your virtual caddie and describe to him/her the type of shot you are going to hit, the shape of it, the ideal distance, the desired target, and so.

Step 3: Go through your full pre-shot routine, step up, and take your shot.

Step 4: Regardless of the outcome of the shot, step back out of the performance zone and mentally review the outcome with your virtual caddie. Did you do what you wanted? If so, mentally note what you did correctly. If not, mentally review what you are going to do better on the next shot.

Step 5: Clear your mind and repeat the same steps before every shot.

The benefits of using this technique are:

➤ You are forced to slow down and take your time before each shot at the practice range.

➤ You create a good habit of doing a pre-shot routine before *every* shot. Remember the top pros don't take a shot, even in practice, without first getting a clear image of it in their minds and doing their routine

➤ You learn more about your distances, shot types, and your game so you can make smarter decisions on the course.

Practice Exercise #2: Play a Virtual Course at the Range:

Another great way to improve the quality of your practice and have fun at the same time on the range is to imagine playing holes of golf instead of just hitting balls. This is an excellent way to simulate performance on the course and develop the habit of doing a pre-shot routine.

Step 1: Create an imaginary hole in your mind and establish the distance of the hole you are playing. For example, determine if the visualized hole is a long par 5, par 4, or a par 3.

Step 2: Create an imaginary fairway or green.

Step 3: Pull out your driver, discuss what your plans are with your virtual caddie, go through your pre-shot routine, and take your shot.

Step 4: Evaluate the results of the shot. Here is an example of how to play the game: If you hit your target, the imaginary fairway, then take your next shot as if you were approaching the green from the short grass. If you missed the target, then add 10 yards onto your approach shot as if you were playing from the first cut of rough. If you hit it really bad shot, then add 20+ yards to your approach shot as if buried in the heavy rough.

Step 5: Determine a target for the green that is the approximate distance away on your imaginary hole.

Step 6: Step back, select the right club for the shot, go through your pre-shot routine, and take your approach shot to the green.

Step 7: Evaluate the results of the shot. Here are examples of how to play in this situation. If your ball landed within a 10-15 ft. radius of your target then you hit the green. If you were outside the radius then you need to chip or pitch to the green. If you miss hit, then take the appropriate shot to get the ball on the green.

Step 8: Once you hit the green, the hole is obviously over since you can't putt at the range. Calculate your score and create another imaginary hole, perhaps a dog leg par 4 this time.

Step 9: Repeat this process until your bucket of balls is finished.

The benefit of using this technique is:

> ➤ You eliminate the "rake and hit" tendency through the simulation of performance. Remember on the course, you will never hit the same shot twice. This teaches you to slow down, stay to your routine, and practice like you will play.

Practice Exercise #3: Visualize Playing Golf Against a Virtual Opponent:

Playing against a virtual opponent is another excellent way to increase your skill level, add fun to your practice, and simulate performance on the course. This technique is one of the ways I developed my skills in basketball growing up. When I had nobody to shoot with, I would play imaginary games of 1-on-1 against my heroes at the time, like Michael Jordan and Chris Webber. Here is how my game worked. I would start at the top of key and pretend to check in the ball. Then I would make a move at full speed and take a jump shot from the area I was working on. If the shot went in I got a point and if I missed my virtual opponent got a point. This game simulation definitely helped me translate my practice into performance on the court.

The same concept can be easily applied to golf and it is a very fun way to practice different shots.

Step 1: Pick a shot that you want to work on. For this example, let's use driving accuracy.

Step 2: Create an imaginary fairway on the range. Maybe a small strip of grass that is between two flags or markers.

Step 3: Create the rules for the game. For example, first one to 10 wins

Step 4: Tee up a ball, take your shot, and if it stays on the imaginary fairway you get a point and if you miss, your virtual opponent gets a point.

Step 5: Step back, do your pre-shot routine, and then take another shot.

Step 6: Repeat till you or your virtual opponent gets to 10 points.

<u>Chapter Review:</u>

In this chapter, you learned basic and advanced ways of using the power of visualization on and off the course to elevate the level of your performance. Visualization is a skill that needs to be developed just like learning your swing. Take time each day to practice these exercises in self-hypnosis to enhance your visualization ability. As you incorporate more and more of these visualization strategies into your game, you will notice a dramatic increase in your execution, confidence, and level of performance from tee to green. Do what the pros do and develop the power of visualization to take your game to the next level.

1. Everybody has the ability to visualize. Some are more naturally gifted than others however everybody can train themselves to develop the skill.

2. Different types of visualization:

   ➢ Associated View (Internal) - Through your own eyes.

   ➢ Dissociated View (External) - Watching yourself on a screen.

   ➢ Standard Trajectory - Visualizing the ball traveling toward the desired target.

➤ Reverse Trajectory - Visualizing the ball traveling backwards from the desired target.

➤ Becoming the Ball - Visualizing traveling with the ball and experiencing the ball flight.

➤ Outcome Visualization - Holding outcome images of the shot in your mind.

➤ Mental Imagery Visualization - Using imagination or mental imagery to assist in your execution of the shot, like imagining a 50 gallon drum over hole to hit when lag putting.

3. NLP experts identified that your subconscious mind stores information in strings of coding the same way a computer does. There are specific ways your subconscious mind codes success and failure. By identifying these differences in your mental coding you can change elements of the code to change your experience and performance.

4. Visualization Perspective Determiner Exercise: This exercise will help you identify the best perspective to visualize from whether that is associated or dissociated.

5. Size and Location of Mental Images: Another way that your subconscious mind codes information is through the size and location of the mental images or visualizations.

➤ Compelling Mental Images are BIG, bold, clear, and in the forefront of your mind.

➤ Uninspiring Mental Images are small, hard to see, and way in the back of your mind.

You can change the experience by changing the size and location of the mental images in your mind.

➤ If you want to make something more compelling, motivating, and appealing then make the images/visualizations bigger, clearer, and move it to the forefront of your mind.

➢ If you want to make something less compelling, appealing, or want to eliminate the compulsion to act upon it then make it very small, harder to see, and move it way into the back part of your mind.

6. The Switch Technique is a technique that is designed to change the size and location of images in your mind and to condition in new, positive and automatic responses to old stress triggers. This is a powerful technique to rewire your mind for success.

7. You can also enhance mental images and visualizations by making these images colorful, brighter, and clearer as well as desensitize negative mental images and visualizations by making these images black-and-white, shades of grey, fuzzy, dark, and dim.

➢ Follow the steps in the exercises for desensitizing negative mental images and enhancing positive mental images to increase your success and performance, and minimize the effects of any negative experiences.

8. Turn your visualizations into experiences that incorporate all of your senses.

➢ Incorporate visual elements into the experience and make them bright, colorful, bold, big, detailed, clear, vivid, etc.

➢ Incorporate feelings into the experience such as the grip of the club, the movements of your body/swing, the feelings of success, the joy of a low round, etc.

➢ Incorporate sounds into the experience and amplify all the sounds such as the sound of your swing, the contact with the ball, the sound of the birds, compliments from playing partners, etc.

9. The Journey of Success Exercise is a technique that will help you intensify and amplify positive experiences of your past as well as help you identify the positive lessons gained from learning experiences, while desensitizing any negative conditioned effects.

10. The Mental Swing Signature Exercise is an in-depth process that determines your specific mental coding of success. When you identify your mental swing signature then you will know the most ideal framework and

coding of success to use so that you can program your mind to perform your best. This is best done with a partner.

11. The 5 Minute Performance Enhancer is a visualization exercise that is designed to increase your ability to focus your mind so that you can maintain a high level of concentration while performing on the course.

12. The Sunday Afternoon Success Generator is a visualization technique designed to help you create new behaviors and elevate your performance by using role modeling and visualization.

13. Incorporating Visualization into Your Pre-Shot Routine

➢ Create an imaginary performance bubble.

➢ Use a double snap to turn on and off focus for the shot, and initiate your pre-shot routine.

➢ Keys for success in your pre-shot routine.

• Affirm it - Mentally affirm to yourself exactly what you want to do in a positive way.

• Visualize it - Pick an ending target and a starting target, and visualize the perfect shot in rich, full detail.

• Feel it- While you are grooving in your swing, keep visualizing the perfect shot and seeing the ball tracing right over the starting target and landing precisely on your end target.

• Commit to it - Cross the commitment line, address the ball, hold onto the outcome image in your mind or the perfect ball flight, and then take your shot.

14. Incorporating Visualization into your putting routine

➢ Get a good read from 3 spots.

• Behind the hole to read the break and slope.

• From the side to determine the speed and distance.

• Behind the ball to determine the line.

➤ Visualize the entire putt.

➤ Visualize the ball coming out of the hole and back to your putter on the perfect line.

➤ Hold the outcome image and putt.

15. Targeting tip for shots and putts: The smaller the target the smaller the margin of error. The bigger the target the bigger the margin of error.

16. Reverse Visualization Course Strategy is a visualization technique that starts at the green and works backwards to the tee.

17. 17. Fun visualization drills for the range to improve quality of practice:

➤ Virtual caddie.

➤ Play a virtual course.

➤ Golf against a virtual opponent.

ELEVEN

MENTAL REHEARSAL

"Mental rehearsal is just as important as physical rehearsal."

-- Phil Mickelson

Throughout this book, we have been discussing that the key to executing your best swing and playing golf in the zone is to use your subconscious mind so you can perform without conscious effort. The problem is most recreational golfer's don't practice or play as often as professional golfers. As a result, they have a harder time consistently performing their correct swing technique and have less mental references to high level performance and success on the course. What typically happens is the recreational golfer tries to change or correct their habits while they are playing on the course and because they forget details of technique, they get them wrong, or slip into old bad habits.

An important rule is you can't change habits while you are performing on the course and, even thinking about what you need to do, will inhibit your ability to play your best. Thinking about swing technique during performance can produce devastating results. This occurs for a number of reasons. First, you are using the "thinking part" of your mind while taking your swing, instead of the "performance part" or your subconscious. Next, when you are thinking about mechanics or technique over the ball during performance, you are slipping back into a lower level of learning as discussed in Chapter Three, and performing at the level of conscious competence instead of unconscious competence, or the state of mastery which utilizes the subconscious mind. Finally, the act of thinking about what you need to do on the course is taking your focus out of the here-and-now, and focuses your mind on the technical aspects of the swing, instead of being fully focused on the execution of the shot, your target, and *"playing"* golf.

Mental rehearsal is way to overcome these challenges and train your subconscious mind to replace negative habits in your performance with positive ones so they become automatic processes on the course. Jack Nicklaus described the process of mental rehearsal as "going to the movies".

In this chapter, you are going to discover the ins and outs of doing mental rehearsal so that you can use this incredible mental training technique to enhance your swing performance, improve your overall course performance, and use it as a way to review a round of golf to boost success and correct mistakes in performance.

What is mental rehearsal? Mental rehearsal is a focused mental drill of visualizing and rehearsing the sequential actions of your swing that occur seamlessly, just like in real life performance.[1] It is a method used to train your subconscious mind to perform at the highest level and develop automatic responses in performance situations. When mental rehearsal is incorporated into your self-hypnosis sessions, it can provide you with some of the best swing practice that you can do. Dr. Thomas Tutko and Umberto Tosi from the Institute of Athletic Motivation at San Jose State University in their book *Sports Psyching* made these comments on mental rehearsal:

> *"The technique should not be confused with wishful thinking or even positive thinking. Wishful thinking is fantasizing about something that you hope is coming true but over which you have little control. Positive thinking is telling yourself that you can do it. Both are concerned with ends rather than with means; you're either hoping for the best or you're attempting to build enough self-confidence to do your best. With mental rehearsal, on the other hand, you are thinking and practicing the doing, the means by which you can give your best possible performance."*[2]

The subconscious mind is the "doing part" of the mind and mental rehearsal is a way to deliberately program the bio-computer between your ears and condition your nervous system to respond in an automatic nature. Mental rehearsal is a way to train your body how to perform by programming the mind with images of the right sequences of behaviors and actions that you want to be doing during your swing and performance. The more vivid, detailed, and life-like the mental rehearsal is, the stronger the mind-body connection becomes and the better your body understands what it has to do to perform. Because your subconscious mind doesn't know the difference between real or imagined events, doing focused mental rehearsal exercises links up the nerves in the mind and body and, as a result, builds muscles memory regardless if you are thinking about performing your swing or actually executing a real swing. The same neurons in the brain are fired and are at work which cause your muscles to subtly respond to your thoughts and it stimulates the motions in your imagination, even if you are not consciously aware of it happening. The more you do mental rehearsal, the more integrated the muscle memory becomes, and the greater the mind-body connection is strengthened due to the nerves in the body getting linked to the thoughts.

Research supports these claims stating that during mental rehearsal and mental practice, the same neuromotor pathways that are involved in the physical execution of a specific motor task are activated and in use. The motor programs in the motor cortex that are responsible for movement in the body, are then strengthened as a result of the activation of the neural pathways during the mental rehearsal exercises. As a result of the mental training, it can improve the appropriate coordination patterns and it primes the corresponding motor neurons of the muscles that are necessary to carry out the task.[3,4]

Even though mental rehearsal and other mental training techniques like visualization are well known in the golf world, the element most often left out of the conversation that dramatically enhances the effectiveness of these techniques, is the use of self-hypnosis.

Self-hypnosis is the missing link that transforms all mental exercises into accelerated learning experiences. To get the most out of the mental rehearsal exercises you are about to learn, be sure to do self-hypnosis prior to starting the exercises.

What Makes Mental Rehearsal Different from Visualization?

Visualization is more of a creative process that conjures up a broad spectrum of mental imagery in the imagination and is more unlimited in its uses. Mental rehearsal is a process that utilizes visualization but it is focused solely on the "how" and the specific, detailed actions of performance needed to produce a successful result. Visualization creates the images and thoughts of the big picture of the swing you want to execute while mental rehearsal focuses on the details of the swing that are important to execute it. Previously in this book, I shared with you a 15 ball drill on how to transition from practice mode to performance mode. Mental rehearsal can be thought of as the mental "practice mode" where each mechanical aspect of your swing is rehearsed in a concentrated way. Visualization could be considered the mental equivalent to the "performance mode".

Keys to Remember for Mental Rehearsal Exercises

It is absolutely crucial that you mentally rehearse all the correct and right actions, and rehearse exactly what you do desire. This is important because mentally rehearsing a bad swing will reinforce the negative actions and behaviors, and increase the likelihood of negative results. You have learned throughout this book the importance of directing your mind in a positive direction, focused on what you do want to achieve. When doing mental rehearsal make every detail of your swing and performance perfect in every way in your mind even if you don't believe it at the moment. Be sure to only create successful shots in your mind and of you executing the most perfect golf swing in the world.

When doing mental rehearsal, the most important part to focus on is the "how" you execute a perfect swing or shot. You want to put your full mental energy into the proper setup, the grip, and all the correct motions of the swing that produces great results. **These exercises are all about rehearsing the means, not the ends.**

You want to over train your mind by rehearsing and conditioning your perfect swing so much that it becomes second nature and so familiar to the mind that it automatically kicks in when you are performing. Be sure to do mental rehearsal in both an associated view, meaning through your own eyes, so that it feels like a real experience in the subconscious mind as well as in a dissociated view, like watching yourself on TV.

Mental Rehearsal Exercises

Now that the basics of mental rehearsal have been covered, let's dive into some exercises so you can begin training your mind for success using this tool. In this section, we are going to cover 3 main ways of using mental rehearsal.

> ➤ First, you will go over the steps to using mental rehearsal to improve swing performance and overcome bad swing habits.

> ➤ Next, you will learn about how to do mental rehearsal to prepare for a competitive round of golf.

> ➤ Finally, you will discover how mental rehearsal can be used in your post-round review process to enhance successful moments as well as correct the poor shots that occurred on the course.

Mental Rehearsal for Swing Performance

Phase 1: Review of the Perfect Swing Sequence (Conscious Mind)

Step 1: Find or Create a Training Aid. The first step in the mental rehearsal process is to prep your mind on the proper mechanics and details of the ideal swing that you want to consistently execute on the course. To do this, use one of the following training aids to assist you:

> ➤ A set of photos from an instructional book that breaks down the sequence of correct actions that produce a perfect swing.

> ➤ A video of a perfect swing that you can watch in slow motion to breakdown the correct mechanics.

> ➤ A video of your role model's swing that clearly shows the mechanics you are working on to improve your swing.

> ➤ A video of you from one of your lessons with a pro/instructor of your best swing or you doing specific mechanics correctly.

If you don't have any of the above then it is recommended that you write out the details of your swing mechanics and all the right actions to produce a perfect swing. For a competitive golfer who has lots of experience and knows their game inside and out, this will be a very descriptive list of detailed actions. If you are a recreational golfer then your steps maybe a little less descriptive. Regardless of your skill level, the goal in this step of the mental rehearsal exercise is to create a detailed description of the correct sequence of behaviors to execute the best swing. If you are writing out the swing sequence be sure to address the following and be as descriptive as possible:

- Your Grip.

- Your Setup and Stance.

- Your Backswing.

- Your Downswing.

- Your Impact Zone and Release.

- Your Follow-Through and Finish.

This is an important step in mental rehearsal. Regardless of which training aid you use to go through the proper swing sequence, be sure to take your time with this step so that you remind yourself of all the proper fundamentals of the ideal swing.

There is a tendency, even with the pros, to forget certain fundamentals from time to time, and old habits can sometimes sneak back into their swing. It can be very valuable for golfers of all levels to review the proper sequences of correct actions and have them in front of you, even if they seem basic, to assist you in doing your mental rehearsal during self-hypnosis as well as to remind you of your swing keys.

Remember the goal of mental rehearsal is to over train your mind so that your subconscious mind becomes so familiar with the correct actions of your swing that it automatically gets released into your performance when you step out on the course.

Step 2: Study the Sequence of Actions. Study and review the pictures, movies, or your detailed list of instructions several times to get all the correct sequence of actions fresh in your mind. Use your conscious mind and really break down, analyze, and study the sequence of actions in great detail.

Phase Two: Mental Rehearsal in Self-Hypnosis (Subconscious Mind)

Step 3: Self-Hypnosis Time. After you have consciously reviewed the perfect sequence of actions to perform your ideal swing, close your eyes, relax your mind and body by following the steps to self-hypnosis, and get into a receptive state of mind to accelerate the learning process and make the experience more vivid and life-like.

Step 4: Slow Motion Mental Rehearsal. Now that you are in a receptive state of mind, you are going to begin mentally rehearsing the sequence of actions of the perfect swing that you have been studying. Be sure to do this mental rehearsal in an associated view, meaning through your own eyes. This first wave of mental rehearsal is to be done in slow motion and as slow, precise, and detailed as possible. Focus your mind on the specific details and components of each phase of your swing: your grip, setup and stance, your backswing, downswing, impact zone, and follow through with a full, balanced finish.

Step 5: Stay in Self-Hypnosis but Open Your Eyes. After you have mentally rehearsed the perfect swing in slow motion and great detail, give yourself this suggestion:

> *In a moment I will open my eyes and remain deep in self-hypnosis. When my eyes open I stay mentally and physically relaxed and the moment I close my eyes I return back into self-hypnosis and more completely and totally relaxed.*

Step 6: Review Photo/Video Sequence in Waking Hypnosis. Once you have given yourself the previous suggestion, open your eyes, remaining in this relaxed state of awareness, and review the pictures or movie again of your perfect swing sequence. Get a clear picture of this sequence in your mind, close your eyes, and continue to relax deeper.

Step 7: Slow Motion Mental Rehearsal. Again, in slow motion and in an associated way, mentally rehearse all the details of the perfect swing sequence. Get into the experience and make it as vivid and real as possible. Mentally rehearse every motion and every aspect of the perfect swing in great detail 3-5 times.

Step 8: Real Time Speed Mental Rehearsal. Repeat the same mental rehearsal process as you have been doing throughout the exercise, but this time rehearse the swing sequence at real time speed. Do this 3-5 times.

Step 9: Emerge from Self-Hypnosis. Take a few deep breaths, reorient to your surroundings, count from 1to 5, and open your eyes feeling refreshed and revitalized.

Remember you can also repeat these same steps in a disassociated view, like performing on TV, as a way to mentally groove your ideal swing. Mental rehearsal is a highly effective way to learn the correct mechanics, train the body how to perform your best, and program consistent patterns of behavior to assist you on the course.

Now that you know the basic process of mental rehearsal, let's go over some other ways of using mental rehearsal to take your game to the next level.

Mental Rehearsal of a Round

When preparing for a competitive round of golf or one where you simply want to play your best, a great habit to get into is mentally rehearsing the entire round of golf prior to performance. If you have played the course before and have a good memory of the layout, then you can use your memory to do this exercise. However, if you don't know the layout of the course, it is recommended to go online and bring up a map of the golf course to assist you with this exercise.

Step 1: Game Plan (Conscious Mind). Having a game plan and strategy for the course and each hole, is an easy way to increase the success you experience on the course. Bring up the map of the course, and using your conscious mind, determine what shots you want to hit, the ideal spots for your approach shots, the best places to attack the greens, and so on. Developing a strategy, instead of just winging it on the course, will help you play to your strengths on each hole which will give you more opportunities to score during the round. Use your conscious mind to study and analyze the course so you have a game plan for each hole.

Step 2: Rehearsing the Details of the Game Plan (Subconscious Mind). Once you have created your strategy of attack, do self-hypnosis and begin mentally rehearsing the details of this game plan to conquering the course. Instead of just visualizing shot outcomes, you must really get focused on the precise details of the swings you want to execute and the actions that produce the results you desire.

Mentally rehearse going through your full pre-shot routine, rehearse all the details of perfect swing mechanics that are needed to execute your game plan. After you mentally rehearse the drive, then do the same thing for your approach shot and go through all the details of the ideal, perfect swing that is needed to attack the green. Then mentally rehearse the perfect putt and all the details of the putting sequence and roll in the birdie putt. Continue this mental rehearsal process for every shot of every hole, staying completely focused on the execution of the details involved in your game plan.

Give your subconscious mind the experience of mentally rehearsing birdies on every hole so that it gets familiar with performing in this way. By mentally rehearsing your entire round, not only are you developing your swing, but you are programming your mind to trigger these thoughts while on the course. The subconscious mind will remember what to do when situations arise on the course and will be pre-programmed to follow through due to the conditioning and association.

If you don't have time to mentally rehearse the entire round then focus on a particular section of the course or phase of your game you consider most important to a great round.

For example you can use mental rehearsal for:

➢ Getting off to a great start to the round.

➢ Making birdies on the hardest stretch of holes on the golf course.

➢ Making the turn with positive momentum.

➢ Executing coming down the stretch and claiming victory.

➢ Scoring well on the pas 3's and par 5's.

One other great way of using mental rehearsal to prepare for a competitive round on your home course is to rehearse your perfect round. I would make a bet that if you are an elite golfer you have already played your home course 18 under par and if you are an average golfer I bet you have already shot your home course even par. Now before you think I am crazy, let me explain. You have already played your home course perfectly, you just didn't do it in the same round. However, if you review your history on that course then chances are great that you birdied or parred each hole at least once at some point in time. When preparing for the round, mentally rehearse the birdies or pars you made on each hole in the past and go through a "hybrid" experience of a perfect round. That way when you step foot on each tee box, you will naturally recall times of success and feel confident as you take on the hole.

Mental Rehearsal as a Post-Round Review Exercise

Regardless of how great a round of golf is, it is inevitable that you will leave happy about some things and wanting to improve other things. Often times, golfers end up focusing more on the things they did wrong versus focusing on the positive things they did right on the course. It is beneficial to be aware of areas of improvement and where one needs to get better. However, most of the time you will find golfers leaving the course and inadvertently using mental rehearsal in a negative direction. They keep playing the negative shots over and over again in their minds which will make these images more compelling in the subconscious and reinforce these negative swings, habits, and outcomes.

Let's go over the steps to using the best of both parts of your mind after your round to do the right type of review process and use your mental energy in a positive and productive way to improve your game. It's time to learn how *not* to fall into this negative mental programming trap many golfers do after their round.

Step 1: Round Assessment (Conscious Mind). It is natural to analyze your performance after a round of golf because the primary function of your conscious mind is to judge, analyze, and critique your experiences to help you refine your choices so you get more of what you want. What is important to remember during the assessment of your round is to focus not just on what you did wrong or need to improve upon, but also on what you did right. In addition, you want to review what you did well in your mental game such as your level of focus, consistency of your pre-shot routine, clarity of visualized pictures, etc., as well as how you handled your emotions on the course. You want to do a complete assessment of the all aspects of your game that you have control over physically, mentally, and emotionally.

You must avoid dwelling on the mistakes you made on the course and refrain from mentally rehearsing the negative shots and swings. This can be devastating to your game because you are strengthening and reinforcing these negative shots into your subconscious mind and using the power of mental rehearsal in a negative direction. Doing this can result in the negative swings becoming a habit and occurring more and more frequently on the golf course.

To overcome this potential problem, it is important to take an honest assessment of what you need to improve and then immediately begin formulating a plan of action to correct the behaviors, actions, or responses. In other words, "What's the solution?" Developing an action plan to correcting the behavior immediately shifts the focus of your mind away from reinforcing the problem to finding solutions and discovering ways to make improvements that produce better results.

Step 2: Correct Problems and Integrate with Mental Rehearsal (Subconscious Mind). Now that you identified some areas that you want to correct and improve on it's time to do mental rehearsal to reprogram the mind with the desired responses. Again, most golfers never correct or update the subconscious mind on the right ways to do things, and as a result keep mentally rehearsing the problem, even if it's at a subconscious level.

Why is it important to correct the mental images in the mind? To answer this question let me provide a real-life example. Imagine a young child who just did something wrong, like write on the walls with a crayon. If the parent just scolds the child and tells them that they did something wrong, but doesn't explain the reasons for why they are upset, the child has no clue what happened or what they did wrong. All it does is create confusion and negative reinforcement, but without correction. The proper way to correct the child so they can learn what is right and wrong, is to explain to the child writing on walls is wrong because we write and draw on pieces of paper. Then the parent brings the child a coloring book and shows them the right use of the crayons and where it's appropriate to use them.

The subconscious mind operates like a child does. It needs to be programmed on the right way to do things. Since most golfers don't correct the mind after poor performance by creating visualizations and mental rehearsal experiences of what they do want to do in that situation, no improvements are made and the negatives are strengthened because it is all the subconscious mind knows.

You must actively go into your mind and deliberately instruct the subconscious mind on what you want it to do in the future, just like you do with a child. Mental rehearsal is the perfect process to do this.

Steps for a Post-Round Mental Rehearsal

The goal of this exercise is to enhance successful behaviors and correct negative behaviors through mental rehearsal. While doing this exercise, it is important to remember to focus more on the means, or the actions and motions of your swing that produce the successful result, rather than just the outcome. Here is what you do:

Step 1: After doing your post-round assessment and you have a good idea of the key improvement areas, close your eyes and follow the steps to self-hypnosis to get into the super learning states of alpha and theta.

Step 2: Once you are in a relaxed and receptive state, beginning with Hole #1 mentally start reviewing each shot. Start with your tee shot and recall the way it occurred on the course. If this was a successful swing which created the desired result then mentally rehearse this shot once more and enhance all the modalities so that it is a very compelling image in your mind. This will embed this successful swing into the subconscious and indicate that it is something to produce more of. If your tee shot didn't go as you planned then use mental rehearsal to update the subconscious mind on the correct and right ways to perform. Mentally take the shot again; however, this time mentally rehearse all the right mechanics and the motions of the correct swing that produces the desired result. Change the shot to be exactly the way you want it to be and mentally experience the results the correct swing produces.

Step 3: Repeat this process for the entire round of golf. Enhance the successful shots and make them more compelling in the subconscious mind, and correct the negative swings through mentally rehearsing the right swing that produces the best results.

If you are too busy to go through your entire round then focus purely on correcting all the negative shots that took place on the course. You must deliberately recondition the mind and provide it new pictures in order to correct the behaviors and begin creating new responses for the next situation. Otherwise, the subconscious mind will maintain these negative pictures and when situations that are similar arise on the course, it will automatically fall back into these patterns since they are more familiar and compelling in the mind's eye. Correct these negative responses by over-training your mind with mental rehearsal and give the subconscious mind correct, compelling images to follow through with. This will make the successful motions of your swing familiar in the mind and replace the old patterns of behaviors so you can have more success in the future.

Chapter Review:

In this chapter, you learned a variety of ways to use mental rehearsal to improve your performance, get prepared for a successful round of golf, and use it as a tool for post-round review. Mental rehearsal is a powerful mental training process that can accelerate the learning process for golfers of any skill level. Train your brain using mental rehearsal and you will be excited with the results it produces in your game.

Mental rehearsal is a focused mental drill of visualizing and rehearsing the sequential actions of your swing that occur seamlessly in real life performance. Jack Nicklaus described this as "going to the movies." Mental rehearsal is a technique used to mentally practice the "doing" or the "means" to achieve a successful swing and outcome. The more vivid and life-like you can make the mental rehearsal the greater the mind-body connection becomes. Mental rehearsal is a way to train your body to perform through your mind.

1. Keys to focus on during mental rehearsal:

    ➤ It is absolutely important that you mentally rehearse all the correct and right actions of your swing and do it exactly as you desire it to be.

    ➤ Keep your focus on "how" your perfect swing is produced and executed.

    ➤ Over train your mind so that it becomes second nature and so familiar to the mind that it automatically kicks in while you are performing due to association.

    ➤ Do your mental rehearsal exercises in both an associated view meaning through your own eyes as well as disassociated view like on a screen.

2. Training aids to assist you in mental rehearsal exercises:

    ➤ Set of photos from an instruction book that show the sequence of correct actions of a perfect swing.

➢ Video of a perfect swing that you can watch in slow motion to break down the correct mechanics.

➢ Video of your role model's swing that show the mechanics of the swing you want to emulate.

➢ Video of you from your lessons with a pro that shows the correct mechanics of your swing.

➢ If you don't have any of these things then you can write out a detailed description of the ideal mechanics of the swing. Focus on these aspects:

• Your grip.

• Your setup and stance.

• Your backswing.

• Your downswing.

• Your impact zone/release.

• Your follow-through and finish.

3. Mental rehearsal of your swing:

➢ Study the sequence.

➢ Self-hypnosis.

➢ Mental rehearsal of swing in slow motion.

➢ Open eyes and review sequence again.

➢ Close eyes, return to self-hypnosis, and do slow motion mental rehearsal again.

➢ Real time speed mental rehearsal.

➢ Emerge from self-hypnosis.

4. Mental rehearsal of a round.

➢ Make a game plan and strategy for each hole of the round.

➤ Mental rehearsal of your game plan and the execution of each shot.

➤ Mental experience of making a birdie on every hole and playing each hole to perfection.

5. Mental rehearsal as a post-round review.

➤ Do an assessment of the round to determine successes and areas of improvement.

➤ Correct the areas of improvement by going into your mind and mentally rehearsing the ideal shot in that situation. It is important that you show your subconscious mind how you want it to perform in order to correct the actions on the course. The subconscious can only support what it knows, so use mental rehearsal to change the pictures and give the subconscious mind a new experience to work towards and create more of.

➤ Enhance all the success of the round by making the mental imagery and experiences bigger, bolder, more colorful, more appealing, compelling, etc. This will increase the likelihood of creating more success in the future.

TWELVE

TROUBLESHOOTING YOUR MENTAL STATE ON THE GOLF COURSE

"Golf is about how well you accept, respond to, and score with your misses much more so than it is a game of your perfect shots."

-Dr. Bob Rotella

Throughout this book, there has been a major emphasis placed on the power of your thoughts and your mind for peak performance on the course. As many golfers are already well aware, changing your thoughts on the course is often easier said than done, especially if the mind hasn't been trained and a positive mental attitude established in the subconscious mind. An interesting thing you are about to discover is you can actually change the way you think and feel on the course, but without having to do more thinking.

In this chapter you will learn how to overcome negative thoughts on the course using your body when it is difficult to change your mental state through positive thinking. You are about to discover some effective ways, to shift from negativity to confidence on the course by changing the way you use your body, and how to maintain a state of empowerment using your body language. In addition, because there is a mind-body connection, I sprinkled in a few extra ways to redirect your mental focus when you need to do some troubleshooting on the course.

The Principle of Congruency

An important fundamental point to understand about the mind-body connection is the principle of congruency. The principle of congruency means that your subconscious mind is always striving to make your thoughts, emotions, and body language congruent with each other. In the next chapter, this principle of congruency will be explained in greater detail. For now, it is important to understand that not only do your thoughts influence your body, your body also influences your thoughts, either positively or negatively.

Let's go over a simple exercise to demonstrate the principle of congruency and how your body influences your thinking. What I would like you to do is look up towards the ceiling and put the biggest smile on your face that you can. Without changing anything and keeping that big smile on your face, try to feel bad about something. If you kept that big smile on your face and didn't change anything, I know you will find it is impossible to feel bad. The opposite is also true. If you put a big frown on your face and hang your head down, it is impossible to feel good. This occurs because of the congruency principle. The thoughts that flow through the mind must be congruent with the way you are using your body. If you are smiling then it is impossible to get upset and vice versa, because everything must be in alignment. LPGA superstar, Yani Tseng, understands the principle of congruency as revealed in her quote, "I like to smile. I smile even when I'm nervous since it calms me down and shows my friendliness."

Now let's take this one step further. I am certain that if you were asked to describe the body language of a confident person, you would be able to provide an accurate description. You would probably describe how tall they are standing, that their shoulders are back, their head is held high, and so on. If you were asked how this confident person moves, then I am sure you would also provide another accurate description. You would probably answer the confident person moves with a sense of purpose and determination, makes powerful and confident gestures, and walks around with an aura of authority.

On the flip side, if I were to ask you to describe a person in a negative state of mind, I am confident your answers would be completely different. You would more than likely describe someone with their head down, slumped shoulders, a scowl across their face, and moving around in a sluggish, lethargic way. If a person carries themselves with this type of body language it is virtually impossible for them to feel good, due to the congruency principle. Thoughts and emotions are always congruent with the body and how it is being used.

Why is it difficult for some golfers to shift their thoughts from positive to negative on the golf course after a poor shot? The answer is simple. It is hard for people because the shot created a shift in their body language. Let's imagine a golfer just hit a bad tee shot into the woods. As they are walking off the tee, most experience one of two things. They either get angry or get down on themselves. Both of these states will immediately be reflected in their body language. While they are using their body in this way, it will shut down all thoughts that aren't congruent with this type of body language. Due to the fact that the body isn't aligned with positive thoughts, these thoughts get rejected by the mind and the thoughts congruent with the negativity reflected in their body, flow easily and without resistance. This consequently reinforces the negative state, which will produce more negativity.

The easiest way to break out of a negative state on the course and get your thoughts back in a positive state after a poor shot, besides positive thinking, is simply by changing your body language. By deliberately changing the way you are holding and using your body, you simultaneously change the internal flow of emotions and thoughts. While on the golf course, it is important to be monitoring both your thoughts and your body language to make sure they are congruent with a state of confidence and self-empowerment. By doing so and making adjustments when needed, you will notice an immediate increase in your confidence while addressing any shot, a boost in your ability to execute at a higher level, and will elevate your enjoyment of the round.

How Your Body Language Affects Your Emotions

Now that you have an understanding of the importance of your body language in controlling your thoughts and emotions on the course, let's take this understanding to the next level of learning: *integration.* Here is an exercise you can do at home that will give you a personal experience of how your body language affects your emotions and help you determine your ideal body language for peak performance. The results of this exercise are immediate and noticeable. After you go through this exercise, you will understand the importance of your body language for maintaining a positive mental attitude on the course.

The Actor Exercise Steps

Step 1: Find a place where there is plenty of space to move around and somewhere you can be alone and completely free to be yourself.

Step 2: Pretend that you are the world's best actor for this exercise. Give yourself full permission to really get into this exercise and act out the roles described below. The more you get into this exercise the more you will benefit from it. Be sure to *exaggerate everything* to feel the full effect of this exercise, just like an actor does when filming a movie.

Step 3: Act out the role of a confident person. Pretend you are filming a movie and you are playing the role of the most confident person in the world. Start by adjusting your body in a standing position to reflect that of a confident person. Ask yourself questions like these and align your body appropriately:

> ➢ How does this person stand?

> ➢ How do they hold their head?

> ➢ How do they hold their shoulders?

> ➢ How do they breathe?

> ➢ How would their face look?

> ➢ What do they do with their hands?

Once you have adjusted your body to reflect this confident person, begin moving around the room as this person would. Ask yourself questions like these to get into the role:

> ➢ How does this person move?

> ➢ What speed do they move at?

➢ What gestures do they make?

➢ How do they express this confidence in themselves?

➢ What are their movements like?

Give yourself at least 5 minutes to act out this role of a confident person and become aware of the way it makes you think and feel. Notice that as you stand and move around as this confident person that it naturally causes you to feel more confident, powerful, unstoppable, and in control. If you are struggling to feel this then get more into the role and make bigger shifts in your body language.

Step 4: Act out the role of a negative and defeated person. Again, pretend you are filming a movie and you are playing the part of a person with a pessimistic attitude. Start by adjusting your body in the standing position to reflect that of a negative person. Ask yourself questions like these and really get into the role:

➢ How does this person stand?

➢ How do they hold their head?

➢ How do they hold their shoulders?

➢ How do they breathe?

➢ How would their face look?

➢ What do they do with their hands?

Once you have adjusted your body to reflect this negative person, begin moving around the room as this person would. Ask yourself questions like these to get into the role:

➢ How does this person move?

➢ What speed do they move at?

➢ What gestures do they make?

➢ How do they express this negativity in themselves?

➢ What are their movements like?

Take at least 5 minutes to act out this role and become aware of the difference in your thoughts and emotions as you play this part. Keep yourself in this pessimistic body language and try to feel confident and positive without changing your body in anyway. It is impossible.

Step 5: Shift your state back to confidence. Clap your hands together forcefully, make a power gesture and shift your body language so that it is back in alignment with the confident self. Once you do this and shift your body language, keep yourself in this position and notice how easy it is to now feel positive, confident, and self-assured.

If you let yourself get into this exercise then you have just learned something extremely valuable about yourself. This information will serve you tremendously on the golf course. First, you have identified the blueprint to how you should be holding and using your body on the golf course to be congruent with confidence and peak performance. By deliberately using your body to reflect confidence at all times, you will notice dramatic increases in your level of confidence on the course. Second, it will give you the awareness if you have shifted to a negative state by monitoring your body language. Finally, it gives you the ability to shift your thoughts and emotions on the course by breaking the pattern and shifting to body language that reflects confidence.

Put this knowledge to the test. You will be amazed at the difference it makes in your level of performance and your enjoyment of the round.

Three Magical Words to Remember on the Course

There are three magical words that can help you in a big way on the course when dealing with adversity as well as to speed up the process of developing confidence in all aspects of your game.

These magical words are **"Act As If."** By incorporating the lessons you learned from the previous example and simply *acting as if* you already are the most confident golfer on the course, you will begin thinking, feeling, and behaving like the role you are acting out.

What tends to occur as you apply this idea and begin *acting as if*, the people around you will start to notice differences in your behavior and attitude. As they observe you doing things differently, oftentimes you will hear them commenting about these changes and making remarks such as, "You sure are playing with confidence," "It's amazing how nothing seems to bother you," or "I wish I was as confident and secure as you are in my game." Even if you aren't feeling confident just by *acting as if* you are, you will start to receive reinforcement from others which after a while will begin to shift your own thinking and feeling. You will start to think "Maybe I really am confident since everybody keeps saying so." This reinforcement combined with the positive feelings that come from using your body in this confident way begin to get linked up in the subconscious mind and true confidence begins to develop.

The "fake it till you make it" approach works. So if you have been struggling to feel confident or positive on the course, start by *acting as if* you already are these things and, in a very short period of time, you will be feeling the confidence and optimism in your game. You can even apply this concept after hitting a bad shot. Even if you don't feel positive about the outcome, by *acting as if* you are, you will set off a chain reaction in your mind, emotions, and body that will shift you faster than doing nothing or wallowing in negativity. Don't wait to feel confident, positive, focused, or any other quality that is connected to high level performance. *Act as if* and speed up the process of internalizing these qualities so you can consistently bring out your best on the course, overcome negative thoughts, and keep yourself in a position to post a great score at the end of your round.

Breaking Negative States with Pattern Interrupts

During the 2010 Honda Classic, Jack Nicklaus was in the booth giving his insights on television with the other commentators. Johnny Miller asked Nicklaus about his experience dealing with adversity during the final holes of a tournament and how he would get back to hitting good shots. Nicklaus responded by saying, "The difference between winning and losing is being able to regroup." Even though the idea of regrouping yourself after a bad shot or a bad hole is common sense and something that golfers have probably heard many times, it isn't the easiest thing to do, especially after ripping a drive into the bottom of the lake or missing an easy putt.

This section is going to breakdown a technique called "pattern interrupts" as a way to rebound after bad shots and overcome negative energy so you can move forward after adversity and play your best on the rest of the course.

A pattern interrupt is a neuro-linguistic programming (NLP) technique that is any action/behavior different from your normal behavior that is done to break a conditioned way of doing things. By doing an unusual behavior it temporarily disrupts the flow of old negative patterns of thoughts and behaviors, and gives you a window of opportunity to shift to a more desired state. This is taking the "cancel that" process described in Chapter Four on self-talk to the next level.

NLP teaches us that human beings run off patterns of behavior based on a cause and effect relationship with the outside world. Tony Robbins, the great motivator, uses a jukebox metaphor to explain how this works. He says that when the world gives you an experience, such as a negative event, your mind searches the jukebox and plays the record that is most congruent with your past experiences. So if a situation makes you angry then your mind plays an angry record, or if it is a positive situation then your mind plays one of your happy records. Robbins expands this metaphor to explain how pattern interrupts work. He asks what would happen if, while an angry record was playing, you took a knife and scratched the record? It would obviously make the record skip when it played over the scratch. What would happen if you kept scratching the record again and again? The answer is the record would get so scratched up that it would make it impossible to play. Pattern interrupts work in the same way to break up our old habitual thoughts and behaviors.[1]

To further explain how pattern interrupts work let's use a real life example. Have you ever been in the situation where you are completely absorbed in a conversation and then someone butts into the conversation and asks a random, off the topic question such as "where is the bathroom?" After you answer the person and they leave, you try to resume your conversation, but you find it is hard to do so and often can't remember what you were talking about even though you were deeply absorbed in the conversation a moment ago. You end up saying, "I just lost my train of thought," or ask, "Where were we?" or "What were we talking about?" This is an example of a pattern interrupt. I think everyone has had an experience like this at one time or another and can relate to this example. What I am getting at here is pattern interrupts have the ability to help you quickly refocus your mind by breaking the negative state, and like the previous example, sometimes we break the pattern so much that you can't even remember what you were thinking or talking about.

So how does all of this apply to golf? Let's imagine that a golfer is teeing it up and has to hit over water. They step up, hit a poor shot, and the ball sinks to the bottom of the lake. What is likely to occur? Typically, this poor result would cause most golfers to search through their mental jukebox, find a congruent record, and their mind releases the patterns of behavior and thought that correspond with this negative experience. If this golfer doesn't actively take control of the situation then what is most likely to occur is an expansion of negative thoughts, self-doubt, and low confidence, all of which will result in more poor shots and missed opportunities on the course. When a bad shot happens, it is important to know that it's not the end of the world. However, if your attitude and mindset get out of control because of the outcome, it can definitely be the end of a good round. In this situation rather than dwelling on negative thoughts or the bad shot, take active control of your mind and body by using a pattern interrupt.

Examples of Pattern Interrupts for Golfers

Clearing Pattern Interrupts: These are pattern interrupts that are to be used after a bad shot to clear negative energy and help you regroup. It is best if these pattern interrupts convey a clearing gesture and something very distinct from normal behavior. Here are some examples:

➢ My personal favorite is wiping my hands 3 times after putting my club in the bag. To me it lets me know to let the shot go, move on to the next one, and it makes me feel like I am ridding myself of the bad shot.

➢ Clapping your hands and/or laughing about it.

➢ Putting your club back in the bag 2 or 3 times to break any patterns.

➢ Smiling on the course.

➢ Snapping your fingers twice to refocus yourself.

➢ Deliberate deep breathing. Changing your breathing creates changes in your physiology and the way you are using your body. I recommend using the 3-6 breathing method described in the relaxation training chapter. This type of deliberate breathing changes the movements of the body, slows the mind down, brings you back to the present moment, and makes it possible to get back to a confident state.

➤ Power Gestures: Power gestures are movements every golfer does when they do something great on the course. Using your power gestures is an excellent way to break a pattern of negativity and give yourself a spark of renewed energy on the course. A power gesture is an easy way to interrupt negative thought patterns and get back to playing great golf.

A good way to discover your power gestures is through the exercise that was described in the last section. As you move around as the "confident you", notice what gestures send electrical waves of excitement through your body. These gestures are your power moves and something that can be useful on the course to break old patterns or to maintain a high level of performance.

Take some time to discover what type of behaviors will disrupt your old patterns. Remember a pattern interrupt is any unique behavior that is different from your old habitual behaviors that breaks up the flow of negativity. The ones that work best for me are pumping my fist (which is a power gesture of mine), deliberate deep breathing (which calms my nerves and body, as well as changes mental focus), and asking myself positive questions (What do I love about playing golf?). Sometimes a simple behavior like changing your breathing will work while other times it might have to be more a dramatic behavior like clapping your hands three times while saying YES, YES, YES! Do whatever works for you to break up the old habits.

The main purpose of a pattern interrupt is to break the state and give you a window of opportunity to shift into a more empowered state. It is important that once you do a pattern interrupt that you take full advantage of this window of time to regain control of your mind and body.

Here are 4 simple steps to follow to mentally/emotionally rebound after a poor shot or hole:

➤ Step 1: Interrupt the pattern.

➤ Step 2: Immediately shift your body language to reflect confidence.

➤ Step 3: Declare positive affirmations or ask positive questions to shift your focus.

➤ Step 4: Go back to basics, do your pre-shot routine, and hit a solid shot.

If the old patterns return, repeat this process as much as necessary until you have made changes in your body language, and saturated your mind with suggestions that make you think and feel like a winner.

Power Questions to Refocus the Mind: Using power questions after doing a clearing pattern interrupt is another great way to interrupt negative patterns on the course. Asking yourself quality questions and taking time to answer them is a powerful way to refocus your mind and shift your mental state. As the timeless adage says, "Ask and you shall receive" and by asking yourself quality questions, your mind immediately goes in search of the answer and, as a result, it breaks the pattern of habitual thoughts by forcing your mind to come up with thoughts congruent to the question.

Here are some of great questions to ask in between shots to keep yourself in a positive mental attitude and shut down negative thoughts in the mind. To benefit the most, be sure to allow yourself to feel the positive emotions generated from the question and follow up question.

➤ What do I love about this day? What about that do I love?

➤ What am I grateful for? What about that makes me feel grateful?

➤ What am I proud of? What about that makes me feel proud?

➤ What do I love about this course? What about that do I love?

➤ What do I love about being with friends? What about that do I love?

➤ What is the funniest thing I can think of? What about that is funny to me?

These types of questions shift the mind from thinking about a poor shot or outcome and get your mind moving again in a positive direction. It interrupts the old pattern and gives you the ability to regroup by giving your mind something different to think about. Making a simple change in focus can make big shifts in your mentality.

Catch Yourself and Correct:

The last way to trouble shoot that I want to mention is to become aware and catch yourself when you say things like the following on the course or range:

> ➤ "I was afraid I was going to do that."

> ➤ "I knew that would happen."

> ➤ That's exactly what I didn't want to do."

> ➤ "I told myself that I wouldn't do that and I did it."

….. or any other variation of this type of remark after a shot.

If you ever catch yourself saying things like this, then immediately stop your-self, and go into your head for a second to become aware of the mental pictures you were holding about the shot. Now be completely honest with yourself and think about what you were holding in your mind and saying to yourself about the shot. What you will discover is there is no need to get upset, frustrated, or angry about the shot because your mind actually produced the shot perfectly. Your mind did exactly what it was instructed to do with the mental images that were in your mind. The only thing that went wrong was you feeding your mind negative pictures.

Remember, your subconscious mind assumes that the pictures you hold in your mind are the desired outcome and relies on you to pick the direction it's to move towards. *Your subconscious mind is the soil that will grow any seed that you plant in the garden regardless of what it is.* You must show it the exact outcome you do want, so the subconscious can direct the body to perform that swing. Be sure to catch yourself anytime you say things like the above while on the course or at the range. When you catch yourself, take an honest examination of your thoughts and self-talk, and it will further validate to you the power of your thoughts and how they influence the way you perform. Then simply start holding in mind positive pictures because you will realize you are in control of your thoughts and simply changing the pictures will change your performance.

Newton's first law of motion says that an object in motion tends to stay in mo-tion. Your mind works in accordance with this law and the subconscious mind is always moving in the direction of your dominant thoughts. In this chapter, you learned how to break the flow of negativity when it occurs on the course so that you can stop the momentum and shift it in back in a positive direction. When you notice a negative state beginning to occur, use the various types of pattern interrupts explained in this chapter so that you can produce better results on the course. Internalize these techniques and you will empower yourself on the course and tap into more of your unlimited potential.

<u>Chapter Review</u>

In this chapter you discovered:

1. One of the reasons it is hard to change negative thoughts on the course is due to maintaining negative body language.

2. The way you use your body affects the way that you think and feel based the principle of congruency.

3. The actor exercise in this chapter demonstrates how your body language can change your state from negative to positive.

4. Three Magical Words - **Act As If**: Once you have determined the body language of the most "confident you", and know the way you move and gesture in that state, then implement it on the course by "acting as if" you already are that person.

5. Pattern Interrupts are unique actions or behaviors outside your normal way of doing things that are done to break conditioned negative patterns of behavior, thoughts, or emotions.

6. The basic steps to using pattern interrupts are:

   ➢ Interrupt the pattern with a unique behavior like a clearing pattern interrupt described in the chapter, i.e., clapping your hands.

   ➢ Immediately shift your body language to reflect confidence.

   ➢ Shift your self-talk with positive affirmations or ask yourself power questions to shift your focus.

   ➢ Go back to basics, do your pre-shot routine, and hit a solid shot.

7. Power Gestures are gestures or movements that you do when something great occurs. Use these power gestures to break old patterns of behavior and get yourself filled with confidence.

8. Power Questions are quality questions designed to refocus your mind in a positive direction and to elicit positive emotions in you i.e. what am I grateful for? Power questions are excellent at refocusing your mind because "ask and you shall receive." By asking good questions your mind will search for answers and fill your mind with positive thoughts.

9. Catch yourself after a poor shot if you use negative language such as "I was afraid I was going to do that." If you catch yourself you will see that you are maintaining negative pictures in your mind, and in fact your body produced that shot perfectly. Use it as a reminder to keep your pictures positive in your mind and focused on the successful outcome. Catching and then correcting is an easy way to boost performance.

10. Newton's first law of motion says that an object in motion tends to stay in motion. The subconscious mind works in accordance to this law and if it gets started on a negative track then it will stay on it until an outside factor breaks the momentum. Use the techniques in this chapter to stop the negative flow of thoughts and emotions, and to shift yourself back into a state of peak performance on the course.

THIRTEEN

THE B.E.T. SYSTEM FOR STATE MANAGEMENT ON THE GOLF COURSE

"Golf is 20 percent talent and 80 percent management."

--Ben Hogan

As you are now aware, success on the golf course is more than just the execution of your swing. A major determiner of success on the course is the way you manage your mental and emotional state so that you give yourself the best opportunity to perform your swing at the highest level on each shot. Many golfers are aware of this fact, however after they tee off on the first hole the vast majority of golfers quickly forget about the importance of state management. Instead, they get so caught up in outcomes and allow the outcome of each shot to determine their level of confidence on the course.

Confidence is something that needs to be intrinsically driven and not based solely on outcomes of shots. Good outcomes can add to your confidence. However, if your confidence comes only from outcomes, then you are setting yourself up for many ups and downs throughout a round of golf. With these fluctuations in your state of confidence, it makes it very difficult to consistently play your best or enter the zone on each shot. In order to bring your "A" game to the course every time out, you need to have a system for managing your state.

Every golfer has the ability to manage their state, but few know how to do it or what to focus on to keep them in a positive mental attitude and in a state of confidence on the course.

In this chapter, you will learn a simple to remember and highly effective method of state management on the course so you can golf with confidence, overcome negative thinking, and maintain mental and emotional control.

You are about to discover the B.E.T. system. Incorporating the B.E.T. system into your game with help take it to the next level in performance.

B.E.T. is an acronym that stands for **B**ody (Movements), **E**motions, and **T**houghts. This seemingly simple acronym holds one of the keys to unlocking peak performance and the ability to make confident golf shots more consistently on the course. The B.E.T. system for state management on the course is effective because it clearly shows the main areas of your golf game that are in your locus of control. You can't control the breaks on the course or the outcomes once you have taken your swing, but you can learn to control your response to them. The B.E.T. system is a way to easily control your *responses* on the course, shift from negativity to confidence in an instant, and maintain a positive mental attitude.

What Makes the B.E.T. System so Effective at State Management on the Course?

In the previous chapter, I mentioned the principle of congruency and how your subconscious mind is always striving to make your thoughts, emotions, and body language congruent with each other. You also went through exercises which demonstrated this principle of congruency and how it is impossible to make shifts when elements are incongruent with each other whereas when everything is aligned you can change your state in an instant.

Now let's take this principle of congruency to the next level. Most people are unaware that your body movements, emotions, and thoughts, while separate from each other, are all interconnected. Your body language, emotions, and thoughts are individual elements but they work together as one unit. Your subconscious mind is constantly at work making sure these elements are in alignment with each other and completely congruent. The interesting thing is when there is a change in one of these elements it simultaneously creates a chain reaction and changes the other two elements.[1]

For example:

> ➤ If you are in a negative state and successfully shift your thoughts back into a positive direction then this action will automatically and naturally change your emotions and your body movement/language to be in alignment and reflect the positive thoughts.

> ➤ If you change your emotional state when feeling negative, consequently you will change your thoughts and body movements to match the positive emotions and become congruent.

> ➤ If you are in a negative state, you can also make a shift back to a positive direction by changing the way you use your body and as a result will change your thoughts and emotions.

The subconscious mind abides by the principle of congruency because it is a part of the operating system innately installed in the bio-computer at birth. When you take control of any of these elements, your subconscious mind has to, because of the principle of congruency, change the other elements in efforts to stay congruent on all levels of being; physically, mentally, and emotionally. This is why the B.E.T. system of state management is so effective.

The Benefits of Incorporating the B.E.T. System in Your Golf Game

The B.E.T. System is powerful and incredibly beneficial to your golf game because this system:

> ➤ Serves as a checklist and guide for you on the course to keep yourself in a state of peak performance: At all times on the course, you want to make sure your B.E.T. system is aligned and congruent with a state of confidence. This way when you step foot on the first tee, you will be in a state of confidence, already feeling unstoppable, and ready to perform at a high level throughout your round.

➢ Serves as a reminder of all the various ways you can shift your state, if and as needed on the golf course: The B.E.T. system empowers you on the course and gives you the ability to overcome obstacles and handle adversity better because you are not limited to just one way of handling things. For example, if you are having a hard time maintaining positive thoughts it doesn't mean it's the end of the world or is something to get hung up on. Simply focus your energy on taking control of a different aspect of the B.E.T. system, such as maintaining confident body language, and you will soon notice that you are thinking in a much more positive way. **Remember *the B.E.T. system works as one unit and changing just one thing will change the whole dynamics of your mind-body connection.***

➢ Helps you elevate your level of swing performance on each shot: You can think of it as a mathematical equation:

Body Language + Emotions + Thoughts = Swing Performance

➢ For this equation to result in a successful swing and positive outcome then it is essential that your B.E.T. system is completely congruent with a state of optimism, confidence, and trust. When it is congruent with a state of confidence, then your physical body will be relaxed, your emotions will be calm and comfortable, and your mind will easily produce positive, clear pictures of success.

All of these things will give you the best ability to perform your swing at your highest level and execute the shot at hand. However, if any one of your B.E.T. system elements are incongruent, off in any way, or in a negative state then it will naturally lower your swing performance. This will cause you to have a body that is tight and tense, have feelings of doubt or insecurity about your ability to execute, or have a hard time getting good clear, and positive pictures in your mind about the shot all of which will inhibit your best swing and abilities.

Throughout this book, you learned a vast number of techniques to use to empower yourself on the golf course physically, mentally, and emotionally. Now you know a system that brings it all together on the course so that you consistently bring out your best, handle adversity in a positive way, and keep performing in the zone.

Embed the B.E.T. system into your brain, write it on your golf glove if you need to remind yourself, and be sure to follow this state management system on the golf course.

I guarantee that by doing so you will feel empowered and in control, consistently swing your best, and most importantly, you will lower your score.

FOURTEEN

GOAL SETTING, SELF-HYPNOSIS AND MENTAL FITNESS

"My ability to concentrate and work toward that goal has been my greatest asset."

--Jack Nicklaus

The most successful people in the world, regardless of the profession, pursuit, or endeavor, all have one thing in common – specific, compelling, and motivating goals. If you want to achieve a high level of success then having clearly defined goals is not optional, it is a requirement. This book wouldn't be complete without discussing the importance, power, and effectiveness of having goals, and their impact on your mind.

Your subconscious mind is a goal achieving machine. When it is properly guided to what it is you want in life, your subconscious mind will work around the clock to bring these goals into reality.

In this chapter, you will learn the process of goal setting, and how to program your mind to achieve more of the goals you set for yourself.

<u>The Difference Between Having Wishful Thoughts and Having Goals</u>

Every day you have thoughts about things that you would like to do, achieve, and experience. However, the majority of these thoughts remain in the realm of wishful thinking, they come and go, and rarely do you achieve these wishful thoughts that flow through your mind. Thoughts by themselves are not goals, they are merely thoughts, intangible ideas, and just one of the 50,000+ that the human mind experiences each day. The way you transform thoughts into goals is by clearly defining what it is you want to achieve and writing them out on paper. If a goal isn't written down then it remains in the realm of wishful thinking, it's simply another random thought, and lacks the power to make an impact on the subconscious mind. When you write out your goals, the intangible idea transforms into an immediate tangible reality because you can now hold the paper, you can read your words, visualize it, and so on. A magical process in your mind begins to happen when you write out your goals on paper; *the mental process of creation.*

An example of this is 2013 Masters Champion, Adam Scott. An article on GolfChannel.com reported that in December 1996, 16-year-old Adam Scott *wrote in a notebook* his ultimate goal in life - "I would like to be a world-class player." Like many golf coaches who have heard this type of wishful thinking before, Scott's head coach at Kooralbyn, Peter Claughton said, "Every kid says I want to be the world's No. 1 or I want to win a major, so you take it with a grain of salt. You would have never imagined it would get it where it is now." Like every champion, Scott's career had both its ups and downs but he stayed committed to his goal and true to his dream. Perseverance pays off and it certainly did for Scott, especially as the priceless green jacket was raised onto his shoulders. At the conclusion of the article, Scott says, "It's amazing that it's my destiny to be the first Aussie to win, just incredible."[1]

What if all that separated Adam Scott from all the others was the fact that he wrote down his goals when others didn't? If that was all that it took to set yourself up for success, would you invest time in writing out your goals? Every kid has wishful thinking, but Adam Scott wrote out a goal. As a result of this action, it made a powerful imprint in his subconscious mind, formed his self-image, and drove him to the top of the game in spite of adversity.

Research shows that having written goals dramatically increases the likelihood of their achievement. Take for instance this commonly referenced 10 year study that was conducted at Harvard's Business School. In 1979, new graduates in the MBA program were interviewed and askcd a simple question, "Have you set clear, written goals for your future and made plans to accomplish them?"

Here were the results that they found:

- 84% had no specific goals at all.

- 13% had goals, but they were not committed to paper.

- 3% had clear, written goals, and plans to accomplish them.

Ten years later, in 1989, the graduates of that class were interviewed again and the results were staggering.

- The 13% of the class who had goals were earning, on average, twice as much as the 84 percent who had no goals at all.

- The 3% who had clear, written goals were earning, on average, ten times as much as the other 97 percent combined!

Perhaps you have heard of this study before, or maybc you heard about it in a slightly different way using Yale instead of Harvard. Turns out that this "study" is just an urban myth according to the research of Gail Matthews, Ph.D., of Dominican University of California, Steven Kraus, social psychologist from Harvard, as well as Fast Company magazine's investigative reporting. They discovered the study had never actually been done. However, due to this study being so "well-known", it inspired Dr. Matthews to conduct her own research into the effectiveness of written goals. You heard the urban myth, now let's look at a real study on the power of goals and achievement.

Here is an excerpt from the document "Brief Summary of Recent Goals Research" posted on: http://www.dominican.edu/academics/ahss/undergraduate-programs-1/psych/faculty/fulltime/gailmatthews/researchsummary2.pdf. by Dr. Matthews in her current research section.[2]

> *"Participants:*
>
> A total of 267 participants were recruited from businesses, organizations, and business networking groups. However, only 149 participants completed the study. The final participants ranged in age from 23 to 72,

with 37 males and 112 females. Participants came from the United States, Belgium, England, India, Australia and Japan and included a variety of entrepreneurs, educators, healthcare professionals, artists, attorneys, bankers, marketers, human services providers, managers, vice presidents, directors of non-profits, etc.

Research Design:

Participants were randomly assigned to one of 5 conditions (groups): Group 1- Unwritten Goal; Group 2- Written Goal; Group 3- Written Goal & Action Commitments; Group 4- Written Goal, Action Commitments to a Friend; Group 5- Written Goal, Action Commitments & Progress Reports to a Friend.

- Participants in **Group 1** were simply asked to **think about their goals (what** they wanted to accomplish over the next 4 weeks) and then asked to rate that goal on the following dimensions: Difficulty, Importance, the extent to which they had the Skills & Resources to accomplish the goal, their Commitment and Motivation to the goal, whether or not they had Pursued this goal before and if so their Prior Success.

- Participants in **Groups 2-5** were asked to **write (type into the online survey) their goals** and then to rate their goals on the same dimensions.

- **Group 3** was also asked to formulate **action commitments**.

- **Group 4** was asked to formulate **action commitments and send their goals and action commitments to a supportive friend**.

- **Group 5** was asked to formulate **action commitments** and **send their goals, action commitments and weekly progress reports to a supportive friend**. Participants in this group were also sent weekly reminders to email quick progress reports to their friend.

At the end of 4 weeks participants were asked to rate their progress and the degree to which they had accomplished their goals.

Results:

1. **Types of goals:** Participants pursued a variety of goals including (in order of frequency reported) completing a project, increasing income, increasing productivity, getting organized, enhancing performance/achievement, enhancing life balance, reducing work anxiety and learning a new skill. Examples of "completing a project" included writing a chapter of a book, updating a website, listing and selling a house, completing a strategic plan, securing a contract, hiring employees and preventing a hostile take-over.

2. **Goal Achievement:** Group 5 achieved significantly more than all the other groups; Group 4 achieved significantly more than Groups 3 and 1; Group 2 achieved significantly more than Group 1.

3. Differences between all writing groups and the non-writing group: Although the previous analysis revealed that Group 2 (written goals) achieved significantly more than Group 1 (unwritten goals), additional analysis were performed to determine whether there were also differences between the group that had not written their goals (Group 1) and all groups

that had written their goals (Groups 2-5). This analysis revealed that the mean achievement score for Groups 2-5 combined was significantly higher than Group 1.

Conclusions:

1. **The positive effect of <u>accountability</u> was supported**: those who sent <u>weekly progress reports</u> to their friend accomplished significantly more than those who had unwritten goals, wrote their goals, formulated action commitments or sent those action commitments to a friend.

2. **There was support for the role of <u>public commitment</u>**: those who sent their <u>commitments to a friend accomplished significantly more</u> than those who wrote action commitments or did not write their goals.

3. **The positive effect of <u>written goals</u>** was supported: Those who <u>wrote their goals accomplished significantly more</u> than those who did not write their goals."

This study provides empirical evidence that supports the "urban myth's" claims about the power of written goals.

Besides helping you to achieve more, let's go over some other reasons why you should commit your goals to writing.

Written Goals Will Help You...

Reverse Engineer Your Success: As you know by now it is very important to be clear on exactly what you want to accomplish. The simple act of writing out your goals causes your mind to think about what you want to achieve and begins with that end in mind. It forces you to think about where you want to go so you can figure out how you will get there. Remember the vacation example in the section on reverse visualization? Well, the same principle is at work with your goals. When you write out your goals you are determining where you ultimately want to go and when you do, it will be easier to determine how you will get there and by when.

Determine Your Daily Actions: Goals serve the same purpose as a thesis statement does for a research paper, and a mission statement does for a company. It serves as a guide to help determine your actions so that you are always moving towards your ultimate destination and the most important things for you. Opportunities can oftentimes be distractions. Clearly defined and written goals help you determine if opportunities that present themselves in your daily life are moving you forward or simply distractions on your path to your goals.

Stay Motivated: Writing down your goals is the first step, the next step is doing a daily review of your written goals to stay motivated and constantly taking action to towards their fulfillment. A great habit to get into is, after reviewing your written goals, take an immediate action step right away, no matter how big or small it may be, that gets you closer to your goal. Even just doing something that makes a 1% improvement, gets you one step closer, and over time, these simple steps create major results. Eventually, reviewing your goals and taking immediate action will get linked in your subconscious mind, and turn you into a goal achieving machine with habits of success.

Overcome Obstacles in Your Path: Having clearly defined written goals will help you when you hit rough patches on your way to your goals. You can use your goals to shift away from thinking about your challenges and problems, and realign your focus back on track to what you want to achieve.

Track Your Progress and Success: When you have written goals you have a method of tracking your success. How do you know if you are making progress without any indicators of improvement? Written goals provide a way of measuring your success, it builds self-esteem as you cross goals off your list, and motivates you to achieve loftier goals each day.

Create Positive Imprints in the Subconscious Mind: When you take the time to write out your goals, it signals to your subconscious mind that these things are important and that they should be focused on. The act of writing your goals embeds positive new pictures in your mind which expands your thinking and what is possible in your life. Handwriting by itself stimulates the subconscious mind and by writing out your goals it imprints these ideas into the subconscious for it to act upon.

Types of Goals for Golfers

According to *The Sport Psychologist's Handbook*, there are generally thought to be three types of effective goals for golfers[3].

> ➤ First are ***outcome goals*** which represent standards of performance and focus on the results of a competition such as beating your friends, getting through a qualifier, or winning an event.

> ➤ Second are ***performance goals*** that focus on improving one's past performances on the golf course such as lowering your score during a round.

> ➤ Third are ***process goals*** that focus on movement procedures that will create improvements such as mechanics goals like transferring your weight, smooth one piece take away, clearing your hips, etc.

There are two other additional types of goals that could also be added to this list: ***mental performance goals and developmental goals.***

Mental performance goals are focused on aspects of your mental game such as executing a consistent pre-shot routine, getting clear pictures before taking your shot, committing to a positive mental attitude, and so on. Since it is a mind-body connection on the golf course, you can also include emotional aspects as well including the way you behave on the course, the type of responses you have to adversity, and the way you want to feel during the round. Having goals for your mental game is a great way to monitor and track improvements. It is also another barometer of success on the course. For example, even if you aren't scoring well but you are able to remain positive, confident, and stick to your routine then you can still chalk it up as a successful day. The score just wasn't there that day, but you succeeded in your mental performance goals and developed greater toughness which is something you can leave the course feeling good about.

Developmental goals are focused on your training goals including: health and nutrition, workouts, mental training, swing coaching, and so on. These are goals for all the behind the scenes activities that develop you as an athlete.

Goal Setting Method #1: S.M.A.R.T. Goals

Greg Norman said, "Setting goals for your game is an art. The trick is in setting them at the right level neither too high nor too low." Perhaps the easiest and most common way to establish goals for yourself is to create **S.M.A.R.T**. goals.[4] **S.M.A.R.T**. is an acronym that stands for:

- ➢ **S**pecific
- ➢ **M**easurable
- ➢ **A**ction Oriented
- ➢ **R**ealistic and Relevant
- ➢ **T**ime Bound

When following this model for goal setting, answer the following questions for each requirement:

- ➢ **Specific:** What exactly do you want to accomplish? Clearly define what you want, where you want it, and why you want it.

- ➢ **Measurable:** How will you measure and evaluate if the goal has been met?

➤ **Action Oriented/Achievable:** Does this goal stretch and challenge me within my ability to achieve this outcome? Be sure to have an action oriented verbs in your goals.

➤ **Realistic and Relevant:** Is this goal realistic and does it align with my main objectives?

➤ **Time Bound:** When will I achieve this goal by? Set your target dates for completion of the goal, include deadlines, dates, and frequency.

Goal Setting Method #2: Creating a Well-Formed Outcome

NLP practitioners use a more in-depth approach at setting well-formed goals to help you determine where you want to go and the steps to get you there. Let's go over the questions you will want to answer to create a well-formed outcome.[5,6]

1. What do you want, specifically? (State in a positive way.)

2. Where are you now? (Clarify and define the present situation.)

3. What will you see, hear, feel, know, etc., when you have it? (Specify your outcome - make this compelling.)

4. How will you know when you have it? (Specify evidence of achievement.)

5. What will this outcome get for you or allow you to do? (Is it congruent with your desires and life?)

6. How will reaching this outcome change your life? (Future pacing.)

7. Where, when, how, and with whom do you want it? (Ecology.)

8. Is it worth what it will take to get it? Why? (Determine level of commitment and motivation.)

9. When you achieve this outcome what else will improve? (Positive side-effects.)

10. What stops you from having the outcome now? (Determine obstacles to success.)

11. Which of the resources you already have available could you use to achieve your result?

    a. Have you ever had or done this before?

    b. Do you know anyone who has?

    c. Can you act as if you have it now?

12. For what purpose do you want this? (The driving force behind the goal.)

13. How are you going to get there? (Action plan and strategy.)

14. What is the first step to begin to achieve this result? (Take immediate action.)

Developing an Action Plan to Achieve Your Goals (Chunking Down Process)

Now that you have accomplished the first step in goal setting which is writing out clearly defined goals, it is now time to take it to the next level and develop your action plan for the achievement of these goals. It is not enough to just create goals, you need a road map in order to get to your destination. Having an action plan will help you with the following:

➢ **Increase Your Progress and Productivity:** Most people set a goal and then wonder what to do next and as a result end up spinning their wheels but don't get any closer to their goal. By having a clearly defined plan of action, it will increase your progress and productivity by eliminating the guesswork on what to do next. An effective action plan maps out the steps to achieving your goal so that you don't waste any time in the day wondering how you will achieve your goal or what the next step is.

➢ **Track Success:** A well mapped out action plan will help you track your progress and success in two ways. First, by writing out what action steps you accomplished in the day, you will be able to refer back to your action plan to confirm whether or not these actions moved you closer to your goals. Second, when you formulate an action plan you will identify milestones of accomplishment that indicate significant progress.

➢ **Build Self-Esteem:** Having an action plan will build your self-esteem in two ways. First, knowing that you have goals and a plan of action, will increase your confidence that achieving this goal is not just possible, but highly probable if you simply follow the steps. Second, with each successful action step forward, it builds confidence, strengthens your positive self-image, and increases your motivation to achieve more.

An effective way to determine a well-defined action plan is to use a process called "Chunking Down". Chunking Down is a process of reverse engineering, meaning you start with the end in mind and slowly move backwards breaking down the steps that came before the others. When you initially start the process of chunking down your goals, it is easiest to start by identifying milestones that indicate great progress and then fill in the gaps with the steps that would help you to reach these milestones.

For example, let's say that your long term goal is to gain status on the PGA Tour. Start by identifying the milestones that come before this goal is reached: Examples of milestones on the road to gaining PGA Tour Status might include:

- Advancing through the stages and qualifying in "Q School" for the Web.Com Tour.

- Competing on a professional mini-tour.

- Finding investors for sponsorship.

- Turning professional.

- Qualifying and competing in amateur competitions.

- Developing the mind to handle competitive pressure.

- Developing a successful, and repeatable swing.

The above are just examples of potential milestones that need to be reached on your way to the goal. Once you have established these milestones continue the "Chunking Down" process and begin to identify the specific steps you need to do to reach the first milestones and eventually the ultimate goal. For example, what is your plan of action to develop a repeatable and successful swing? How do you plan to accomplish this? When do you want to achieve this by? What is your development schedule going to include?

Here is an example of a milestone that is chunked down appropriately:

Milestone: Develop a Repeatable and Successful Swing

Action Plan Steps:

1. Find an instructor that I respect and enjoy working with to get the necessary lessons to improve my swing.

2. Commit to weekly lessons with my instructor to keep fine tuning my swing.

3. Daily practice for at least one hour devoted to working on the proper swing mechanics at the range.

4. Daily self-hypnosis exercises to mentally rehearse my swing, develop confidence, and train my mind to have a positive mental attitude that maintains pictures of my success.

5. Play golf at least once a week on the course to fine tune my swing in a performance setting.

6. Daily morning and night self-talk to keep me motivated, focused on my goals, and determined to succeed.

Obviously, this list could include a lot of other things, but I am sure you are getting the idea on what is being asked of you. Take the time to create a solid action plan for the achievement of your goals. This investment of time and energy planning out your action steps will save you more time in the long run, will accelerate you to your goals, and keep you consistently taking action.

When you are finished creating your action plan, it should have the following:

➤ A clearly defined goal that starts with the end in mind.

➤ A series of major milestones along the journey that indicate big progress steps in the pursuit of your goal.

➤ A series of smaller steps and action plans that will get you to these milestones and ultimately to your final goal.

Time to Take Action

The final and most important step in achieving your goals is taking action. Your goals cannot be reached with just wishful thinking. Taking consistent and persistent action combined with a positive mental attitude is the only way to achieve your goals and dreams. Nobody will do the work for you, it is up to you to put in the time to achieve what you desire. It is natural that you will encounter some mental obstacles when pursuing your goals that keep you from taking action and cause you to procrastinate. To help you overcome any mental blocks that produce procrastination, let's go over some effective suggestions to keep you motivated and taking consistent action.

Commit to the T.N.T. Club

T.N.T. is an acronym that stands for "Today Not Tomorrow". The most deceptive form of procrastination that can creep into the mind is the idea, "I will do it tomorrow." An important thing to remind yourself is tomorrow never comes. Every time that you put off action till tomorrow, you will never do it or you're one day behind. When you feel inspired, take action right away.

The Thought is Always Bigger and More Overwhelming than the Actual Task

It can sometimes take mental toughness to plow past procrastination and get yourself taking action. The reason this occurs is the thoughts we have about taking action are often made out to be bigger and more daunting in our imagination than what it really is. Earlier in the book, I shared with you the psychological law that *"Your imagination is more powerful than your will and when these two come into conflict the imagination will always win."*

When you are thinking about taking action instead of just acting upon the inspiration, the imagination can kick in and make the task out to be bigger than it is. If this occurs remind yourself that the thought is always bigger than the action. When you get past the imagined thoughts that can overwhelm you and just take a step forward, you will realize that task was much simpler to achieve than you initially thought. Keep this in mind as you pursue your goals and you will get much more done in a faster and easier way.

Champions Are Made When Nobody is Around

More time will always be spent on the practice range developing your skills compared to times competing of the course. You can't improve your swing, or any aspect of your game while you are in the heat of the moment performing during a round. Champions in golf are chiseled out when nobody is around on the practice range and in private mental training sessions. It is this behind the scenes work that gives you the ability to shine when the spotlight is on. If you are struggling to take action to go practice or do mental training, remind yourself of this fact and go hone your skills so that you can perform like a champion the next time out on the golf course. Use your downtime, to develop the skills needed to succeed because champions are made when nobody is around.

Fail Forward Fast

At first glance, this saying may appear to be negative. However if you really absorb what this means, you will discover that it is a very positive and effective motivator. Many people worry about making things perfect, fear failure, or want to know exactly what to do in order to succeed. Instead of concerning oneself with these things, it is more important to just take action and see what happens.

Remember the only failure in life is not taking action. Every time you take action you succeed, because you will either produce the desired result or learn something that will get one step closer to what does. So instead of staying stuck with illusions and fears of failure, dive right in and you will discover that you have what it takes to succeed or you will get a great education. Irrespective of the result, you are moving forward and getting closer to the achievement of your goal.

Mind Expander Exercises

Besides writing out your goals and formulating action plans for their achievement, there are other great ways to expand your subconscious mind and get it moving towards your goals and dreams. It is important to understand that what you focus on expands and a mind in motion tends to stay in motion. Once the mind has seen what is possible it can never shrink back down in size. These next exercises are designed to expand your mind and what is possible in your golf game and life.

When doing these exercises for mind expansion, give yourself permission to be like a child again where all things are possible and there are no limits to what can be created. Let your imagination run wild and have fun with these exercises. Dream as big as you want and refrain from judging or analyzing what's possible. Be sure to write out everything that is asked of you in order to make the greatest impact on your mind. Simply doing the exercises in your mind is not enough.

Mind Expander #1: The Dream Sheet

For this exercise find a notebook or bring up a new document on your computer, and find a place where you won't be disturbed for 10 minutes. Take a few minutes before starting to do some deep breathing to clear your mind and relax your body. Next, set a timer for 10 minutes and make a commitment to yourself that you are going to keep writing or typing for the entire 10 minutes without stopping. For these 10 minutes, you are to write out all your dreams, ambitions, and goals. Remember, during this exercise there are no limits to what is possible and the goal is to just keep writing down everything you want to do, accomplish, experience, and so on. Here is a sample list of things to possibly include:

➢ Lifelong dreams.

➢ Places you want to go.

➢ Experiences you want to have.

➢ People you want to meet.

➢ Things you want to do.

Now press start on your timer and write out all your dreams, goals, and desires for 10 minutes. Make the commitment that no matter what happens you will keep writing. Expand your mind past all old limitations and create your dream sheet.

Once you have completed the 10 minutes of writing, notice how incredible you feel. Notice how your mind is now flowing with new possibilities, ideas, and excitement. Do you feel more empowered? Are you more motivated to take your golf game and life to the next level now you are more aware of what's possible? Keep this dream sheet in a handy place so that you can refer to it if you need a boost of energy, want more excitement or motivation to take action on your goals, and to simply remind yourself of what is possible in your life.

Mind Expander #2: Your Perfect Round of Golf

This is another writing exercise designed to expand your mind and can be used to program your subconscious mind with positive pictures of success when it's completed. In this exercise, you are to write out your perfect round of golf in great detail. The more specific and detailed you make it, the more it will stimulate your imagination and, as a result, the greater the impact it has on the subconscious mind. Remember there are no limits while doing this exercise, so have fun and let your imagination run wild as you write out your perfect round of golf.

To help you with this exercise, below you will find a series of questions to ask yourself as well as some suggestions to get your pen flowing on the paper.

> ➢ **Where are you playing golf and who are you playing with?** Write down things like: The name of the course, where it is, what is your tee time, who you are playing golf with, what you are wearing, what's in your bag, what is the temperature and the weather like. Do your best to be specific.

> ➢ **How do you feel warming up for the round?** Write down things like: How does your body feel, how relaxed and loose are you, what is your attitude, what kind of thoughts do you have in your mind, what type of energy level do you have. Do your best to be specific.

> ➢ **What is your attitude on the first tee?** Write down things like: What is your mental state, what are you thinking or saying to yourself, how are you holding your body (body language), how do you feel around these golfers, what are you visualizing, how does your body feel. Do your best to be specific.

> ➢ **What is your swing like?** Write down things like: How does your swing feel, how well do you strike the ball, what type of contact do you make, how rhythmic is your swing, what is your back swing like, where are you at impact, how do you finish your swing, what types of

shots do you hit, how relaxed are you over the ball, what is your attitude addressing the ball. Do your best to be specific.

➢ **How accurate are you?** Write down things like: How accurate is your drive, how accurate are your second shots, how many fairways do you hit, how many greens in regulation, how close are you to your targets, what are you visualizing to increase execution. Do your best to be specific.

➢ **What is your attitude on the greens?** Write down things like: What is my attitude on the greens, what is my mental state, what am I thinking or saying to myself, how do I move on the green (body language), what do I do to read the putts, how well do I read putts, what am I visualizing. Do your best to be specific.

➢ **What do you putt like?** Write down things like: How many 1-putts do you make, how many saves, how much distance of putts do you make, how accurate are you, what is your putting stroke like, what is going through your mind as you are standing over the putt, how do you visualize the line, what is the entire putting process like. Do your best to be specific.

➢ **Describe events of your perfect round.** Write down things like: What exciting things happened in this round, what amazing shots did you hit, what incredible putts did you make, how did you handle the other golfers, did you play your game, what are the highlights of the perfect round. Do your best to be specific

➢ **How do you handle adversity during this perfect round?** Write down things like: How did you overcome poor shots, how did you stay positive, how did you stay focused, how did you let negativity go, how did you handle the competition, how did you stay relaxed. Do your best to be specific.

➢ **What is the end result of the round?** Write down things like: What was your final score, what milestones did you achieve, what did you win, how do you feel, what was the day like, what did you learn. Do your best to be specific.

➢ **Who am I?** Write down things like: Describe the type of golfer you are, how you feel, how you look, what is your energy level like, what is your confidence like, what mental states give you the edge, what makes you worthy of great success, what champion qualities do you possess. Do you best to be specific.

➢ **What do I need to do to make this round a reality?** Write down action steps that move you towards this dream round of golf.

Now that you have completed writing out your perfect round of golf, take a few minutes to close your eyes, do self-hypnosis, and imagine this experience unfolding on the course. You can also record what you wrote so you can play it during your self-hypnosis sessions to guide your imagination through the experience of playing your perfect round of golf. This is a fun way to do positive mental programming and keep expanding your mind on what is possible. Keep your perfect round of golf in a place you can refer to it often, to refresh your level of excitement pursuing your goals, to become aware of what aspects have manifested into your golf game, and as a reminder to keep dreaming big.

Mind Expander #3: Vision/Dream Board

The last mind expander exercise makes use of your imagination, it expands your mind on what's possible, and best of all it doesn't require any writing to do it. For this exercise, you will need either a poster board, or a large piece of cardboard so that you can use it to create your vision/dream board. Once you have your poster board, begin going through magazines, and catalogues as well as doing image searches online, and find pictures of things that you want to achieve, have, or do. For example, if your dream is to win the Masters then find a picture of the green jacket, cut it or print it out, and then glue it to your dream board. Fill up this entire board of pictures that represent your goals, your dreams, your rewards for your hard work, the things you want to have, the places you want to go, and so on. Once you have filled up your board, put it in a place that you will see it every day to serve as a reminder to your subconscious mind of your goals and dreams, to keep your mind moving towards these desires, and to inspire you to keep taking action.

Creating a dream board is a fun and powerful way to direct your subconscious mind to success and the accomplishment of your goals. Each time you see your dream board your mind will keep expanding on what is possible in your life.

Self-Hypnosis Exercise for Goal Achievement

Now that you have clearly defined and written goals, it is time to bring these goals to life in a self-hypnosis session to program your subconscious mind for their achievement. This exercise takes into consideration the two key aspects of goal setting: It starts with the end in mind and action steps to get there.

Let's go over the steps to this exercise now so you can use it to accomplish more in your golf game and your life.

Step 1: Find a quiet place where you can relax and won't be disturbed. Once you have found this place, relax your mind and body using your favorite self-hypnosis method.

Step 2: Once in a relaxed state of awareness, begin to visualize and think about you successfully achieving a goal such as winning a golf tournament. Begin to visualize and imagine, as real as possible, you with the trophy in your hand and experience what it would be like during the moment you achieved your goal. Incorporate all your senses into the experience and notice the sights, the sounds, and the feelings of the moment. Make it real in your mind and enhance it in every way so that it is appealing, compelling, motivating, and better than you could ever imagine.

Step 3: Now as you focus on this scene of success and achievement, begin to imagine that the scene is becoming transparent to the point where you can see through it. As you imagine looking through this scene, you can see yourself doing all the things that helped you achieve your goal. For example, you might see yourself practicing on the range and putting in the time to improve your swing. You might see yourself doing your mental training exercises to condition your mind for success on the course. You notice yourself performing on the course in the most ideal fashion, executing confident swings, handling adversity like a champ, going low on the course, and all other actions and behaviors that got you to the goal. Take a few minutes to visualize yourself doing the things that made it possible to achieve the success.

Step 4: After you have taken in the details that lead you to great success, become aware again of the end result and the experience of you holding the trophy. Imagine walking up to that person, the one who evolved way beyond all challenges, who performed on the course in the best possible way, and who achieved the goal that they set for themselves. Go up to that person and shake their hand. Compliment and praise them on their success. And, ask them for advice or anything you need to know to make this goal a reality. After receiving that advice, imagine giving them the biggest hug you have every given anybody in your life, and squeeze them so tight that you merge together and become one.

Step 5: As you merge together and become one, begin to experience life as this empowered you. Notice what they notice, do what they do, and experience life through this lens of viewing the world. Experience what it is like to achieve this goal. Become aware that you are this person, that you have what it takes to achieve your dreams, and that you have everything you need inside to make this goal a reality. Let this experience make a major impression in your mind and the more real you make the experience the more powerful it will be. Mentally store this experience into your mind and body.

Step 6: Finish up this exercise with a few minutes of mental programming and giving yourself positive suggestions to internalize this experience, learn from it, and apply it in your golf game. You can also provide your subconscious mind with any other positive suggestions that motivate you to act on your dreams.

Step 7: Emerge from self-hypnosis by counting forward from 1to5, open your eyes feeling rejuvenated and energized, and take an action step towards the achievement of this goal.

I highly recommend that you use this self-hypnosis exercise as often as possible because it is one of the most effective ways to make positive impressions in the subconscious mind to achieve your goals. This process can be used for short-term and long-term goals, sometimes with amazing and immediate results. Remember Paul Woodbury from the forward? This is one of the processes I guided Paul through each day during the NGA Tour's 2013 Palmetto State Open. It resulted in Paul's first professional win. Another example of the power of visualizing short-term goals comes from Jason Day. After the 2014 WGC-Accenture Match Play Championship, champion Jason Day revealed a little bit of his thought process the night before the final match. Day told CBS, "It's, 'How much do I want it? How much do I want to win? He continued, "I kept saying that last night and visualizing myself with the trophy." Jason Day didn't do the exact process described above but demonstrates the same concept. One last example of the power of visualizing your goals is 2014 Kraft Nabisco Championship winner, Lexi Thompson. Before doing the famous Poppy's Pond jump, Lexi Thompson said in her post round interview, "This was my main goal coming into this year...to win a major. I have always seen myself winning the Kraft Nabisco Championship and taking a leap into Poppy's Pond." She continues, "This one is so special to me with the history behind the tournament, I always visualized myself jumping into that pond."

All three of these examples demonstrate the power of bringing your goals to life through self-talk, visualization, and self-hypnosis. Be like the pros by following the steps above and start making your goals a reality.

Two Pitfalls of Goal Setting That Must Be Avoided

Now that you are aware of the importance of having well defined goals and action plans to achieve them, it is important to bring up two common pitfalls or traps you want to avoid falling into. Goals, if used improperly, can actually result in and cause a great deal of unhappiness in life.

In all the years I have been studying goal setting, rarely have I heard any mention of these two pitfalls of goal setting that comes with improper use. Let's go over these pitfalls now so that you can avoid them and use your goals successfully.

The first pitfall that can occur is a shift in thinking from the present moment to more future oriented thinking. When we create goals, it is best to start with the end in mind. However, if we get trapped in this future thinking, it can create anxiety, frustration, and negativity because we end up constantly thinking about all the things we haven't achieved yet. Then your imagination kicks in and makes everything bigger than what it is and, as a result, we stay stuck in a vicious cycle of procrastination, frustration, and unhappiness.

The other trap that can occur is that so many people think when they achieve a specific goal, *then* they will be happy. This mentality can lead to a tremendous amount of unhappiness, because more time will always be spent on the journey to the achievement of the goal than in the actual moment the goal is reached. With this mindset, the ultimate tragedy is likely to occur. The person reaches their goal and it doesn't bring them the fulfillment that they were hoping for. They end up thinking "Is this all there is?" or are surprised when the goal didn't fill the void that they thought it would. Since there is always something bigger than what was just achieved, they assume that it must be the next thing that will ultimately make the happy. This is a cycle that always leads to unhappiness.

To overcome these potential pitfalls of goal setting, it is important that you are clear on your goals and then make the commitment to finding enjoyment in the journey as much as the destination. Fulfillment comes from the process of reaching your goals, and not solely from their achievement. If you are relying on goal achievement to make you happy, then you will be searching for it all your life. It is vitally important that you know where you are going, and to enjoy every step that you take to get there.

Let me give you another sports example outside of golf to drive this point home. If you have ever gone bowling then you know that a perfect game is a score of 300. With this in mind, why don't people just go to the bowling alley and write down 300 on their scorecard, and simply enjoy the success of doing that? The reason is the enjoyment doesn't come just from the score or the end result. The enjoyment from bowling, or any other sport, comes from playing the game and doing your best to reach the ultimate goal.

Learning how to enjoy the process is the key to happiness, greater goal achievement, and fulfillment. If you are too focused on the future, constantly anxious and stressed because you haven't reached the goal yet, or will be only happy when the goal is reached then you run the ultimate risk of missing out on the beauty of the journey and life. When you learn to be happy now and with each step of the process, it will make it easier to achieve more and make the achieved goals much more fulfilling.

Let's conclude this chapter with some words of wisdom from Ben Hogan, "As you walk down the fairway of life you must smell the roses, for you only get to play one round."

Chapter Review

In this chapter you discovered ways to get clear on your goals, create action plans for their achievement, and how to embed your goals into your subconscious mind to fast track your success. To be a great success in any endeavor of life, written and clearly defined goals are a requirement. If you haven't done so already then take some time now to go through the exercises, get clear on your goals, and write them out. Put goal setting to the test. You will be happy and amazed at the results it will help you produce in life and how much more you accomplish.

1. To achieve the greatest success you can, written goals are a requirement, not simply an option.

2. A goal is not a goal until it is written out. If it just stays in your head, then it remains in the realm of wishful thinking, positive thinking, or remains a mere thought.

3. Research from Dominican University of California validated the effectiveness of written goals, plans of achievement, and being accountable.

4. Written goals will help you:

    ➢ Reverse engineer your success.

    ➢ Determine your daily actions.

    ➢ Stay motivated.

    ➢ Overcome obstacles in your path.

    ➢ Track progress and success.

    ➢ Create positive imprints in your subconscious mind.

5. Types of Goals:

    ➢ Outcome Goals: Focused on standards of performance and results of competition.

    ➢ Performance Goals: Focused on improving past performances.

    ➢ Process Goals: Focused on movement procedures and mechanics to improve skills.

> ➢ Mental Performance Goals: Focused on mental and emotional aspects of course performance.

> ➢ Developmental Goals: Focused on training, including workouts, mental training, swing development, etc.

6. Goal Setting: Method 1 - S.M.A.R.T. Goals

> ➢ Specific

> ➢ Measurable

> ➢ Action oriented

> ➢ Realistic and Relevant

> ➢ Time Bound

7. Goal Setting: Method 2 - Well-Formed Outcomes

> ➢ This is an in-depth approach to determining your goals; please follow the steps outlined in the chapter.

8. Developing an action plan to achieve goals will help you:

> ➢ Increase progress and productivity.

> ➢ Track your success and milestones.

> ➢ Build self-esteem.

9. "Chunk Down" your goals to determine your action plan.

> ➢ Start with the end in mind.

> ➢ Identify milestones along the journey to reach your main goal.

> ➢ Determine actions to achieve each of the milestones and ultimately your big goal.

> ➢ Take action each day to keep getting closer to your dreams.

10. Helpful ideas to keep you taking action and staying motivated.

> ➢ Commit to the T.N.T. Club - Today Not Tomorrow.

➤ The thought is always bigger and more overwhelming than the actual task.

➤ Champions are made when nobody is around.

➤ Fail forward fast.

11. Mind expander exercises:

➤ The dream sheet exercise.

➤ Your perfect round of golf.

➤ Creating a vision/dream board.

12. Self-hypnosis for goal achievement: Follow the outlined steps for this exercise to program your subconscious mind for goal achievement.

13. Pitfalls of goal setting that need to avoided:

➤ Getting too caught up in future oriented thinking which can emphasize all the uncompleted tasks and create anxiety and frustration.

➤ The idea that I will only be happy when I achieve this goal. This will set you up for a lot of unhappiness because the journey to the goal is much longer than the moments of triumph.

14. Overcome these pitfalls by making the commitment to enjoy the journey as much as, or more than, the destination. Learning to enjoy the moment will keep you enjoying the process, keep you motivated, and make the achievement of the goal much more fulfilling.

CONCLUSION

YOUR JOURNEY TO ACHIEVING MENTAL FITNESS IN GOLF

"Once an athlete overcomes a mental or physical barrier, suddenly the barrier no longer exists and new expectations or limits of what is possible are formed."

--Patrick Cohn, Ph.D.

A common question that tends to emerge at this point in time is "How do I measure success and know I am making improvements in my mental game as I move forward?" Remember that regardless of what you set out to learn in life, there are four levels of learning that everyone must progress through in order to establish new positive habits and completely integrate the new understandings. Let's review the four levels of learning from Chapter 3 so that you can know what to expect as you begin developing the mental side of your golf game.

Review of the Levels of Learning:

> **Level 1**: Unconscious Incompetence

> **Level 2**: Conscious Incompetence

> **Level 3**: Conscious Competence

> **Level 4**: Unconscious Competence

Level 1: When beginning the journey towards mental development, everyone starts at the first level of learning or what's called unconscious incompetence. What this means is "You don't know what you don't know." Most golfers have no idea at this level of learning how the mind functions, its influence on performance, the various roles the two parts of the mind play on the course, how to train their mind effectively, and so much more. In order to advance to the next level of learning, you need to get informed in this area of mental fitness for golf. As you discover more information, you are no longer unaware or unconsciously incompetent because now you know there is lots to learn about the mental game that you didn't know before.

Goals at Level 1 of Learning:

1. Get informed about the mental game of golf.

2. Learn how your mind functions, the various roles of the mind on the course, and how it is influencing performance.

3. Discover the right information on how to develop this side of your golf game.

After completing this book, you have more than likely already progressed from this level of learning and to the next phase of development.

Level 2: After you have started gathering new information, you start becoming more aware of the mind's influence on performance. In this level of learning, you start to notice the game differently and pick up on many new things. You might become more aware of stressors or negative thoughts that are affecting you on the course. Perhaps you are more aware of the power of visualization, the importance of performance routines, and other positive aspects. However, you are still at a learning level of "incompetence" and haven't as of yet gained proficiency in applying the new strategies.

To progress out of this level of learning two key things are needed; awareness and recognition. During this level of learning, it is important to become aware of old patterns of behavior that are inhibiting success and begin to recognize how these patterns are influencing performance negatively. While working through this level, it may first appear like an internal battle has begun and as if you are fighting with yourself on the course. Say for example, you started to become aware of negative self-talk and thoughts of doubt during performance. But now, because you know more about the benefits of positive thinking from your learning in Level 1, you start to fight these old thoughts by using self-talk that conveys confidence and optimism. Then the old programming kicks back in and once again you have to fight it by forcing yourself to think positive.

Believe it or not, this is an excellent sign of progress and advancement in learning. Recognizing the negative thoughts is a major success in and of itself, because it means you are getting off of mental auto-pilot and recognizing conditioned patterns of thought and behavior that were getting in your way. Even though you might struggle overcoming the old programming at first, the very fact that you are *"aware"* means that your thoughts are changing and you are learning a new way of doing things. Every golfer must go through this stage of learning whether it's related to the mental game, a new move in their swing, or any other aspect of the game in order to advance their skills. So avoid resisting this stage because you need to become aware and recognize things that aren't working in order to make improvements. Take everything in stride in Level 2 and trust that you are succeeding even though it may not look like that at first. A simple thought that has helped my golfers through this phase of learning is: *"Gradually leads to sudden"*. Keep working your plan, even if it feels like progress is slow because you never know when the breakthrough will occur, and, when it does you will know!

Goals at Level 2 of Learning:

1. Get off mental auto-pilot by gaining awareness and recognition of old negative patterns of behavior, thought, and emotion.

2. Start to work on changing the old patterns and fighting back the negative thoughts and ways.

3. Not accepting the old ways any longer. This also indicates a positive boost of self-esteem.

Level 3: When you get to Level 3, you now have the right information about the mind and its influence on performance, you are now recognizing and aware of old patterns from the past, and no longer accepting the negative programming that was inhibiting your success. Now you have progressed to the level of conscious competence. At this level of learning, you know what to do, how to do, and are successfully producing results, but it still requires conscious effort to implement your new mental strategies for success. Signs of success at this level are not based on score. Success in the mental game at this level of learning is measured by things such as the way you feel over the ball, new positive behaviors like a consistent pre-shot routine, the way you are thinking on the course, the way you rebound and handle adversity, and so on. This all indicates success because, just like your golf swing, when you do the right things mentally and behaviorally on the course, the improvement in score will follow.

To progress through this level of learning, you need consistent reinforcement and conditioning of the new patterns of behaviors, thoughts, and emotions so that they become a natural part of your game. This level of learning is when you are forming the foundation for new positive habits of success on the golf course.

Goals at Level 3 of Learning:

1. Put conscious effort into implementing your new mental strategies.

2. Reinforce and condition the new behaviors, thoughts, and emotions.

3. Do it consistently enough to form a habit.

Level 4: When you reach Level 4, you have obtained a state of mastery in what you were learning. You have now successfully established new habits on the golf course and are performing in a state of unconscious competence. At this level, all the new thoughts, behaviors, and strategies, have now become second nature and very little thought is required to implement these keys to success effectively and consistently. The old ways of being on the course now seem foreign or totally forgotten all together. At this level, real results are showing on the scorecard and lower scores on the golf course begin to happen on a regular basis. Even though scores are significantly improving now, the score is no longer the dominate thought on the course when this level has been reached. The main focus is now on executing the specific keys to success on each shot and throughout the round that naturally lead to great swings and low scores.

Bottom line when you reach this level of learning, habit integration has occurred and your subconscious mind has been conditioned with new patterns that naturally occur on the course each time you play golf.

Goals at Level 4 of Learning:

1. Have fun enjoying the fruits of your labor with low rounds of golf and pushing yourself to higher levels of performance with your new positive habits and mental strategies for success.

This Moment Marks a Turning Point

Even though this book is now coming to an end, it marks the beginning of your journey towards mental fitness in the game of golf.

The greats in the game all understood the importance of the mind to play golf at an elite level. You now know the secrets of self-hypnosis to harness the power of your subconscious mind to take your game and life as far as you wish to go. Self-hypnosis is the key to developing the mind for success because it is the vehicle that enables you to integrate information so it is not just understood, but acted upon consistently and naturally in your golf game.

I have cited just a few of the rigorous university-led research trials and results which substantiate my opinion that self-hypnosis and the techniques outlined in this book work. All the techniques, the self-hypnosis examples, and step-by-step instructions, have proven to be effective with golfers of all skill levels and will transform your golf game as long as you implement them. Best of all, the results of self-hypnosis and these mental fitness techniques are cumulative in nature so the more you do them the more you will benefit from them.

Your Commitment To Mental Fitness

To be your best it requires constant and never-ending improvement both physically and mentally. As you embark on your journey to achieving mental mastery, you must make the following commitments to fully realize the power of your mind:

> ➤ **A burning desire to be your best.** Desire is the starting point of all achievement and is a requirement if you are to discover your full potential.

> ➤ **An undying faith and belief in yourself**. Success is an inside-out process, meaning it starts inside of you. Many people say "When I see it,

I will believe it" and more often than not, these same people end up waiting their entire life to take action on their dreams. This statement needs to be flipped to read, "When I believe it, I will see it."

➢ **Have faith that what you can conceive in your mind and believe in, will in fact be achieved**. Also, have faith in the power of your mind. Until you consistently start training your subconscious mind, you have no idea what your mind is capable of. As you incorporate self-hypnosis into your training program you will be amazed at the level of success you can achieve with this tool.

➢ **Commitment to mental training.** Developing mental toughness and the mind of a championship golfer doesn't happen overnight. It takes consistent and persistent effort to master these skills and realize their full benefits in your golf game.

You now know that it is impossible to separate the mind from performance. Your mind goes with you everywhere, it directs your every move, and is constantly at work creating your most dominate thoughts. Now that you are fully aware of these facts, it is important that you make the commitment to maximizing the power of your mind for your success.

Trust me, it is worth the commitment to do daily mental training and self-hypnosis because not only will you improve your golf game, you will be able to apply these skills to all areas of your life.

Gary Player said, "We know so much about technique that the last frontier in golf is mastering the mind."

THAT LAST FRONTIER IS HERE NOW.

AFTERWORD FROM THE AUTHOR

I want to sincerely thank you for giving me the opportunity to share this information about the power of the mind with you and for your investment of time and energy in reading this book. Refer back to it often because each time you read it you will notice new ways to apply the information.

Enjoy your journey of improving your mental fitness and *have fun reaping the rewards*. You have the most powerful computer between your ears and now you have a user manual to tapping into more of its unlimited potential. Wishing you tremendous and ongoing success as you discover the champion within.

With gratitude,

J. Weir

2014

APPENDIXES

APPENDIX I

Chevreul's Pendulum Experiment

As discussed in Chapter One, The Mind-Body Connection in Golf, the following exercise will give you a first-hand experience of the mind-body connection. Every thought that you have affects the body and creates a psychosomatic response.

One exercise that demonstrates the mind-body connection is called Chevreul's Pendulum Experiment. In order to do this exercise you will need a pendulum and a sheet of paper with a big circle on it with a vertical and a horizontal line intersecting in the middle.

If you don't have a pendulum then you can easily make one. To do so what you will need is a piece of string or a shoe lace, and a ring, washer, or even a key. Take the shoe lace, put the ring or washer through it, and you are good to go.

Chevreul's Pendulum Experiment Chart for the Exercise:

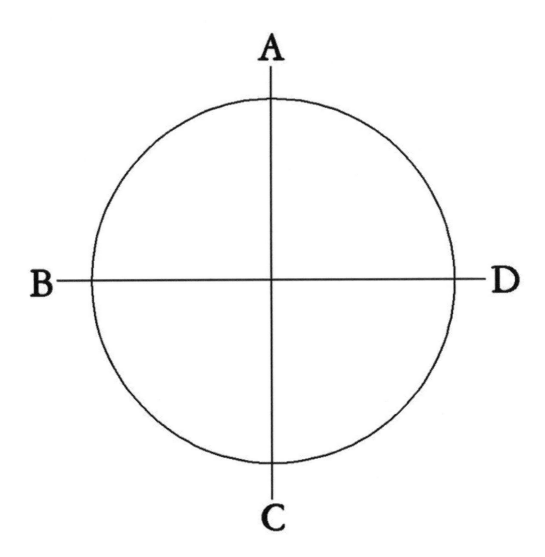

Follow the four simple steps as outlined in the chapter. This simple experiment, when done correctly, powerfully demonstrates how the mind influences the body. So what makes the pendulum move during this experiment? Is it some mystical force or the power of intention? Not likely. The reason the pendulum moves, seemingly on its own, is due to psychosomatic responses taking place. If you breakdown the word psychosomatic into its root words, you get psyche which is the mind, and soma, which is the body. A psychosomatic response relates to the effects of the mind on the body, and how the thoughts held in the mind create physical responses and muscle movements. While you imagine the pendulum moving in your mind, this is sending signals through the body, and subtly influences the micro muscles of the body to respond in alignment with the thoughts.

APPENDIX II

Bonus Article: Why Your Handicap Is Handicapping Your Performance On the Golf Course

Attention golfers, did you know that your believed handicap is actually handicapping your ability to bring out your full potential on the course? ***In this article, I will explain 3 reasons why your handicap is holding you back on the course and why it is essential to eliminate the internal belief in the idea of a handicap index in your golf game forever.*** The time has come to end the negative programming that the idea of a handicap index has created in your golf game so you can play your best on golf course and lower your score.

The first way your handicap is limiting your performance is because the word handicap is actually a negative programming word to your subconscious mind. Let's take the word handicap out of a golf context for a moment. When you hear the word handicap what types of thoughts get conjured up in your mind? If you are like most people when you think about the word "handicap" you probably think about things like a physical or mental disability, or restrictions and limitations to do certain things in life. The next question to ask yourself is, when you hear the word handicap does it make you feel positive or negative inside? I have no doubt that the word "handicap" invokes negative feelings inside of you that are linked to that word at the subconscious level.

My background is in the areas of hypnosis and maximizing human potential. One of my jobs is to help my clients identify negative programming words they are using that are holding them back in life and to then help them to make a shift in their language so they can begin producing a new result. An acronym that can be used to explain how a seemingly simple word or a thought can effect results in life as well as on the golf course is T.F.A.R. T.F.A.R. stands for **T**houghts, **F**eelings, **A**ctions, and **R**esults. This acronym provides a simple framework that shows the chain reaction that occurs in you with every thought you have.

Your thoughts about something create feelings. Your feeling towards something will determine your actions and your actions will determine your results. Positive thoughts create positive feelings. When you feel positive then you take positive actions. Positive actions lead to the results you desire. The opposite is also true. If you insert the word or idea of having a "handicap" in any area of life (including your golf game) into the beginning of this formula, then you will become aware, at the simplest level, how the word "handicap" is affecting your performance, score, and abilities on the course. When you think about the word handicap it creates negative images in the mind. These images then conjure up negative feelings and emotions. When you are in a negative state you tend to take no action, or wrong actions that are in alignment with the negative thought. No action or wrong action produce results that are less than what you are capable of.

Don't underestimate the power of the words you use and their impact on your subconscious mind. It is important to know the subconscious mind always moves towards your dominant thought, but it doesn't discern the difference between good or bad thoughts, it just supports the compelling and powerful thoughts. *It is your job to program your inner mind **to work for you instead of against you.** The starting point is making shifts in your language.*

Let's now take it to the next level. The words that you consistently use form your internal belief systems and these belief systems govern your behaviors. Belief systems are much more powerful than words because they are things that you believe to be true about yourself and ideas from others that have been accepted by the subconscious mind. These accepted ideas then become mental programs that direct your behaviors, thoughts, and feelings.

Unfortunately for most golfers, the consistent use of the word handicap in their language and in their thoughts has formed negative and limiting beliefs that holds the golfer back from tapping into their best more often.

The subconscious mind is nothing more than a bio-computer and can only operate on the programs that have been installed. It must follow the belief systems that are in place because that is all the inner mind knows to be true and its job is to make sure that these beliefs come into fruition. When you have accepted limiting beliefs as what is true for your experience on the golf course, then you tend to find and create situations that validate your beliefs and reinforce the negative thoughts in the mind, which only makes the belief system stronger. The words you use on a consistent basis form your belief systems. In the same way, the belief systems you maintain on a consistent basis reinforce your thoughts and behaviors which form the next level, your self-image Your self-image, or the internal picture of yourself, is a combination of all your belief systems that form the framework in your subconscious mind of who you are. The self-image, in my opinion, is a greater determiner of success and performance on the course, much more than your swing or physical mechanics. Physical ability will only take you so far and, at the level of the PGA Tour players, very little separates them in regards to their golf swing and physical skill level. *What separates the champions from the rest of the pack is the self-image.*

Trust, belief, confidence, focus, and all the intangible qualities of a champion can only be developed so much at the range and from lessons. The pros all work on their minds and their internal picture of themselves in order to bring forth and develop these mental qualities so they can perform at the highest level on the course. However, most amateur golfers never take into consideration that how they are thinking, the words they use, and the way they view themselves internally are just as important, if not more important than what they are doing with their physical body or with their swing.

Why is the self-image so crucial and how does this relate to a golfer's handicap? As mentioned earlier, the word handicap conjures up negative feelings and thoughts. These thoughts over time form your belief systems and these belief systems form your self-image. The idea of having a handicap is a direct mental program to the subconscious mind that sets limitations on performance to match that number. It is important to know that your subconscious MUST fulfill the self-image and make it right. The subconscious mind only supports what it knows. If you have been consistently telling yourself "I am a 10 handicap golfer" then it is your subconscious mind's job to make that right every single time. In other words, it becomes a self-fulfilling prophecy.

How can you trust that what I am saying is true? Let me answer this question by providing you three examples. Chances are you have experienced all of them.

The first validation can come by asking yourself the question, "How long have I been at this handicap even though I play golf all the time and put in lots of work at the range?" If physical practice was enough, then more golfers would break through their handicaps and make consistent improvements in their golf game. However, since most golfers maintain a self-image that is capped by the idea of a handicap, it makes it very difficult to break through the ceiling that's created in the inner mind.

Next, how many times on the course have you performed at a high level through the first nine holes only to find yourself falling apart on a hole or two which resulted in you scoring right at your handicap? Have you ever wondered why this happens? Now you know it is a result of the subconscious mind fulfilling the self-image. *Your score will reflect what your mind believes to be true.*

Finally, I know there have been times that you scored better than your handicap in a round of golf and you leave the course scratching your head wondering why you can't play golf like this all the time. The next time you go out on the course, you expect yourself to continue the success and play golf at that high level, only to find the opposite occurs, and you end up shooting a round higher than your handicap. If you look at the two scores and take the average you will amaze yourself when you discover that you indeed still shot your handicap. This is a powerful example of how the handicap limits performance and more validation that the subconscious mind always supports the self-image.

To transform your golf game and consistently make improvements it is absolutely vital you understand that success in golf is an "inside out" process. Most approach golf improvement in the wrong way and with an "outside in" mentality, meaning they try to change external things to change their results. Golfers can work on the physical side of the game all they want but it won't make a difference on the course if they neglect their thoughts and self-image. They will always stay limited, always score their handicap, and never breakthrough due to the self-image and the limits of the handicap.

Your self-image is the determiner of success on the golf course. When you understand this and work on releasing your old limiting beliefs then will you start seeing the breakthroughs you have been waiting for in your golf game.

APPENDIX III

More Information on Brain Wave Development from Emory University

Dr. Philip Holt and researchers from Emory University School of Medicine used EEG's to monitor electrical brain wave activity through the various stages of mental development. For this book and appendix I will only present their findings on the electrical activity during the "waking state," or when fully alert and awake. If you want more details and information on additional findings then click this link: http://www.pediatrics.emory.edu/divisions/neurology/pedeeg.html.

Here is what Emory University discovered about the stages of mental development as it relates to electrical brain wave activity:

Infancy Age 1 month to 12 months: The dominate brain wave rhythm in the mind is at 3-4 Hz or Delta Waves.

Toddler/Early Childhood Age 1-3 years old: The dominate brain wave rhythm increases gradually to 6-8 Hz by the age of 3. Children in this period operate primarily in Theta and Delta waves.

Pre-school and Early Childhood 3-6 years old: The dominate brain wave rhythm is at 8 Hz and is a mixture between theta and alpha waves. The amount of alpha waves experienced increases with age and the majority of children are operating at 8-9 Hz by the age of 6.

Elementary School/ Late Childhood 6-12 years old: The dominate brain wave rhythms are alpha. Alpha waves keep increasing during this period and by the age of 10 the main rhythm is around 10 Hz.

Adolescence: During the period of 13-19 years of age, the alpha waves are still the dominate brain rhythm and have become very well defined at a range of 9-11 Hz. Beta brain rhythms begin to occasionally appear in the later stages of adolescence usually in the range of 12-13 Hz.

Adulthood: As the mind matures and becomes fully developed, the adult minds dominant brain wave rhythm is beta at a range of 13 Hz-30 Hz. Alpha waves in adults typically occur when their eyes are closed and relaxed, but not as a dominant brain wave rhythm at full maturity.

As you can see from the above research, children are operating in a "hypnotic" state for 19 years of their life since their brains are oscillating between alpha and theta rhythms. During this period, the subconscious mind absorbs information non-critically and works to piece all the information together to form the self-image which will direct thoughts, behaviors, and emotions as an adult. This is also the time of super learning that enables a child to understand language, how to talk, read, write, and all the other amazing feats of learning. What is important to understand is all of this learning is done subconsciously and without conscious effort.

Once our minds have matured fully and beta brainwaves have been established, our minds shift from pre-dominant right hemisphere functioning (subconscious) to pre-dominantly left hemisphere functioning that includes critical thinking and analysis. Now what happens is instead of information going directly into the bio-computer, it gets filtered and analyzed by the critical factor based on the self-image established during the developmental period.

APPENDIX IV

100 Golf Affirmations for Self-Talk Scripts

Review and experiment with some of the golf affirmations and experience how your golf game changes with consistent positive self-talk.

1. I am a great golfer and always getting better.

2. I swing with confidence.

3. My swing has great tempo, and rhythm.

4. My swing is effortless.

5. I step up to take every shot with self-assurance.

6. My swing flows perfectly.

7. My swing is powerful and precise.

8. I hit all shots with tremendous accuracy.

9. I strike the ball on the sweet spot.

10. I hit the sweet spot more often.

11. I am confident while pitching and chipping.

12. I am accurate, precise, and on target around the greens.

13. I target all shots and visualize the path of the ball.

14. My body projects confidence on the golf course.

15. My game is always improving.

16. My score is constantly getting lower.

17. I concentrate on all shots.

18. I focus completely on the ball during every shot.

19. Every shot gets my full attention.

20. I play golf in the moment.

21. I know the shot I am taking is the most important one of the round.

22. I play consistently great.

23. My swing produces great results.

24. My swing is automatic.

25. I am confident off of the tee.

26. My tee shots are long, accurate, and powerful.

27. I make great contact on every tee shot.

28. I play with greatness.

29. My confidence in my drive constantly improves.

30. I hit every shot better than the last.

31. I play with self-assurance and courage.

32. When it's my shot, I know I will hit a great shot.

33. All old distractions now help me to concentrate more fully on my shot.

34. I always play like a winner.

35. I always stay positive on the course.

36. I know that being positive is a key to success.

37. I focus on the successes I have on each hole.

38. I focus on my success and create more success.

39. I am an optimistic golfer who is superior to negative thinking on the golf course.

40. I love golf and always play with a happy, upbeat attitude.

41. I relax into my game, and let my best performance to flow out.

42. I play in the moment.

43. I play within my game.

44. I always make smart decisions on the course.

45. I gain more confidence with every swing.

46. I am amazed at my new improvements.

47. I notice myself swinging better, making more putts, and producing lower scores.

48. I have fun while golfing.

49. I putt better now that I'm more focused.

50. I can make any putt long, or short.

51. I focus completely on every putt, even on the "gimmies".

52. My putting ability has now improved by leaps and bounds.

53. It's so easy for me to read greens.

54. It's so easy for me to play with greatness every round.

55. I strike the ball cleanly every time.

56. I play my best every time on the course.

57. I maintain a confident attitude the entire round.

58. I play with precision.

59. I concentrate on every shot.

60. I swing with the right tempo.

61. I play better than ever because I am focused.

62. I have a great time playing golf.

63. Today I have more confidence in my swing than ever before.

64. I am focused on every tee shot.

65. I lock my eyes on the ball.

66. My concentration is unbreakable.

67. I play like a pro.

68. I am mentally prepared to play my best.

69. I make incredible shots.

70. I can read any green correctly.

71. I make more putts.

72. I always putt straight toward the target.

73. I take fewer putts every round.

74. It's easy for me to make plays out of the sand.

75. I am a smart golfer.

76. I make wise decisions on the course.

77. When I grip my club confidence fills my body.

78. When I step foot on the course I get in the zone.

79. I easily find my swing's tempo, and rhythm.

80. All distractions help me to focus more on my game.

81. I play my game, and never let other golfers distract me.

82. I impress people with my golfing talents.

83. I notice big improvements every time on the course.

84. I conquer any hole.

85. I am superior to negative thinking on the course.

86. My attitude is in one of a winner.

87. I expect to produce great results with my swing.

88. I always visualize the path of the path before every shot.

89. I do lots of mental practicing.

90. I hit perfect golf balls all day in my mind.

91. I am more accurate.

92. I am more powerful.

93. I am playing better than ever.

94. I'm a winner.

95. I'm unstoppable.

96. I am a great golfer, and I'm always getting better.

97. I have trained my mind for success.

98. I am prepared to play great.

99. I play my best today.

100. Today's my day to succeed better than ever before on the golf course.

APPENDIX V

Self-Talk Scripts

Below you will find more examples of self-talk scripts that you can use for am/pm mental programming time. Use these scripts as is or to help you create your own personal self-talk scripts.

Motivation Self-Talk:

I, (INSERT NAME) am a golfer who has unlimited talent, skill, and ability. I am determined, disciplined, and focused on achieving all of my goals in golf. I have a great work ethic, I love putting in time on my game, and all my hard work pays off with better and better results on the golf course. I am motivated and excited to take my game to the next level of performance. I consistently take action each day to sharpen my skills and discover more of my unlimited potential. I am a fast learner and integrate new skills into my game seamlessly. It is easy for me to make positive changes and produce better results.

Each day I practice, I produce successful results or I learn new things that help me make progress. I am committed to excellence so I train my mind and body every day to be the best on the course. I am a champion and do the things that champions do. I am positive, focused, and motivated to succeed. I am committed, consistent, and confident. I am driven, determined, and dedicated to enhancing my game. I am excited and enthusiastic to achieve all of my goals.

Today is the first day of the rest of my life and I am fully committed to developing the skills that bring forth my greatness on the course.

Positive Mental Attitude Self-Talk Script:

I, (INSERT NAME) am an empowered golfer who is full of confidence, optimism, and excitement. I know that a positive mental attitude is a key ingredient to success and I am committed to being the most positive golfer each and every time on the course. On the golf course, I am my own motivator and booster. I constantly encourage myself to greater and greater success. My positive self-talk fuels my confidence and keeps me performing at my highest level. I am inspired and energized on the course by my positive thoughts. I am committed to being the most positive golfer on the course at all times.

I make the decision to handle adversity in a positive way and use my self-talk to keep me confident, fearless, and determined. This makes me unstoppable on the course, a fierce competitor, and a high level performer. Positive thoughts produce positive results so I make the commitment to being the most positive golfer on the course every time out and I succeed.

Champion Self-Talk Script

I, (INSERT NAME) am a born winner. I am a champion through and through. I think, act, walk, talk, and perform like a champion. I believe in myself. I believe in my game. I believe that I have the power to achieve all of my goals because I am a winner, a champion, victorious in all ways. I take great pride in being the best me that I can be. I cultivate my gifts, talents, and skills on a daily basis. I do what the champions do and I succeed in surprising and wonderful ways. I am mentally tough, my body is strong and powerful. I am in control of my thoughts and emotions, and I perform every shot in the zone. I have the game to dominate every course I play. I am a champion who conquers every hole by making confident swings and fearless putts. I can do anything I set my mind to and achieve my goals because that is what a winner does.

Every day I get better, more motivated, and more successful. I am determined to always be at my best and take action each day to make my dreams a reality. Today is the first day of the rest of my life and I am committed to being my best.

Confident Swing Self-Talk

I, (INSERT NAME) have an excellent golf swing that is getting better and better every day. The moment I grip any club, I feel surges of confidence, empowerment, and determination flowing through all parts of my mind and body. I am extremely confident with every club and I know I have the skills to execute any shot on the course. I know I can execute every shot because I have perfect muscle memory of my best swing and I trust it. My confidence and trust in my swing gives me the power to perform without conscious effort. I let my subconscious mind produce my smooth, perfect, and effortless swing on every shot. When I address the ball, my mind is calm, focused on success, and my body follows through perfectly. My awesome swing produces precise, accurate, and successful results. With every swing of my club my confidence grows and grows and grows.

I have the power to make the correct adjustments when needed which allows me to consistently perform in the zone. Every time I grip any club, my best swing simply flows out of me and I love the results it produces. I am confident from tee to green and with all clubs, because my subconscious mind produces my best swing consistently on the course. I trust my swing, I trust all the hard work, and I trust my mind and body to execute in the perfect way. I have an awesome swing that is getting better and better every day.

APPENDIX VI

Progressive Relaxation Script and/or an Induction Script

This is my suggested progressive relaxation script, which can also be used as an induction script. Please review and adapt to what is optimal and comfortable for you.

Recommended Progressive Relaxation Script by John Weir:

It is time to relax now and as I close my eyes I give my mind and body full permission to enjoy this time of deep relaxation. From this point forward every breath that I take calms and relaxes me more and more on every level. I am happy to have this time to relax and I value this time away from the world that is all for me. The deeper I relax the better I feel and the better I feel the easier it is to relax completely and totally.

As I focus my attention on my feet all muscles begin to relax deeply and completely. All muscles in my feet are relaxing and going loose, limp, and relaxed. My feet have supported me all day long, and I give all muscles permission to let go now and enjoy the feeling of deep, soothing relaxation. The muscles of my feet are now relaxing and letting go. With every breath I take it increases the sensations of deep relaxation in my feet and all parts of my body. All the muscles in my feet are now completely relaxed.

As I breathe in deeply now, the relaxation begins moving into my lower legs and circulating through all the muscles, tendons, and fibers in my calves. Every breath

I breathe causes my muscles to relax more and more. The warmth of this deep relaxing energy is melting away all tension and stress in my lower legs and causes my legs to feel completely at peace. The muscles in my lower legs are letting go completely. They are completely relaxed now.

The relaxation is now moving into my upper legs and all the muscles have already started to relax completely. All tension is unlocking and melting away in my upper legs. The warmth of the relaxation washes through every muscle, tendon, fiber, and cell of my legs. My legs are completely letting go. I can feel my legs relaxing deeply now. All tension is gone and my legs are loose, limp, and completely relaxed.

My hips and buttocks are now releasing all tension as the relaxation swirls through this area. All the muscles are releasing, letting go, and becoming free of all tensions. I can feel the warmth of the relaxation calming and soothing all the muscles. My hips and buttocks are completely relaxed now and all parts of my body continue to relax deeper with every breath I take.

As the relaxation moves into my abdomen and lower back, it instantly and automatically begins to release all tension and completely fills this region of my body with peace, comfort, and relaxation. The warmth of this deep relaxation is unlocking all the muscles and all muscles let go completely into total comfort. My abdomen and lower back are relaxing so completely. These muscles are now completely relaxed and becoming more and more relaxed with every breath I take.

My chest and upper back are being consumed by the relaxation and all muscles are letting go so completely now. Every breath I take invokes greater and greater levels of relaxation in this part of my body. The relaxing energy is swirling through all the muscles, organs, tendons, fibers, and cells of my chest and upper back. The relaxation moves up my spinal column releasing all tensions and flooding my body with total comfort and complete relaxation. All muscles are letting go into relaxation so quickly and deeply now. All parts of my chest and upper back are completely relaxed now and feel peaceful, warm, and comfortable.

The relaxation is now spreading through my shoulders, down my arms, and to my fingertips. All remaining tension in the body is being pushed out now through the tips of my fingers as the relaxation takes over completely. All stored tension is leaving now going out and away, out and away, out and away through my fingertips. Relaxation is now spreading through every inch of my arms and shoulders, calming, and relaxing me deeply. All tension is now gone and replaced by peace, comfort, and relaxing energy. My shoulders and arms are now completely relaxed and peaceful.

The relaxation is now working its magic on all the muscles of my neck, loosing and relaxing all muscles completely. My neck has done an excellent job supporting my head and it now has permission to completely relax and enjoy time off. It feels as if my neck is being massaged and all the muscles of my neck are going loose and relaxed. My neck muscles are relaxing now and peace is flowing into these muscles. The warm relaxation is soothing away all tensions now. My neck muscles are now completely relaxed and relaxing more and more with every breath I take.

The warm relaxation is now moving into my head, face, and scalp smoothing out all the muscles. My jaws are relaxing and loosening causing my mouth to separate as the peace settles in. My facial muscles are unlocking now and returning to a state of pure relaxation. All the muscles in my head and face are releasing all tension and melting into the comforting relaxation that has taken over. My face, scalp, and head muscles are now completely and totally relaxed. I am in a state of perfect relaxation.

My entire body is now completely blanketed in deep, soothing relaxation. Every breath I breathe keeps increasing the state of relaxation I am now feeling. My entire body is now at peace. Each and every time I have the intention of relaxing it gets easier and easier to enter into deeper and deeper levels of relaxation.

At this point, you will want to insert the deepener or go straight into suggestions/mental exercises. Then finish with a count out.

APPENDIX VII

Hypnosis Induction Tips and Scripts

Self-Hypnosis Tips:

1. It is strongly recommended that you use the self-hypnosis starter audio when starting the process of learning self-hypnosis. This audio will help you out tremendously at first because it will teach you through experience as well as get you familiar with the process before doing it yourself. You can get this free audio by going to www.golfersguide-tomentalfitness.com and you can download a full length hypnosis session free at www.mentalcaddie.com.

2. Make recordings of your self-hypnosis sessions. Recording audios is easier than ever before, and there are free smart phone apps for voice recording that you can use. By recording your sessions, it gives you the ability to get more into the experience since you don't have to actively deliver suggestions to yourself. This will increase the effectiveness of your self-hypnosis sessions because you can remain passive and simply absorb the positive messages you have predetermined and wrote out.

3. Use the scripts in the appendix to help you create your recordings. Remember the key components of every self-hypnosis session include: Hypnosis Induction, Deepener, Positive Suggestions, and finally the Count Out. Be sure to include these elements in your recording to get maximum benefit.

4. The induction scripts found in this book use the word "You" instead of "I." While doing your induction, think of it as you directing yourself into self-hypnosis. After the induction and deepener are done, shift your language to "I" when giving yourself suggestions to make them more personal.

5. When recording your script take your time. Be sure to pace yourself and speak in a calm and soothing voice. Pretend to be an actor and use your voice to convey the messages you want to get across.

The Elman Induction Script - Self-Hypnosis Version

Find a spot on the ceiling to focus on and allow your mind to imagine a beautiful and relaxing scene. As you continue to focus on that spot and begin to relax...take a nice soothing deep breath in…hold it for a moment…and as you slowly exhale allow your eyes to close down. Take another long deep breath in…hold it…and as you exhale let yourself relax completely. When you are ready breathe in deeply one last time…hold it…and as you exhale simply let go…and embrace this time away from the world to simply relax. As you continue to breathe peacefully and easily now, simply let every healthy breath you take guide you deeper inside to a perfect state of peace.

Now become aware of how nice it is to have your eyes closed right now…giving yourself full permission in this moment...to enjoy this time that is just for you. Begin now...by relaxing all the little muscles around your eyes. Allow all those muscles to relax so completely that all those muscles *just won't work.* Go ahead and do that now…relax all those little muscles around your eyes so much that *they just won't work*…it feels so good to do so. In a moment I will have you give yourself a quick check to make sure you have relaxed your eyelids so much *they won't work.* You might find that you can maybe manage to move your eyebrows but your eyelids are becoming so relaxed now they just refuse to work. Once you have done that and you have convinced yourself that you have relaxed those eyelids so much *they just won't work*…give them a quick test now and make sure they won't work. Perfect…stop testing and let yourself go deeper relaxed.

Now take that beautiful feeling of relaxation that you have allowed in your eyes and send it down through your entire body. Imagine and let yourself experience a wave of relaxation starting at the top of your head and washing down, down, down to the tips of your toes. Letting every muscle, fiber, and cell in your body… *completely relax and let go*. The more you relax the better you feel and the better you feel causes you to continue to relax more completely…as all sounds, thoughts, and sensations guide you into deeper and deeper levels of hypnosis…allowing yourself today to relax as deeply into hypnosis as you need to go…*to create the success you desire.*

Now we are going to deepen this beautiful feeling of relaxation…and…it is so easy to do. In a moment I will have you open and close your eyes. When you open your eyes, you will immediately find that spot on the ceiling you focused on earlier and the moment you close your eyes that is your cue and signal to allow this relaxation and peace to become twice as complete. All you have to do is want that to happen and it will happen naturally and easily. Imagine how great it will feel to double this relaxation…now…open your eyes…close your eyes…and let go twice as deep into this peace and comfort.

In a moment I will have you open and close your eyes again. When your eyes open find that spot and as you close your eyes this time…it is your cue to allow this relaxation…you now have…to become ten times deeper. Just imagine the euphoria of relaxing 10 times deeper and now open your eyes…close your eyes and let go 10 times deeper into this state of peace and openness.

In a moment I will have you open and close your eyes one last time. This time when you close your eyes it is your mind's cue to relax deeper than ever before. When you close your eyes you drift into the perfect state of relaxation and receptivity for you to…accept all suggestions for your success. Now open your eyes and close your eyes…allowing yourself to…now go into that perfect state of mind and body…that's just right for you.

You are doing perfect…and…as you continue to relax more and more with every gentle breath you take…you notice that all you care to think about it is the sound of my voice. Simply listening to the sound of my voice takes you deeper relaxed… and you will find…that all other sounds besides my voice…the sounds in and outside the room…the sounds of the people around you…and any other sound besides my voice…takes you deeper relaxed and enhances your ability to focus…only upon the sound of my voice.

As you relax so deeply and easily...I want you to know...that there are two ways to relax. You can relax physically and you can relax mentally. You have already proven that you can relax physically so easily and effortlessly which is often most difficult for people...relaxing your mind will be so simple for you to do because you have already relaxed the body so deeply and completely.

Now here is the secret to mental relaxation. In a moment I am going to have you begin silently counting backwards in your mind starting with the number 100...in this way. On your inhale mentally say "100" and on the exhale mentally say "deeper relaxed"...99 deeper relaxed...98 deeper relaxed and so. With each number you say...take a deep breath in and double your mental relaxation as you exhale...let every number relax your mind more completely. You will find...that after you say just a few numbers...that your mind will become so relaxed and so peaceful...that all numbers will just disappear and vanish...*the numbers will just leave...* and... when all the numbers are gone...your mind and body will be...deep in hypnosis... and...*open and receptive*...to all beneficial suggestions to you.

As you do this...I will continue to communicate with your subconscious mind... however keep your focus on the task until all numbers have vanished. When all the numbers have vanished and disappeared completely... you will be much deeper into hypnosis and feeling even more comfortable. Begin the process of mental relaxation now by silently counting backwards from 100 now and double your mental relaxation with each number you say...after just a few numbers...when you are ready to feel even more euphoric...the numbers will simply disappear...your mind will then be open and receptive...and you can return to the sound of my voice.

Now, insert the deepener here or go right into suggestions/mental exercises. Finish your session with a count out.

Self-Hypnosis Induction Script 2:

Find a spot on the ceiling to focus on now...as you quietly listen to my voice...and you find...as my words enter your mind through your ears...a pleasant heaviness develops in your eyelids...you may notice it happening now or in just a moment... maybe when you least expect it...but you can notice a heavy, heavy feeling coming over your eyes...wanting to close. You don't have to try or force this to happen... it will happen naturally...automatically...without any conscious effort on your part…the same way without even trying…your breathing has **now slowed down**, and feelings of peace have entered your body…this all occurs…not because I say so…but because your unconscious…mind…has been given permission…**to now respond** to the sound of my voice.

As you now breathe in deeply…allow that feeling of heaviness in your eyelids to become **more absolute now**, and as you exhale you may notice a strong desire to close those heavy, heavy, tired eyes…or not…whatever is right for you, and if your eyes aren't closed completely yet…your unconscious mind can close them… when **you are ready** to feel even more comfortable, peaceful, and serene. Let your conscious mind wander…drift anywhere it wishes…for it doesn't even have to... listen to the sound of my voice …because your unconscious…mind is now at the forefront…listening and now responding perfectly to my words…delivering the message that is right and perfect for you…that's right…you hear the words that create the changes you desire now as your eyes close, or remain shut more peacefully.

Oh, how nice it feels to have your eyes closed…allowing relaxation to flow through your body…and as it does…all muscles, large and small, naturally let go and relax…all muscles embracing this well-deserved relaxation away from all the pressures and demands of society…for this is your time…now releasing from your mind and body any stress or tension that was built up or stored…and as you allow yourself to breathe in deeply…all stress and tension gets collected…exhale…now releasing it from your life forever, or at least for our time together…so you can fully take pleasure in this time that is all for you.

As you become aware of the chair you are sitting in…all muscles just sink deeper and deeper relaxed…just comfortably melting into the chair. With your eyes closed and while listening with your unconscious…that's right…your unconscious mind makes it easy to learn in many different ways. You can learn simply by using your ears and listening to my voice…relaxing into my voice causes your mind and body to feel more and more euphoric. As the sound of my voice goes in your ears… it enters into your mind…creating **new ways** of feeling, doing, and thinking… thinking is the second way **you can learn** in this state of mind. You find without any effort…you can visualize, picture, imagine or think about anything I suggest to you. For example, I know that you weren't thinking about this a moment ago… but for no other reason…only because **you are** using your mind in a new way…

you are able to picture, imagine, or think about what your home looks likes. You may notice the color…maybe the material it's made out of…or maybe you notice one of the rooms inside your house…that's right, relaxing deeper as that image comes to mind…feeling right at home with this serene, wonderful moment. As the image of your home entered into your mind you may have noticed it crystal clear behind your eyelids like watching TV…maybe a movie…or maybe you had to pretend or imagine it to be there. It doesn't matter which way you experienced it…because there is no right or wrong while in this state of mind…the same purpose is served either way…however…you notice with each passing moment and with each healthy beat of your heart …your imagination becomes more powerful…now creating more vivid, detailed, and lifelike thoughts…using your mind now…similar to the same way you did as a kid. Maybe you used to pretend to be an astronaut, or a sports hero...no matter what you imagined yourself to be… you allowed your imagination to work so beautifully…that you **really were** those things you were imagining to be. By the time we are finished together…the same thing occurs. All the success, improvement and the change you envision…using this dynamic part of your mind…is your new reality. Einstein said…our imagination is more powerful than knowledge and with this **now firmly in mind**…you allow your imagination… to take over now…and create the changes you want. For your unconscious…is your imagination…and your imagination is childlike, playful, happy, fun…and for the next few moments we have together…your mind goes back to being childlike, becoming curious again…opening your mind to all the new possibilities in your life…easily discovering new distinctions that enable greater happiness, abundance, and success.

Now, insert the deepener or go right into suggestions / mental exercises. Finish your session with a count out.

Self-Hypnosis Induction Script 3 (Includes Deepener):

To begin this experience, you need to find a place that makes you feel the most comfortable and relaxed. It's best to find a quiet place…free of disturbances and excess noise. Once you have found your relaxation area, you can either sit or lay down whatever is more comfortable for you.

If you decide you want to stay seated, please uncross your legs and place your feet flat on the floor. Just allow your hands to rest comfortably in your lap. If you chose to lie down, uncross your legs and rest your arms comfortably along the side of your body. Now that your body is in this relaxed position, let's begin.

All relaxation starts with a peaceful thought and a nice deep breath. Do it now… take a nice deep breath in…and hold it for a moment… now exhale all the air out of your lungs and begin inviting relaxation into this moment. When you are ready, take another long deep breath in…hold it…and exhale all tension away from your body. Letting it all go, leaving your body more at ease. Again take another long deep breath in and hold it. And this time as you exhale allow your eyes to close now and drift deeper into relaxation.

As you are sitting there, become aware of how nice it is to have your eyes closed, right now, because you know that this is time just for you. Time now to just let go, time now to relax completely, time for a mental vacation away from the world. And as you now breathe in deeply…exhaling all stress and tension out and away from you, you may even feel a little lighter now as you let go even more in this moment. Giving you this opportunity to completely enjoy this time, that's just for you.

As you relax further, you value this time because it is your time, the present time is what everyone has to create what they want...and that is what you do…create what you want **now** as you relax into this receptive state of consciousness where you feel safe and secure with this relaxation. It's so natural and comfortable to you because you easily relax and let go completely. Become aware of your peaceful and easy breathing...and as you do...understand that as I count down from 7 to 1 you go deeper into relaxation with each lower number. On the last count, 1, you will activate within yourself the receptive mindset that effortlessly accepts the powerful changes you now *desire* in your life.

7… As you concentrate more on the sound of my voice, all other sounds, like the sound in and outside the room, relax you deeper, deeper and deeper. Listening to my words and following my instructions creates continuous good feelings of re-laxation and comfort. Allow my words to relax you and begin stimulating change. My words inspire the best in you as you now begin to realize and utilize your true potential. Quietly listening to my voice, all other sounds begin to fade away, only background noise to you, as you keep going deeper into relaxation.

6… Inviting deep relaxation into this present moment like a long lost friend, takes your body and mind to a more comfortable state of peace. Because this deep relaxation is encompassing every cell of your body, you are able to think, picture, or imagine anything I suggest to you. For example, I would like you to picture or think about an image of a perfectly formed rose. As that thought or picture enters your mind, drift deeper relaxed because *this* is so easy for you. Now I would like for you to picture or imagine what a beautiful sunset would look like and as that image enters your consciousness, relax further, deeper and deeper.

5… These peaceful feelings in your body continue to grow as you relax. Your subconscious mind is becoming more fully available and receptive with each and every lower number and since we are at a lower number than the one before you must be deeper relaxed right now. And when you find that you are you also realize that because you are deeper in relaxation you are able to become aware of any feelings I suggest to you instantly. You will find that your subconscious will do all the work for you and no effort is needed now on your part to respond to the suggestions. Notice how easily this works. Since you are deep in hypnosis, you now become vividly aware of the material beneath your fingertips. When that material is realized by your mind, go deeper relaxed. Now you become aware of the weight of your legs. Becoming aware of that sensation relaxes you more. Finally, you become aware of your calm and gentle breathing. So peaceful that every breath you exhale calms you more into relaxation. Because it was so easy for you to be receptive to these past instructions and respond perfectly, you now have made it easier for you to create the changes you want.

4… This is working. This thought that has now entered your mind, whether it was there earlier or not, is put on a continuous loop in your subconscious and the confidence of **knowing** sets in. You may or may not be aware of this, but the idea… this is working…plays continuously in your mind, just like your favorite song that you can't stop singing. Each time you have the thought…this is working…you find yourself relaxing deeper.

3... Knowing that the light at the end of your tunnel is here upon you now. And because your subconscious can hear...now... change can be easy. As you relax into this moment, you feel great...going deeper the better you feel.

2... Take a deep breathe in now...and as you slowly exhale allow your entire body to completely embrace deeper relaxation. Soon you may realize how much deeper you are now compared to when you were at 7 and 6 and 5...4...3...and now even deeper than you were a mere moment ago. On the next count, you drift deeper in relaxation shifting into a more receptive state of consciousness...as you are now entering this super learning state it is easy to make the changes you desire...

1... Let go completely now.

Now begin positive suggestions / mental exercises. Finish your session with a count out.

APPENDIX VIII

Deepener Examples

The following are examples of hypnotic deepeners. Hypnotic deepeners follow the induction and are designed to guide you into deeper states of relaxation.

Deepener Example 1:

In a moment I will begin counting from 5 down to 1, and with each lower number let yourself relax more and more completely.

Now at the count of 5...deeper and deeper relaxed...just letting go now...and the first way that you can learn in hypnosis is by listening to my voice and following my instructions. In fact, all sounds other than the sound of my voice take you deeper relaxed. The sounds in the room, the sounds outside, the sounds in your body, and in your mind all help you to relax...because the only sound you care to think about is the sound of my voice.

Now at 4...deeper...deeper...so calm and relaxed...and the second way you can learn in hypnosis is by picturing, visualizing, or thinking about anything I suggest to you. For example right now, even though you weren't thinking about it a moment ago, you become aware of the thought, image or picture of your home. That's right and as that image or thought enters into your mind go deeper relaxed. You may have noticed your home very vividly behind your eyes like watching TV or a movie...or maybe all you saw was black and you had to imagine what it looked like...it doesn't really matter which way you experienced it because the same purpose is served either way. So do what is right for you.

Now …3…Even deeper now. No longer needing to try or think because the subconscious mind is firmly locked down upon the sound of my voice…responding perfectly, automatically and instantly to my suggestions. The third way you learn in hypnosis is through your feelings…notice how easily your mind is now responding. Even though you weren't thinking about it…you become vividly aware of the feelings of the material beneath your fingertips…that's right and as you become aware of the feelings beneath your fingertips go deeper relaxed. Now you become aware of how calm and gentle your breathing has become…reminding you that every breath takes you deeper.

Now on 2…Take a deep breathe in and as you exhale relax even deeper. On the next count you enter into the super learning state where you subconscious is at the forefront ready to and willing to accept these helpful suggestions for you. In this state of mind it is easy for you to…create the changes you desire.

Now… 1….. (Begin positive suggestions / mental exercises.)

Staircase Deepener Example:

Imagine standing on top of the most beautiful staircase in the world...the one that takes you deeper and deeper into peace and relaxation. In a moment I will begin counting from 5 down to 1, and with each lower number imagine taking another step down that beautiful staircase into greater relaxation and comfort. Each step down takes you deeper and deeper and deeper relaxed.

Now…. 5...taking that first step and feeling the relaxation becoming more and more complete.

Now… 4...each step taking you deeper and deeper as you descend down the staircase.

Now… 3...really letting go now as you take another step down the staircase toward greater relaxation.

Now… 2...so relaxed, so comfortable, so peaceful, as you go deeper and deeper into relaxation.

And now… 1...you are now in a state perfect peace and absolute comfort...going deeper and deeper with every breath you take. **(Begin positive suggestions / mental exercises)**

APPENDIX IX

Count Out Examples

The count out is the process for emerging from self-hypnosis. Count out suggestions come after your positive mental programming or mental training processes, and when you are ready to end the session.

Count Out Example 1:

In a moment I am going to count from 1to 5. At the count of 5, your eyes will open…bringing forth a feeling of happiness, renewed energy, and peace of mind knowing that change has occurred in the right way for you. Even though we just had a few minutes of hypnosis today you realize that today is the day success has occurred and you can go about living your life in a happy and positive way. Even though it was just a few minutes of hypnosis…you created tremendous success today.

Now… **1**…The next time you get hypnotized by yourself or anybody you trust… you enter this wonderful state of mind deeper and deeper. Any time in the future you get hypnotized by someone you trust or by yourself you immediately enter this level of depth and deeper.

Now… **2**…Over the next few days longer if you like the color red, red, red, red, red will catch your eye. The color red… red…. red …seems brighter, sharper, and clearer to you. Every time you see the color red, red, red…more vividly now…it will reinforce and strengthen all suggestions delivered to you today. The color red will seem to just catch your eye and as it does all positive and beneficial suggestions get reinforced deeper into your subconscious mind whether consciously aware of it or not.

Now… **3**…Take a deep breath in and as you do feel a renewed sense of energy returning back into your body. Wiggle your fingers and toes…now beginning to return to the here and now. It feels as if your mind and body has been bathed in a brook of knowledge…now full of clarity, peace, and energy.

And… **4**…Take another deep breath in, locking in the changes, and feeling more and more energized. On the next count your eyes will open, feeling amazing and successful. However, unable to open your eyes no matter how hard you try until all positive suggestions have been accepted by your inner mind and you are absolutely ready to…now be more a successful.

And… **5**…Eyes opening…locking in the changes…feeling amazing in every way.

The Count Out Example 2:

The next time I relax in this way I will quickly and easily relax this completely and continue to relax deeper every time. I enjoy these feeling of deep relaxation and my body feels rejuvenated, restored, and back in a perfect state of peace. In a moment I will count from 1 to 5. At the count of 5 my eyes will open and I will feel refreshed, revitalized, and full of energy.

Let's start….**1**…The next time I do self-hypnosis or get hypnotized I get into deeper states of relaxation quicker and easier than the time before.

Now … **2**…Coming up more and more now. I can feel the positive energy surging into my body.

And … **3**…Feeling completely rejuvenated now as if I was coming up from a refreshing nap.

And … **4**…All suggestions are accepted in my mind and I am ready to create more success. I am energized, excited, and feeling great.

And … **5**…eyes open full of energy and motivated to succeed.

ACKNOWLEDGMENTS

I want to give a special thanks to Ted Frick of The Classic Swing Golf School in Myrtle Beach, SC. Ted, I can't thank you enough for your belief and support of my work over the years. You have been a great contributor, inspiration, and friend. Thank you so much for giving me an opportunity to be of service and supporting me along this journey.

I also want to say thank you to all the golfers who I have had the great privilege of working with over the years. Special thanks to Paul Woodbury and Austin "Freebird" Frick. Thank you for being a big part of this journey with me and I wish you both massive and ongoing success in all that you do.

This book would not be possible without the priceless help, guidance, and work of my dear friend Alison Falls. Ali, the work you have done on this book has been nothing short of pure genius. I am so grateful and appreciative for everything you have done and it is difficult to put into words how much it means to me. Thank you so much for being such a light in my life and for your invaluable contributions.

Finally, I want to thank my loving and supportive parents. From day one, both of you have been the best parents a son could ask for. Thank you for your never-ending encouragement, all the time you have spent listening to me ramble about my new ideas, and for always believing in me and the work I am doing. I am forever grateful for all that you have done for me over the years. I love you both so much.

-- *J. Weir*

NOTES

Chapter One: The Mind-Body Connection in Golf

1. Web Resource: *Golf Magazine Top 100 Teachers 2011,* http://www.golf.com/node/154300.

2. Dr. David Wright Recorded Interview with John Weir, 2012

3. Kay Porter and Judy Foster, *Visual Athletics Visualization for Peak Sports Performance.* (Dubuque, IA: William C Brown Publishing, 1990), 17.

4. Jon Finn, An Introduction to Using Mental Skills to Enhance Performance in Golf: Beyond the Bounds of Positive and Negative Thinking. *Annual Review of Golf Coaching*, 2008, 255-269.

5. Hope Hamashige, Train Your Brain. *Chanhassen, MN: Experience Life Magazine,* Nov. Issue, 2006, http://experiencelife.com/article/train-your-brain/.

6. Robert Woolfork, Mark Parrish, Shane Murphy, The Effects of Positive and Negative Imagery on Motor Skill Performance. *Cognitive Therapy and Research*, Volume 9, Issue 3, June 1985, 335-341.

7. J.A. Taylor and D.F. Shaw, The Effects of Outcome Imagery on Putting Performance. *Journal of Sports Sciences,* 20, 2002, 607-613.

8. *Annie Plessinger, The Effects of Mental Imagery on Athletic Performance* (Vanderbilt University Psychology Department) http://healthpsych.psy.vanderbilt.edu/HealthPsych/mentalimagery.html.

9. Kathleen Martin, & Craig Hall, Using Mental Imagery to Enhance Intrinsic Motivation. *Journal of Sport & Exercise Psychology*, 17, 1995, 54-69.

10. Jack Nicklaus, & Ken Bowden, *Golf My Way.* (New York, NY: Simon and Schuster. 1974),79.

11. Gerald Kein, Rules of the Mind (Privately published manuscript, 1985), 1-2.

12. Zali Segal, *Hypnotize This!* (New York, NY: BooksRYou, 2004), 62-63.

Chapter Two: The Truth About Hypnosis

1.   John K. Williams, *The Knack of Using Your Subconscious Mind* (Englewood Cliffs, NJ: Prentice Hall Inc., 1952), 47-48.

2.   Emile Coué, *My Method* (Garden City, NY: Doubleday, Page & Co., 1923), 13.

3.   Harry Arons, *Master Course in Hypnotism* (S. Orange, NJ: Power Publishers, 1961), 11.

4.   Web Resource for EEG: http://en.wikipedia.org/wiki/Electroencephalogra phy/#Wavepatterns.

5.   Philip Holt M.D., *Introduction to Pediatric EEG* (Emory University School of Medicine - Pediatric Neurology, Website 2013). http://www. pediatrics.emory.edu/divisions/neurology/education/pedeeg.html

6.   Suzanne Evans Morris, Ph.D., *The Facilitation of Learning.* (Privately published manuscript, 1989), 16-17.

7.   Thomas Budzynski, Turning on the Twilight Zone. *Psychology Today*, August 1977.

8.   Thomas Budzynski, *A Brain Lateralization Model for REST* (Denver, CO: Paper from First International Conference on REST and Self-Regulation, 1983).

9.   Suzanne Evans Morris, Ph.D., *The Facilitation of Learning.* (Privately published manuscript, 1989),16-17

10. Tom Silver & Ormond McGill, *Hypnotism: A Hypnosis Training and Techniques Manual* (Newbury Park, CA: Silver Institute Publishing Co., 2003), 18.

Chapter Three: How Your Mind Functions on the Course

1. Nicole Schneider and Steven Cocks, *NLP Practitioner Program Manual* (Privately published manuscript, Global NLP Training Institute, 2008), 8, Section 1.

2. John Pates, Andrew Cowen, & Costas Karageorghis, The Effect of Client-Centered Approach on Flow States and the Performance of Three Elite Golfers. *International Journal of Golf Science*, 1, 2012, 113-126.

3. Pia Nilsson, Lynn Marriott, and Ron Sirak, *Every Shot Must Have A Purpose* (New York, NY: Gotham, 2005), 28-29.

4. Joaquin Dosil, *The Sport Psychologist's Handbook: A Guide for Sport-Specific Performance Enhancement* (Hoboken, NJ: John Wiley & Sons Inc. 2006), 305.

5. Owens, D., & Bunker, L., *Advanced Golf: Steps to Success* (Champaign, IL: Human Kinetics, 1992).

6. Ruth E Schneider & David S Prudhomme, *FROM STRESSED TO BEST: A Proven Program for Reducing Everyday Stress,* (Port Clinton, OH: MW Press, 2014), 49.

7. Jose Silva, *The Silva Mind Control Method* (New York, NY: Pocket Books, 1978), 30.

8. Dr. David Wright Recorded Interview with John Weir 2012

9. Weinberg, Seabourne, & Jackson, Effects of Visuo-motor Behavior Rehearsal, Relaxation, and Imagery on Karate Performance. *Journal of Sport Psychology*, v3, 1981, 228-238.

10. Beauchamp, P.H., Halliwell, W.R., Fournier, J.F., & Koestner, R., Effects of Cognitive-behavioral Psychological Skills Training on the Motivation, Preparation, and Putting Performance of Novice Golfers. *The Sport Psychologist*, v.10, 1996, 157-170.

11. John Pates, The Effects of Hypnosis on an Elite Senior European Tour Golfer: A Single-Subject Design. *International Journal of Clinical and Experimental Hypnosis*, 61-2: 2013, 1-12.

12. Robert C. Eklund & Susan A. Jackson, Assessing Flow in Physical Activity: The Flow State Scale-2 and Dispositional Flow Scale-2. *Journal of Sport and Exercise Psychology* 24, 2002, 133-150.

13. John Pates, Rachael Oliver, and Ian Maynard, The Effects of Hypnosis on Flow States and Golf-Putting Performance. *Journal of Applied Sport Psychology* 13, 2001, 341-354.

14. Gayle Privette, Peak Experience, Peak Performance, Flow: A Comparative Analysis of Positive Human Experience. *Journal of Personality and Social Psychology*, 45, 1983, 1361-1368.

15. Lars-Eric Unestahl, *Inner Mental Training* (Orebro, Sweden: Veje Publications, 1983).

16. John Kihlstrom, *Hypnosis*. (Annual Review Of Psychology, 36, 1985), 385–418.

17. John Pates, Rachael Oliver, and Ian Maynard, The Effects of Hypnosis on Flow States and Golf-Putting Performance. *Journal of Applied Sport Psychology* 13, 2001, 341-354.

18. Web Resource: Louie Oosthuizen YouTube Clip: http://www.youtube.com/watch?v=ndqDfAZrurU.

19. Web Resource: Tiger Woods YouTube Clip: http://www.youtube.com/watch?v=QEaWv0SBp3A.

Chapter Four: Self-Talk, Affirmations and Autosuggestion

1. Rosemary Tator & Alesia Latson, *More Time for You: A Powerful System to Organize Your Work and Get Things Done* (New York, NY: Amacom, 2010), 79.

2. Web Resource: Blog of Member of LONI and Author of *Mind Your Own Fitness,* http://bobchoat.com/2013/06/24/what-are-your-thoughts-doing-to-you-each-day/.

3. The Golf Club Radio Show, Host Danielle Tucker Interview with Lynn Marriott March 4, 2013, http://www.youtube.com/watch?v=JduYnI5aWcI.

4. Amir Dana, Mohammad VaezMousavi, & Pouneh Mokhtari, Belief in Self Talk and Motor Performance in Basketball Shooting. *International Research Journal of Applied and Basic Sciences,* Vol., 3 (3), 2012, 493-498.

5. Seyed Abbas Afsanepurak, Abbas Bahram, The Effect of Self-talk and Mental Imagery on Motor Performance in Adolescents. *International Research Journal of Applied and Basic Sciences*, Vol., 3 (3), 2012), 601-607.

6. Emile Coue, *My Method* (Garden City, NY: Doubleday, Page & Co., 1923), 13.

7. Emile Coue, *My Method* (Garden City, NY: Doubleday, Page & Co., 1923), 24.

Chapter Five: Relaxation Training

1. Dr. Brian M Alman & Dr. Peter Lambrou, *Self-Hypnosis: The Complete Manual for Health and Self-Change 2nd Edition* (New York, NY: Brunner-Routeledge, 1992), 16-17.

2. Sharon Salzberg & Joseph Goldstein, *Insight Meditation: A Step by Step Course in How to Meditate* (Boulder, CO: Sounds True, 2001), 33.

3. Thich Nhat Hanh, *The Art of Mindful Living* (Boulder, CO: Sounds True, 2000), Audio Program.

4. Khasky, A.D., & Smith, J.C., *Stress, Relaxation States and Creativity* (Perceptual and Motor Skills, 88 (2), 1999), 409-416.

Chapter Six: Steps to Self-Hypnosis

1. Gerald Kein, *Rules of the Mind* (Privately published manuscript, 1985), 3.

2. Dave Elman, *Hypnotherapy* (Glendale, CA: Westwood Publishing Co., 1964), 58-66.

3. Harry Arons, *Handbook of Self-Hypnosis* (Irvington, NJ: Power Publishers, Inc., 1969), 71-74.

4. The National Guild of Hypnotists *Hypnotism Certification Course Book 1* (Merrimack, NH: National Guild of Hypnotists Inc., 2004), 20.

Chapter Seven: Other Methods of Self-Hypnosis

1. Norbert Bakas, *Self-Hypnosis: Your Golden Key To Self-Improvement and Self-Healing* (Charleston, SC: Dr. Norbert Bakas, 2010), 54-57.

2. Silva, J., *The Silva Mind Control Method* (New York, NY: Pocket Books, 1978), 30-31.

Chapter Eight: Hypnotic Suggestions and Positive Mental Programming

1. Norbert Bakas, *Self-Hypnosis Your Golden Key to Self-Improvement and Self-Healing* (Charleston, SC: Dr. Norbert Bakas, 2010), 85.

2. Charles Tebbetts, *Self-Hypnosis and Other Mind Expanding Techniques* (Glendale, CA: Westwood Publishing Co., 1977), 42-48.

3. Zali Segal, *Hypnotize This!* (New York, NY: BooksRYou, 2004), 96.

4. Calvin Banyan & Gerald Kein, *Hypnosis and Hypnotherapy: Basic to Advanced Techniques and Procedures for the Professional* (St. Paul, MN: Abbot Publishing House, Inc., 2001), 96.

5. Dave Elman, *Hypnotherapy* (Glendale, CA: Westwood Publishing Co., 1964), 104.

6. Gerald Kein, *Basic-Intermediate-Advanced Hypnosis Training Manual* (Deland, FL: Omni Hypnosis Training Center, 1999), 7.

Chapter Nine: Conditioning and Anchoring

1. Web Resource: Ivan Pavlov and Classical Conditioning Video, http://www.youtube.com/watch?v=hhqumfpxuzI.

2. Nicole Schneider & Steve Cocks, *NLP Practitioner Program Manual* (Privately published manuscript by Global NLP Training Institute, 2008), 19-20, Section 2.

3. Nicole Schneider & Steve Cocks, *NLP Practitioner Program Manual* (Privately published manuscript by Global NLP Training Institute, 2008), 20, Section 2.

Chapter Ten: The Power of Visualization: Exercises and Applications

1. Richard Bandler, John Grinder, Robert Dilts, Leslie C, Bandler, Judith DeLozier, *Neuro-Linguistic Programming Volume 1: The Study of the Structure of Subjective Experience* (Cupertino, CA: Meta Publications, 1980), 17.

2. Tad James, *The Accelerated NLP Practitioner Certification Training Manual (*Privately published manuscript by Tad James & Advanced Neuro Dynamics, Ver. 5.8 4/04, 2004), 27.

3. Allison Yancey, Daniel Czech, Barry Joyner, Drew Zwald, & Noah Gentner, The Experience of Pre-Shot Routines among Professional Golfers: An Existential Phenomenological Investigation. *Journal of Excellence*, Issue 14, 2011, 48.

4. Czech, D., Ploszay, A., & Burke, K., *An Examination of the Maintenance of Pre Shot Routines in Basketball Free Throw Shooting.* Journal of Sport Behavior, 27, 2004, 323-329.

5. Dr. Bob Rotella, *Golf is Not a Game of Perfect* (New York, NY: Simon and Schuster, 2007), 65.

6. Mark Fairchild, Garrett Johnson, Jason Babcock, & Jeff Pelz, *Is Your Eye on the Ball?: Eye Tracking Golfers while Putting* (Rochester, NY: Rochester Institute of Technology Chester F. Carlson Center for Imaging Science, 2001), http://www.cis.rit.edu/fairchild/putting.html

7. Gary McGuire, *Realizing Your Potential* (Delhi, India: Readworthy Publications Pvt. Ltd., 2009), 84.

Chapter Eleven: Mental Rehearsal

1. Douglas Juola, *GolfNosis* (Lake Forest, CA: Advanced Enterprise Solutions Inc., 2010), 243.

2. Dr. Thomas Tutko & Umberto Tosi, *Sports Psyching* (New York, NY: Tarcher/Putnam, 1976), 144.

3.   Kosslyn, S., Ganis, G., & Thompson, W., *Neural Foundations of Imagery* (Nature Reviews Neuroscience, 2, 2001), 635-642.

4.   MacKay, D., *The Problem of Rehearsal or Mental Practice* (Journal of Motor Behavior, 13, 1981), 274-285.

Chapter Twelve: Troubleshooting Your Mental State on the Golf Course

1.   Anthony Robbins, *Personal Power II: The Driving Force* (Santa Monica, CA: Guthy-Renker Corporation, 1996), Audiobook CD, Disc 4: The Science of Success Conditioning.

Chapter Thirteen: The B.E.T. System for State Management on the Golf Course

1.   Nicole Schneider & Steve Cocks, *NLP Practitioner Program Manual* (Privately published manuscript by Global NLP Training Institute, 2008), 9, Section 1.

Chapter Fourteen: Goal Setting, Self-Hypnosis and Mental Fitness

1.   Rex Hoggard, Article on Adam Scott, April 7, 2014, posted 11 am., http://www.golfchannel.com/news/rex-hoggard/rise-and-fall-and-rise-adam-scott/?cid=twitter-gc-a-rise-and-fall-of-adam-scott-040714.

2.   Gail Matthews, Ph.D., *Brief Summary of Recent Goals Research* (Dominican University of California, 2013), http://www.dominican.edu/academics/ahss/undergraduate-programs-1/psych/faculty/fulltime/gail-matthews/researchsummary2.pdf.

3.   Joaquin Dosil, *The Sport Psychologist's Handbook: A Guide for Sport-Specific Performance Enhancement* (Hoboken, NJ: John Wiley & Sons Inc., 2006), 314.

4.   George T. Doran, *There's a S.M.A.R.T. Way to Write Management's Goals and Objectives* (Management Review, Volume 70, Issue 11, 1981), 35-36.

5. Nicole Schneider & Steve Cocks, *NLP Practitioner Program Manual* (Privately published manuscript by Global NLP Training Institute, 2008), 21, Section 3.

6. John Kappas, *Hypnosis Motivation Institute: Clinical Hypnosis 201Training Manual* (Tarzana, CA: Panorama Publishing, 2003), 24-25, Section 1.

BIBLIOGRAPHY

Afsanepurak, S., & Bahram, A., The Effect of Self-talk and Mental Imagery on Motor Performance in Adolescents. *International Research Journal of Applied and Basic Sciences,* Vol. 3 (3), 2012.

Alman, B. & Lambrou, P., *Self-Hypnosis: The Complete Manual for Health and Self-Change,* 2nd Edition, (New York, NY: Brunner-Routeledge, 1992).

Arons, H., *Handbook of Self-Hypnosis* (Irvington, NJ: Power Publishers, Inc., 1969).

Arons, H., *Master Course in Hypnotism* (S. Orange, NJ: Power Publishers, 1961).

Bakas, N., *Self-Hypnosis Your Golden Key to Self-Improvement and Self-Healing* (Charleston, SC: Dr. Norbert Bakas, 2010).

Bandler, R., Grinder, J., Dilts, R., Bandler, L., & DeLozier, J., *Neuro-Linguistic Programming Volume 1: The Study of the Structure of Subjective Experience* (Cupertino, CA: Meta Publications, 1980).

Banyan, C., & Kein, G., *Hypnosis and Hypnotherapy: Basic to Advanced Techniques and Procedures for the Professional* (St. Paul, MN: Abbot Publishing House, Inc., 2001).

Beauchamp, P.H., Halliwell, W.R., Fournier, J.F., & Koestner, R., Effects of Cognitive-behavioral Psychological Skills Training on the Motivation, Preparation, and Putting Performance of Novice Golfers. *The Sport Psychologist*, 10, 1996.

Budzynski, T., Turning on the Twilight Zone. *Psychology Today*, Aug., 1977.

Coué, E., *My Method* (Garden City, NY: Doubleday, Page & Co., 1923).

Czech, D., Ploszay, A., & Burke, K., An Examination of the Maintenance of Pre-shot Routines in Basketball Free Throw Shooting. *Journal of Sport Behavior*, 27, 2004.

Dana, A., Mousavi, M., & Mokhtari, P., Belief in Self Talk and Motor Performance in Basketball Shooting. *International Research Journal of Applied and Basic Sciences*, Vol. 3 (3), 2012.

Doran, G., There's a S.M.A.R.T. Way to Write Management's Goals and Objectives. *Management Review*, Volume 70, Issue 11, 1981.

Dosil, J., *The Sport Psychologist's Handbook: A Guide for Sport-Specific Performance Enhancement* (Hoboken, NJ: John Wiley & Sons Inc., 2006).

Eklund, R.C. & Jackson, S.A., Assessing Flow in Physical Activity: the Flow State Scale-2 and Dispositional Flow Scale-2. *Journal of Sport and Exercise Psychology*, 24, 2002.

Elman, D., *Hypnotherapy* (Glendale, CA: Westwood Publishing Co., 1964).

Fairchild, M., Johnson, G., Babcock, J., & Pelz, J., *Is Your Eye on the Ball? Eye Tracking Golfers while Putting* (Rochester Institute of Technology Chester F. Carlson Center for Imaging Science, 2001.

Finn, J., An Introduction to Using Mental Skills to Enhance Performance in Golf: Beyond the Bounds of Positive and Negative Thinking. *Annual Review of Golf Coaching*, 2008.

Hanh, T. N., *The Art of Mindful Living* (Boulder, CO: Sounds True, 2000).

Hamashige, H., Train Your Brain. *Chanhassen, MN: Experience Life Magazine*, November Issue, 2006.

Hoggard, Rex, Article on Adam Scott, April 7, 2014, posted 11 am., http://www.golfchannel.com/news/rex-hoggard/rise-and-fall-and-rise-adam-scott/?cid=twitter-gc-a-rise-and-fall-of-adam-scott-040714.

Holt, P., Introduction to Pediatric EEG. *Emory University School of Medicine - Pediatric Neurology, Website*, 2013.

James, T., *The Accelerated NLP Practitioner Certification Training Manual* (Privately published manuscript by Tad James & Advanced Neuro Dynamics Ver., 5.8 4/04, 2004).

Juola, D., *GolfNosis* (Lake Forest, CA: Advanced Enterprise Solutions Inc., 2010).

Kappas, J., *Hypnosis Motivation Institute: Clinical Hypnosis 201 Training Manual* (Tarzana, CA: Panorama Publishing, 2003).

Kein, G., *Basic-Intermediate-Advanced Hypnosis Training Manual* (Deland, FL: Omni Hypnosis Training Center, 1999).

Kein, G., *Rules of the Mind* (Privately published manuscript, 1985).

Khasky, A., & Smith, J., Stress, Relaxation States and Creativity. *Perceptual and Motor Skills*, 88 (2), 1999.

Kihlstrom, J., Hypnosis. *Annual Review of Psychology*, 36, 1985.

Kosslyn, S., Ganis, G., & Thompson, W., Neural Foundations of Imagery. *Nature Reviews Neuroscience*, 2, 2001.

MacKay, D., The Problem of Rehearsal or Mental Practice. *Journal of Motor Behavior*, 13, 1981.

Martin, K., & Hall, C., Using Mental Imagery to Enhance Intrinsic Motivation. *Journal of Sport & Exercise Psychology*, 17, 1995.

Matthews, G., *Brief Summary of Recent Goals Research* (Dominican University of California, 2013).

McGuire, G., *Realizing Your Potential* (Delhi, India: Readworthy Publications Pvt. Ltd., 2009).

Morris, S., *The Facilitation of Learning (Privately* published manuscript, 1989).

National Guild of Hypnotists, *Hypnotism Certification Course Book 1* (Merrimack, NH: National Guild of Hypnotists Inc., 2004).

Nicklaus, J., & Bowden, K., *Golf My Way (*New York, NY: Simon and Schuster: 1974).

Nilsson, P., Marriott, L., Sirak, R., Every *Shot Must Have a Purpose* (New York, NY: Gotham, 2005).

Owens, D., & Bunker, L., *Advanced Golf: Steps to Success* (Champaign, IL: Human Kinetics, 1992).

Pates, J., The Effects of Hypnosis on an Elite Senior European Tour Golfer: A Single-Subject Design. *International Journal of Clinical and Experimental Hypnosis*, 61-2, 2013.

Pates, J., Cowen, A., & Karageorghis, C., The Effect of Client-Centered Approach on Flow States and the Performance of Three Elite Golfers. *International Journal of Golf Science*, 1, 2012.

Pates, J., Oliver, R., & Maynard, I., The Effects of Hypnosis on Flow States and Golf-Putting Performance. *Journal of Applied Sport Psychology*, 13, 2001.

Plessinger, A., *The Effects of Mental Imagery on Athletic Performance.* (Vanderbilt University Psychology Department).

Porter, K., & Foster, J., *Visual Athletics: Visualization for Peak Sports Performance* (Dubuque, IA: William C Brown Publishing, 1990).

Privette, G., Peak Experience, Peak performance, Flow: A Comparative Analysis of Positive Human Experience. *Journal of Personality and Social Psychology*, 45, 1983.

Robbins, A., *Personal Power II The Driving Force,* (Santa Monica, CA: Guthy-Renker Corporation, 1996).

Rotella, B., *Golf is Not a Game of Perfect,* (New York, NY: Simon and Schuster, 2007).

Salzberg, S., & Goldstein, J., *Insight Meditation - A Step by Step Course in How to Meditate* (Boulder, CO: Sounds True, 2001).

Schneider, N & Cocks, S., *NLP Practitioner Program Manual,* (Privately published manuscript by Global NLP Training Institute, 2008).

Schneider, R., & Prudhomme, D., *From Stressed to Best: A Proven Program for Reducing Everyday Stress,* (Port Clinton, OH. MW Press, 2014).

Segal, Z., *Hypnotize This!* (New York, NY: BooksRYou, 2004).

Silva, J., *The Silva Mind Control Method*, (New York, NY: Pocket Books, 1978).

Silver, T., & McGill, O., *Hypnotism: A Hypnosis Training and Techniques Manual*, (Newbury Park, CA: Silver Institute Publishing Co., 2003).

Tator, R., & Latson, A., *More Time for You: A Powerful System to Organize Your Work and Get Things Done*, (New York, NY: Amacom, 2010).

Taylor, J., & Shaw, D., The Effects of Outcome Imagery on Putting Performance, *Journal of Sports Sciences*, 20, 2002.

Tebbetts, C., *Self-Hypnosis and Other Mind Expanding Techniques*, (Glendale, CA: Westwood Publishing Co., 1977).

Tucker, D., The Golf Club Radio Show Interview with Lynn Marriott, 2013.

Tutko, T. & Tosi, U., *Sports Psyching*, (New York, NY: Tarcher/Putnam, 1976).

Unestahl, L.E., *Inner Mental Training*, (Orebro, Sweden: Veje Publications, 1983).

Weinberg, R. S., Seabourne, T.G., & Jasckon, A., Effects of Visuo-motor Behavior Rehearsal, Relaxation, and Imagery on Karate Performance. *Journal of Sport Psychology*, 3, 1981.

Williams, J.K., *The Knack of Using Your Subconscious Mind* (Englewood Cliffs, NJ: Prentice Hall Inc., 1952).

Woolfork, R., Parrish, M., & Murphy, S., The Effects of Positive and Negative Imagery on Motor Skill Performance, *Cognitive Therapy and Research*, Volume 9, Issue 3, June 1985.

Wright, D., Recorded Interview with John Weir, 2012.

Yancey, A., Czech, D., Joyner, B., Zwald, D., & Gentner, N., The Experience of Pre-Shot Routines among Professional Golfers: An Existential Phenomenological Investigation. *Journal of Excellence*, Issue 14, 2011.

ABOUT THE AUTHOR

John Weir is founder of the Mental Golf Academy in Orlando, creator of the Mental Caddie, and performance coach to collegiate and professional golfers worldwide. There are ongoing breakthroughs in the mental golf game, and Weir stands at the forefront of discovery.

For nearly fifteen years, Weir has been helping clients learn how to take control of their minds to live healthier and happier lives through clinical hypnosis. Today, he combines this passion with his favorite pastime: golf. He is the youngest person in the National Guild of Hypnotists' history to be inducted into their Order of Braid—the highest honor given for lifetime achievement.

Weir is a psychology alumnus from Point Park University, a board certified hypnotist, certified instructor through the NGH, NLP Master Practitioner, and peak performance coach. His Golf Hypnosis Specialist Certification Course is offered to hypnotists and coaches from over sixty countries.

Made in the USA
San Bernardino, CA
18 February 2015